MAD ABOUT MYSTERY:

100 Wonderful Television Mysteries from the Seventies

by Donna Marie Nowak

With an Introduction by Stefanie Powers

Published in the USA by:
BearManor Media
P O Box 71426
Albany, Georgia 31708
www.bearmanormedia.com

Printed in the United States of America
ISBN   978-1-62933-255-0 (paperback)

Book & cover design and layout by Darlene Swanson • www.van-garde.com

Cover Photo: Stefanie Powers and Peter Lawford with director Barry Shear in *Ellery Queen: Don't Look Behind You (1971)*. Photo courtesy of Universal Television.

Back Cover Photos: *(top)* Peter Falk as Lieutenant Columbo with Jose Ferrer in "Mind Over Mayhem" (1974). Photo courtesy of Universal Television and Studios USA. *(bottom)* Lynda Carter as Wonder Woman. Photo courtesy of Warner Brothers Television.

To my wonderful sisters Julie and Kathy

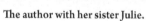

The author with her sister Julie.

The author's sister Kathy.

and my beloved Maltipoo Scrappy

Scrappy Doodle Nowak.

Contents

Acknowledgments ix

Introduction by Stefanie Powers xi

The Made-for-Television Movies 1

Adventures of Nick Carter (1972) 2

Along Came a Spider (1970) 3

Bad Ronald (1974) 3

Baffled (1972) 4

Cat Creature, The (1973) 6

Cold Night's Death, A (1973) 7

Crowhaven Farm (1970) 8

Curse of the Black Widow (1977) 9

Dead Don't Die, The (1975) 10

Dear Detective (1979) 11

Death at Love House (1976) 12

Death Cruise (1974) 13

Do Not Fold, Spindle or Mutilate (1971) 14

Dracula (1974) 15

Duel (1971) 16

Dying Room Only (1973) 17

Ellery Queen: Don't Look Behind You (1971) 18

Escape (1971) 19

Eyes of Charles Sand, The (1972) 20

Five Desperate Women (1971) 21

Get Christie Love (1974) 23

Golden Gate Murders, The (1979) 23

Goodnight My Love (1972) 24

Helter Skelter (1976) 25

Hit Lady (1974) 27

Home for the Holidays (1972) 28

House on Greenapple Road, The (1970) 29

House that Would Not Die, The (1970). 29

How Awful About Allan (1970) 30

Howling in the Woods, A (1971). 31

I Love a Mystery (1973) 32

Isn't It Shocking? (1973). 33

Judge and Jake Wyler, The (1972) 34

Legend of Lizzie Borden, The (1975) 35

Little Game, A (1971). 36

Live Again, Die Again (1974) 38

Log of the Black Pearl, The (1975) 38

Longstreet (1971) 39

Maneater (1973) 40

Mind Over Murder (1979) 41

Murder by Natural Causes (1979) 42

Murder on Flight 502 (1975) 43

Murder Once Removed (1971). 44

Nero Wolfe (1979) 45

Night Slaves (1970) 46

Night Stalker, The (1972) 47

Norliss Tapes, The (1973) 48

Old Man Who Cried Wolf, The (1970) 49

One of My Wives is Missing (1976) 50

Paper Man (1971). 51

President's Plane is Missing, The (1973) 52

Reflections of Murder (1974). 53

Return of Charlie Chan, The (1973). 54

Revenge (1971) 55

Ritual of Evil (1970). 56

Salem's Lot (1979). 58

Satan's School for Girls (1973) 60

Satan's Triangle (1975) 61

Savages (1974) 62

Scream, Pretty Peggy (1973) 63

Screaming Woman, The (1972) 64

She Cried Murder (1973) 66

She Waits (1972). 67

She's Dressed to Kill (1979) 68

Sherlock Holmes in New York (1976). 69

Skyway to Death (1974) 70

Someone's Watching Me! (1978). 71

Stonestreet: Who Killed the Centerfold Model? (1977) 72

Sweet, Sweet Rachel (1971). 73

Taste of Evil, A (1971) 75

They Call It Murder (1971) 75

Trilogy of Terror (1975) 76

Twin Detectives (1976) 78

Two for the Money (1972) 78

Very Missing Person, A (1972) 80

Victim, The (1972) 81

Weekend of Terror (1970). 82

When Michael Calls (1972). 83

Who is the Black Dahlia? (1975). 83

Woman Hunter, The (1972). 84

The Television Series 87

Cannon (1971-1976). 88

Charlie's Angels (1976-1981) 92

Columbo (1971-2003) 96

Ellery Queen (1975-1976). 100

Hardy Boys/Nancy Drew Mysteries (1977-1979) 104

Hart to Hart (1979-1984) 108

Hawaii Five-O (1968-1980). 112

Ironside (1967-1975). 116

Kojak (1973-1978) 120

Kolchak: The Night Stalker (1974-1975). 124

Mannix (1967-1975) 128

McCloud (1970-1977) 132

McMillan & Wife (1971-1977) 136

Police Woman (1974-1978) 140

Quincy, M.E. (1976-1983) 144

Rockford Files (1974-1980) 148

Scooby Doo: Where Are You? (1969-1970) (1978) 152

The Streets of San Francisco (1972-1977) 156

VEGA$ (1978-1981) 160

Wonder Woman (1975-1979) 164

Memories of Those Who Were There 169

Sharon Farrell – Actor 171

Peter S. Fischer – Producer/Writer 181

Robert Herron – Stuntman 194

Lance Kerwin – Child/Teen Actor 198

Diana Muldaur – Actor 209

Tom Sawyer – Writer/Producer 220

Harriett Weiss – Writer (as told by her daughter Michele Weiss) 234

Just One More Thing: Epilogue by Donna Marie Nowak 237

About the Author 245

Index 247

Acknowledgments

My thanks and gratitude to:

My wonderful publisher Ben Ohmart who keeps the flame alive for the classics of film, television and radio; the divine Stefanie Powers, my idol since childhood, who so generously and kindly contributed the introduction to my book and made me feel as if all roads and dreams lead home – as Lionel Stander said in the voiceover of *Hart to Hart*, "She's quite a lady"; Darlene Swanson for her behind-the-scenes wizardry; Sharon Farrell, Peter S. Fischer, Bob Herring, Lance Kerwin, Diana Muldaur and Tom Sawyer, all magnificently talented and prolific individuals who know the industry inside out, for contributing their memories and experiences so kindly and generously for this book; Peter S. Fischer for sending me an autographed copy of his delicious and moving book *Me and Murder, She Wrote* which has so many tales and insights into the television industry; the witty and wonderful Michele Weiss for her generosity in sharing memories of her witty and wonderful mother, television writer Harriett Weiss; Jim Dykes and Alison Arngrim (Nellie Oleson of *Little House on the Prairie*) for kindly lending their advice; Wikipedia and the International Movie Database for so faithfully cataloguing the production credits for every television show and film known to man; the Movie Store for photos of television shows found in this book; Marianne Weldon for her assistance with photos of Ms. Powers; Eva Alfhild Jonsson for her assistance and generosity regarding photos of Ms. Muldaur; JoAnn Paul for her assistance with *Mannix* photos; and my beloved Maltipoo Scrappy who supervised the whole project from the vantage point of my lap.

Stefanie Powers: "I've always been more interested in the world around me than I have been in myself." Photo courtesy of the Movie Store.

Stefanie Powers Talks About HART TO HART and Her Experience in the Television Industry

*L*ovely Stefanie Powers, widely known as glamorous Jennifer Hart in Hart to Hart *and as* The Girl From U.N.C.L.E., *was born in Hollywood and is a graduate of Hollywood High. A trained dancer, she began her career in motion pictures as a teenager and has over 200 television appearances to her credit, along with numerous appearances on the British and U.S. stage and in film. Her decade-long relationship with actor William Holden led to her creation of the William Holden Wildlife Foundation in 1982 which offers conservation programs and education as a backup to the species conservation ongoing at the Mount Kenya Game Ranch in Africa. Among the many awards and honors she has received for her commitment to wildlife preservation and the humane treatment of animals are a Lowell Thomas Award by the venerable Explorers Club and a Fellowship to the Royal Geographic Society. She wrote the memoir* One from the Hart *and as a member of the Screen Writers' Guild of America, has written and produced several screenplays. Along with acting and animal preservation, she also recorded a CD with legendary jazz artist Page Cavanaugh and is an independent board member of three mutual funds. Currently she divides her time between Los Angeles, Kenya and London.*

Q. I wanted to start with how you got your start in the business and touch on something you've said in a number of interviews about feeling like your career might not have happened quite so accidentally if you were starting out today.

A. Well, the world was smaller in the days when I started. There were three television networks. There were major studios and there were very few independents—independent producers. Television was something that you didn't go on if you wanted a movie career. (*laughs*) And so when I actually was put under contract to a studio, I was exclusive to motion pictures and was not allowed to do television. After 15 films, three films a year for five years that I was under contract to Columbia, ironically, they sold my contract to MGM for me to be able to do a television series. It was called *The Girl From U.N.C.L.E.* and it was the first time a woman had ever been the lead in an hour-long television series.

This cover illustration from the February 1983 issue of Mike Shayne Mystery Magazine was clearly based on a photo of Stefanie Powers as The Girl From U.N.C.L.E. with co-star Noel Harrison in the background.

Q. I loved that show. I know you were very busy in TV in the 70's – all those great movies of the week. What was the atmosphere of TV like during that period?

A. Well, [in] the 70's, I did a lot of miniseries, a lot of episodics and things like that. But I was spending a great deal of time traveling around the world with William Holden. We spent most of the '70's together. He died in '81.

Q. I know you did Five Desperate Women and Sweet, Sweet Rachel.

A. Yes, all those. I did many, many miniseries to the point where I think I had done more miniseries than anybody at that time, starting with the first long form miniseries which was called *Washington Behind Closed Doors*, which was, I believe, 12 hours long. It was hugely popular – an internationally popular miniseries that was patterned after a book that Haldeman had written after the Nixon scandal about the CIA. It was called *The Company*.

Q. How long did it take to shoot a series like that?

A. Oh, quite a few months. Jason Robards played the President. Most of what I did was opposite Cliff Robertson who I knew very well. We had done three other movies together. He was under contract to Columbia and so was I. Of course, I was with Bill at the time and he had done *Picnic* with Bill. The biggest difference in then and now is that the corporations hadn't taken over the world. People who were the heads of studios actually knew how to make movies, because they weren't part of the corporate world, they weren't making corporate decisions based on safe ideas that were somebody else's first or a "branded" something that comes off a comic strip. They were moviemakers. Samuel Goldwyn would watch the rushes of every movie that was filming at his studio and if he didn't like the day's work, he would ask them to shoot it over and he knew every script that was going on. It was very different. Now they're corporations. They're run with business models. The biggest thing that changed was in the 1980's when all of these sort of geniuses popped out of business schools all around the world with the same kind of mantra that they were going to take over the world with business models that could be superimposed on any industry. It didn't matter if you were making widgets or you were making movies. You didn't have to know anything about the business you were in, all you had to do was know the business model.

Q. Okay.

A. That's the difference. That's the biggest difference that changed everything.

But also the population. Suddenly we were in a world where baby boomers were now hot on the scene. It was the largest generation in the world. We were fighting an unhappy war in Vietnam and there were social movements and all sorts of things that were changing in the world and the motion picture companies were breaking up as a result of the sanctions that were put on them in the late 1940's to divest all of their holdings, and television was becoming more of a force of nature. Television sets and technology had advanced to be able to have not only one, but two televisions in every household, so all those changes.

Plus, at the time there was some other little part of history that very few people will tell you about. Currency control was in effect all over the world. I remember being in Europe in the 1960's and into the 1970's where if you were an English person traveling abroad, you couldn't take more than 50 pounds in cash out of the country. When the movies would be distributed around the world, most of the money they earned in each country had to remain in that country. In the 1960's, Hollywood movies began to be made in Europe, using their frozen funds earned by movies they had distributed there. There were some great filmmakers in Europe and great technicians and so while television was taking a cut into the motion picture ticket sales, movies started to be made abroad. And that lasted all the way into the 1970's.

Q. Wow.

A.   Yes. So very interesting little sideline. I can't tell you how many people, even people who are old enough to have remembered, don't know that.

Q.   Did you often go on location to shoot some of the television movies? There were fabulous homes and estates in so many of them.

A.   Yes. In many instances, yes. It was too expensive to build a set, so when it was necessary, we'd shoot in actual locations or locations that would be dressed to be appropriate.

Q.   Okay. I wanted to talk about another of your mystery-oriented series before I get into Hart to Hart -- The Girl From U.N.C.L.E. What were the demands of doing the series as opposed to – say, the telemovie or movie of the week?

A.   Well, just to give you an idea of our shooting schedule with *Girl From U.N.C.L.E.,* we did 29 shows in one year – one TV year. Today they do, I believe, 22 maximum. Most of the time only about twelve and then, of course, all the series that are now on Showtime and Netflix and all that – I think they do eight or ten or something like that. They spend a great deal more per episode than even when we shot *Hart to Hart.* With *Hart to Hart,* we did 23 episodes a year. We worked nonstop, because in those days, the technology wasn't as great. We were still using big 35 mm cameras, the film was much slower when we were doing *The Girl From U.N.C.L.E.,* you needed more light to light the sets, and more people on the set to service the greater amount of equipment. We weren't quite as nimble as shooting became when the speed of the film changed and the lights were smaller and easier to manipulate.

So we would work 13-hour days, 14-hour days almost constantly and I remember one day shooting *The Girl From U.N.C.L.E.* where we had three location changes, location moves. We started on Lot 2 at MGM Studios. We then moved to Lot 3 which was about two miles down the road, then we moved back to the main lot, Lot 1, and we did 57 set-ups in one day. That means every time you move the camera, it's called a set up.

Q. **Oh, my goodness. My goodness.**

A.   And that was with all of our cumbersome equipment.

Stefanie Powers on the set of The Girl From U.N.C.L.E. with Man From U.N.C.L.E. star Robert Vaughn. The name April Dancer was suggested by James Bond creator Ian Fleming shortly before his death. Photo courtesy of Arena Productions and MGM Television.

Q. When you got Hart to Hart, what do you think made Hart to Hart such a success, in your opinion?

A. If I knew, I'd know the most valuable secret in the world. In hindsight, I hope it was chemistry. I think it was chemistry. It was like the perfect storm; a lot of good things came together at the same time and we were on for five years. By the time the fifth year was there, we were on our 4th group of writers. It was always more difficult to get that kind of humor because it was fast disappearing and it's almost completely disappeared at this moment. There are a couple of people who still have wit, but not very many.

Q. I totally agree with you. What was it like for you working as a producer on Hart to Hart for the TV movies as opposed to an actor?

A. Well, I was already working as a producer. In many cases when you see an actor go on as a producer, there's really a logical reason why. Because in the practical aspect of shooting the show, an involved actor – someone who is concerned about the production -- understands the restraints of filming and so becomes an asset to the production. By the time we were into our third year, Robert Wagner, who was already one of the producers, and I knew more about our characters and knew more about the framework of the show and what it should be than anyone. We read every first draft, we had script meetings and discussed production issues, so we were in effect very much hands on with the day-to-day production of the show.

Q. Is there any character you've played who was very similar to who you are? Did you work aspects of yourself into Hart to Hart?

A. Well, I hope and pray (*laughs*) that I am not an actor who looks at a role to find out what's similar about it to myself. Obviously, there are only so many situations an actor can find themselves in. They can play a role that is like themselves in a situation that's familiar to them. They can play a role that is not like themselves in a situation that is familiar to them. Or they can play a role that is not like themselves in a situation that is not familiar to them.

That is the most challenging for all actors and the one we hope to play most of all. That is the *ultimate* for all actors.

Q. Okay.

A.   Those are the most fun, those are the parts that we look for wherever we can. But there are certain things that prevent that from happening a great deal of the time, mainly, in many cases, decisions from the network. I remember when I was hired to play in a miniseries called *Mistral's Daughter* and the character I was playing was a French woman, so when I assumed an accent that would be accurately a French woman speaking in English, notes came back from the network saying, "Oh, she's speaking with an accent." And in that instance, my producer was wonderful and he went back to them and said, "Yes, it's appropriate." Because the boys in the suits at the networks were business men. They hadn't an artistic bone in their bodies.

I did have the same battle at CBS when I was one of the producers on a miniseries which I also helped to develop about the life of the aviatrix Beryl Markham who was the first person ever to fly west across the Atlantic. She grew up in Kenya. I was living in Kenya a great deal of the time and many people that I knew in Kenya had known her. I did a lot of research about her there and we put together actually a much more accurate portrayal of her than was in the book she wrote that contained embellishments from her husband who had been a screenwriter. The book was called *West with the Night*.

Q. I read that. And you also got your pilot's license. Is that true?

A.   A long time ago. I do some flying, but I always have a pilot in the other seat, so I don't screw up because I don't fly enough to be safe on my own. But I love flying.

Q. What's your philosophy of life, if you have one?

A.   I don't really have a philosophy. I don't really like to encapsulate things or institutionalize things. I suppose I derive a great deal of the way I conduct my life from things that I read, studied, the people I've known, the experiences I've had. I grew up with an insatiable curiosity and I've always been more interested in the world around me than I have been in myself. I have really never put myself in front of an issue or in front of most of the things in life. My primary concerns when I wake up in the morning are other things —my dogs, other people, other obligations. So I suppose I have to practice at being more self-centered.

Q. I know you do a lot of work with the William Holden Wildlife Foundation.

A. Well, I created it.

Q. And you're operating it.

A. Yes. I'm the chief fund raiser and on the ground, I create the programs and institute them. I direct most everything because it was, in fact, my baby. But I would like to see the baby walk on its own, because one day I might not be there to pick it up if it falls.

Q. What do you look for now when you're choosing a project as an actor?

A. Well, I obviously look for something that's going to stretch me. The place where I find that is usually in the theater. I have the great joy of working consistently in England in the theater. And that door opened to me some years ago and I kept my foot in that door. I kept my boot in that door, because I certainly didn't want it to close. Last year I did a play called *84 Charing Cross Road* which we're hoping to bring to the West End.

Q. Let's get back to Hart to Hart.

A. Okay. Let me say something about the construction of *Hart to Hart*. Unlike most mysteries, what made it very difficult to write *Hart to Hart* was the fact that we had to maintain the thing we did best and what created the environment where we could do that was the construction of the stories.

Accidents had to happen to us, so that we were reactive more than proactive. Because that's not what the Harts were. They weren't detectives. They wound up being detectives because of incidents that happened to them and as long as that was put into that perspective, we could have the sort of life that we had, we could have the rapport that we had, we could have the frivolity and the fun and the romance and still solve the crime. So the ideal template for the ideal show would be given to some of the writers at the beginning of the season and usually it was Tom Mankiewicz who really took the material that he was given and created *Hart to Hart* from something that Sidney Sheldon had written called *Double Switch* which was sold to Aaron Spelling. Mankiewicz made it into Jonathan and Jennifer and the dog and Max and what we became. Mank always kept an eagle eye out for us and even when he moved on to direct movies, he would come back to have the pep talk with the new writers. He would tell the writers that the ideal template for a show was: Jonathan and Jennifer emerge from a lovely restaurant in New York City dressed in evening clothes. Max is at the curb, opening the door to their car. Jennifer says to Jonathan, "Oh, darling, it's such a beautiful night out. Why don't we take a walk through the park?" Jonathan says, "Right. Max, meet us on the other side of 67th Street, blah, blah, blah." We start walking through the park, it's a beautiful evening, we stop to kiss underneath a tree and Bingo! – a dead body falls out of the tree. Jonathan bends down to see if the man is alive and the flashlights go on – it's the police. "You're arrested for the murder of this man." That's an ideal set-up for Jonathan and Jennifer and you can see it, can't you?

Q. Yes.

A.   And that's what made that show different in the scheme of mysteries because they weren't straight-forward sleuths. Everything happened to them, so that they became personally involved.

Powers with her co-star Robert Wagner in Hart to Hart, a glamorous and gorgeous power couple. Photo courtesy of Rona II, Spelling-Goldberg Productions, and Columbia Pictures Television.

Q. Did you ever get involved in the writing of any scripts, putting your input in?

A. We had different concept ideas for stories that we would discuss with the producers. Some of them were taken and absorbed, but during the development period when we were on hiatus from *Hart to Hart*, both R.J. and myself were involved in other productions. At the time that we were informed that we were not being picked up for the next season, I was in Paris filming a miniseries called *Mistral's Daughter*. Knowing that I was going to be in Paris, the *Hart to Hart* team, R.J. and myself had discussed two story concepts to be filmed in Paris at the beginning of the next season. But sadly, on that fateful Sunday night, I received a phone call from Mr. Spelling, Mr. Goldberg and R.J. to tell us we were not picked up for the next season, so our story ideas were obviously not made.

Q. And then you came back to the States.

A. Well, when I finished *Mistral's Daughter*, I went to London because I always spent a great deal of time in London. I didn't really have to go back to L.A. I was going to eventually go to Kenya. So while I was in London, I was having lunch at the House of Lords with a very dear friend of mine, Lord Buxton who started Anglia Television (ITV Anglia). As we were having lunch in this very private and exclusive luncheon area just for the Lords and their guests, in walks an ensemble of people which included Aaron Spelling and his wife. For a start, it was bizarre to see them in those circumstances because Aaron never traveled and didn't fly, so they had made this incredible journey by boat and by train to come to England. It was highly unusual to see them out of the United States, let alone California. I walked over to them. They obviously didn't see me. I tapped on Aaron's shoulder and said (*lowers voice*), "I didn't know they allowed Hollywood people in here" and of course, his jaw just fell to the floor, because they had pulled so many strings -- every string that they could -- to get into that exclusive domain so they were shocked to see *me* there and then Aaron said, "Well, this is our last night here. We're having a party. You must come." I went to the party that he was having. He told me, "I'm doing a project. It's a Jackie Collins book, *Hollywood Wives* and I've got a part in there for you. You've got to do it." And that's how I got the role of Montana Gray. Interesting how life is.

Made-for-Television Movies

Roger Moore as Sherlock Holmes and Patrick Macnee as Dr. Watson in Sherlock Holmes in New York (1976). Photo courtesy of 20th Century Fox Television.

Adventures of Nick Carter (1972) 73 min.; Network: ABC; D: Paul Krasny; Universal Television; Release Date: February 20, 1972; Stars: Robert Conrad; Shelley Winters, Broderick Crawford, Neville Brand, Pernell Roberts, Pat O'Brien, Sean Garrison, Laraine Stephens, Dean Stockwell, Brooke Bundy, Jaye P. Morgan, Sorrell Booke, Ned Glass, Paul Mantee.

One of three pilots that were introduced for a proposed revolving or "wheel" series called *The Great Detectives,* each featuring great detectives of literature, this telemovie involved adventurer Nick Carter (Robert Conrad) who was created in Street & Smith private detective dime novels by John Russell Coryell in 1886. Carter first appeared in *New York Weekly* in a 13-week serial and had several other incarnations, including in radio. This sets the story in New York City circa the early 1900's and Conrad plays him tough, a product of the Tenderloin. As was par for "period" television shows or movies in the 70's, the production is filled with colorful and broadly drawn characters. Everything and everyone looks right out of Central Casting or the backlot and a world of early New York with horse-drawn carriages, steam engines and the Hippodrome is faithfully recreated. Carter's colleague is murdered and during the investigation he undertakes with his pretty assistant Roxy O'Rourke (Brooke Bundy), he discovers the murder was tied in with a wealthy playboy Freddy Duncan's missing wife Ivy. Wild-eyed Dean Stockwell plays the squirrely and arrogant Duncan who doesn't seem to care about Ivy, although his father Otis Duncan (Broderick Crawford), a robber baron, wants to see the culprit hanged and feels she was worth more than all of them. Meanwhile Carter recognizes one of Ivy's earrings on Bess Tucker (Shelley Winters), the proprietress of a nightclub and brothel of sorts and determines to find out what happened. His sleuthing takes him through the high and low points of society and various facets of early New York, including a hotel run by Chinese tongs. Like Sherlock Holmes, he dons several disguises. He also gets into plenty of fist fights and altercations. (Stunts were performed by veteran stuntman Bob Herron – see "Memories of Those Who Were There.") This is a fine production with some twists and turns, if an unremarkable mystery, and should have been successful, but the series unfortunately never was picked up. Interestingly, Chicago-born Conrad's Chicago accent is clearly discernible here.

Along Came a Spider (**1970**) 75 min.; Network: ABC; D: Lee H. Katzin; 20th Century Fox Television; Release Date: February 3, 1970; Stars: Suzanne Pleshette, Ed Nelson, Andrew Prine, Brooke Bundy, Richard Anderson, Wright King, Barry Atwater, Milton Selzer, Frank Ferguson, Virginia Gregg, Joe E. Tata.

Based upon the play *Sweet Poison* by Leonard Lee, this mystery/drama stars the very beautiful and talented Suzanne Pleshette as Janet Furie, the widow of a research scientist who assumes a fake identity to get close to Dr. Martin Becker (Ed Nelson), the professor she holds responsible for her husband's death. Although it was allegedly an accidental death during a high-risk experiment, Janet believes it was murder. Under her alias as Anne Banning, student, Janet hatches her devious plan, first becoming romantically involved with Martin and then disappearing and setting the scene to implicate Martin in Anne's "murder." She resurfaces again as a blonde to assume her old life. But was Martin really responsible? This is a competent and involving story that keeps one guessing with solid acting by Pleshette. Aside from Pleshette, the great and ubiquitous character actor Milton Selzer is also a welcome presence as Dr. Leonard Schuster. Dig Pleshette's kicky bright red vinyl coat (very 60's), the hair flips and ponchos. There is also ample evidence of the hippie culture on the college campus and beach.

Bad Ronald (**1974**) 74 min.; Network: ABC; D: Buzz Kulik; Lorimar Productions; Release Date: October 23, 1974; Stars: Scott Jacoby, Pippa Scott, John Larch, Dabney Coleman, Kim Hunter, John Fiedler, Linda Watkins, Cindy Fisher, Cindy Eilbacher, Lisa Eilbacher, Ted Eccles, Roger Aaron Brown, Aneta Corsaut, Angela Hoffman, Karen Purcil, Shelley Spurlock, Lesley Woods.

Scott Jacoby plays the ultimate outcast in this thriller and horror film about an unpopular and bullied teenage boy, Ronald Wilby, who accidentally kills a girl who was taunting him. When he tells his mother (Kim Hunter), she insists that he go into hiding and keeps him hidden behind a wall over the bathroom in their Victorian house. The ghoulish part comes when his mother dies and he remains hidden inside the house when the new family moves in with three comely teenage girls (two of whom are the Eilbacher sisters, Cindy and Lisa, fixtures in 70's TV, playing Althea and Ellen). Meanwhile Ronald has taken a fancy to the eldest girl, Babs (Cindy Fisher), even as he is going increasingly mad. There were a few movies that touched on the idea of people living inside crawlspaces, which is always an unsettling concept, and this one has its share of creepiness. The jolting scene when Babs discovers one of the holes Ronald has drilled in the wall and finds his dark eye watching her is actually reminiscent of Hitchcock's *Psycho* (1960) when proprietor Norman Bates (Anthony Perkins) watches Marion Crane (Janet Leigh) undress through a peephole into her room at the Bates motel. Ronald naturally has to come out to raid the refrigerator, although he doesn't bother to bathe, and the Wood girls fear there are ghosts in the house. Meanwhile there is a very nosy neighbor, Mrs. Schumacher (Linda Watkins) who suspects something is up. Things are not going to go well. Although *Bad Ronald* has to end quickly to accommodate its short running time, it is distinguished by fine acting from Jacoby and Hunter. Jacoby had been nominated for a Tony Award at age twelve for the Broadway musical *Golden Rainbow* and won an Emmy Award for his role in the 1972 made-for-television film *That Certain Summer*.

Baffled (**1973**) 90 min.; Network: NBC; D: Philip Leacock; ITC Productions; Release Date: January 30, 1973; Stars: Leonard Nimoy, Susan Hampshire, Rachel Roberts, Vera Miles, Jewel Blanch, Valerie Taylor, Ray Brooks, Angharad Rees, Christopher Benjamin, Mike Murray, Ewan Roberts, Milton Johns, Al Mancini, Patsy Smart.

Baffled is another of my top favorite telemovies of the 70's with two wonderful stars, lovely Susan Hampshire (who has a doppelganger in Sandra Bullock) and Leonard Nimoy. It's a fascinating cast and story involving mystery and the occult with high production values and wonderful on-location shots of London and the British countryside. Intended as a series which never materialized, it has more of a feature film feeling, aside from the opening credits which spell series, and pleasantly recalls the old-fashioned mysteries from the Disney studio at its height. It had been released theatrically, in fact, before premiering on American television. When race car driver Tom Kovack (Leonard Nimoy) reveals on television that a psychic vision caused him to lose control of his vehicle during a competition, he receives a visit from pretty Michele Brent (Susan Hampshire), an expert on the occult and psychic phenomena. She encourages him to follow up on his vision of a manor house in England and the phrase "Wyndham in Devon." After sketching the house, Kovack discovers there is an actual place in Britain called Wyndham in Devon which has rooms available during the tourist season. He and Brent travel to England to stay there where they encounter movie star Andrea Glenn (Vera Miles) and her daughter Jennifer (Jewel Blanch). Kovack recognizes Jennifer as the girl in his vision. Andrea is hoping for a reconciliation with her estranged husband who lives in a nearby village and Jennifer desperately misses her father. Something strange is going on at Wyndham, however. Jennifer's personality suddenly changes; she begins acting sophisticated and hostile to her mother. Meanwhile the landlady Mrs. Farraday (Rachel Roberts) seems to be getting younger every day. Hampshire and Nimoy make a fun and likeable pair of sleuths with believable romantic chemistry and Roberts is wonderfully sinister. Blanch who resembles Marcia Mae Jones (Clara in Shirley Temple's *Heidi* (1937)) has the ability to play sweet and sneeringly nasty like Ann Blyth in *Mildred Pierce* (1945). She is perhaps best-remembered for a *Night Gallery* segment called "The Doll." Although *Baffled* unfortunately never developed into a series, it remains a solidly entertaining and absorbing standalone mystery.

5

The Cat Creature (1973) 72 min.; Network: ABC; D: Curtis Harrington; Douglas S. Cramer Company; Release Date: December 11, 1973; Stars: Meredith Baxter, David Hedison, Gale Sondergaard, Keye Luke, John Carradine, Renne Jarrett, Stuart Whitman, Kent Smith, Virgil Frye, William Sims, John Abbott and Peter Lorre, Jr.

The Cat Creature is a tribute to the Val Lewton films of the 40's and the feeling of the 40's permeates it visually. It also features some delicious supporting players from Old Hollywood who make it special, along with high production values. Scripted by Robert Bloch of *Psycho* fame, it opens with appraiser Frank Lucas (Kent Smith of the original "Cat People" films) cataloguing a private collection of Egyptian antiquities in the dead of night and discovering a sarcophagus in the basement (where else?) that holds a mummy wearing an amulet. The amulet is a solid gold cat's head with emerald eyes (Looks more like something found in a cereal box, but that's part of the fun of made-for-television). Smith is the first to die. A thief Joe Sung (Keye Luke, "Number One Son" from the old *Charlie Chan* series) steals the amulet and tries to pawn it at The Sorcerer's Shop, which specializes in the occult, but the proprietress Hester Black (the divine Gale Sondergaard) throws him out. Meanwhile Lt. Marco (Stuart Whitman) is investigating the murder with the expert advice of Roger Edmonds (David Hedison), a professor who specializes in archeology. The theft of the amulet sets off a murderous chain of events involving Black, Lt. Marco, Edmonds, Sung, a salesgirl Rena Carter (a young and fresh Meredith Baxter) and a black cat with glowing eyes. *The Cat Creature* has some quirky features like a colorfully-dressed prostitute dwarf named Mabel who propositions Lt. Marco. Dwarves were a staple in 70's television and movies. The gleaming white Nouveau exterior of the building in which Carter lives is shot at night at a distorted angle, making it very impressive indeed, like the Dakota in the opening credits of *Rosemary's Baby* (1968), and there is nice cinematography throughout. Best of all are the wonderful mystery film veterans like Sondergaard (so memorable as the mysterious Spider Woman in the Sherlock Holmes entry of the same name), John Carradine, Keye Luke and Kent Smith. They give this telefilm a unique touch of presence and class.

A Cold Night's Death (1973) 74 min.; Network: ABC; D: Jerrold Freedman; Spelling-Goldberg Productions; Release Date: January 30, 1973; Stars: Robert Culp, Eli Wallach, Michael C. Gwynne.

This tense, claustrophobic sci fi mystery is set in an isolated arctic research lab, Tower Mountain Research Station, and involves two scientists, Robert Jones (Robert Culp) and Frank Enari (Eli Wallach) who are sent to investigate when radio transmissions from the lab stop. Dr. Vogel's communications were growing increasingly irrational until snowstorms caused the base to lose contact altogether. Upon arriving at Tower Mountain, the two men discover Vogel frozen to the radio and the lab in disarray. The monkeys who are used in altitude experiments are barely alive and it's assumed that Vogel lost his mind and allowed everything to atrophy. But as Jones and Enari set out salvaging the base and continuing on with the work, they begin to experience the same sense of paranoia that afflicted Vogel and realize that something terribly wrong is going on there. One of the astounding things about this telefilm is how effectively arctic conditions are captured, since the actual filming was done in California. The snow and chill factors are palpable and it's never less than believable that the setting is an arctic wasteland. Although *A Cold's Night Death* offers a tour de force opportunity for the two leads who are the entire show, the script is relatively thin and not quite as effective as a *Twilight Zone* story which it resembles. Without much action beyond the growing paranoia of the men and the increasing agitation of the primates, the interest becomes as strained as the nerves of the two protagonists. The story might pose as a meditation on scientists being tricked up by their own experiments and the perils of isolation, but it is essentially a one-trick pony. What happened to Dr. Vogel becomes clear fairly quickly and the idea isn't a new one. Although not an exciting exercise to my mind, *A Cold*

Night's Death remains well-regarded and may be just the thing to watch on a sweltering summer night.

Crowhaven Farm (1970) 74 min.; Network: ABC; D: Walter Grauman; Aaron Spelling Productions; Release Date: November 24, 1970; Stars: Hope Lange, Paul Burke, Lloyd Bochner, John Carradine, Cindy Eilbacher, Cyril Delevanti, Milton Selzer, Patricia Barry, Woodrow Parfrey, June Dayton, Virginia Gregg, Louise Troy, Pitt Herbert, Ross Elliott, Dennis Cross, William Smith.

One of the most unsettling and justly well-remembered offerings from ABC's Movie of the Week, *Crowhaven Farm* is also one of the best supernatural thrillers ever made about witchcraft in New England. Clearly it is heavily influenced by *Rosemary's Baby*, which came out two years prior in 1968, many of the characters and situations running parallel, but it has its own distinction and merit. Maggie Porter (Hope Lange) and her husband Ben (Paul Burke) inherit a farm in Brampton, Massachusetts after Maggie's uncle dies in a car crash. He actually encounters a strange, little, blonde girl (Cindy Eilbacher) on the road whose abrupt appearance causes the crash (she will enter the plot again later). Immediately Maggie feels a disturbing sense of déjà vu and foreboding and wants to leave Crowhaven Farm, but Ben, an artist, begs her to stay. Their marriage has been troubled by Ben's jealousy and their inability to have a child and Ben feels farm life will heal them. Maggie is soon beset by visions involving bonneted Pilgrims and stones and strange rituals and begins to believe she is a reincarnated witch. Harold Dane (Cyril Delevanti), the local historian (evoking "Hutch" from *Rosemary's Baby*), explains that the house dates from the Puritan era and tells of the area's witchy past involving targeted females being crushed by stones placed over a wooden panel. This is in line with Maggie's visions. When the Porters take in a little blonde girl named Jennifer after her aunt dies, she proves disturbingly precocious beyond her years despite her angelic looks. She is actually the child who caused Maggie's uncle to fatally crash on the road. As in *Rosemary's Baby*, no one is who they seem to be and at this time Maggie learns she is pregnant. Something wicked this way has come. *Crowhaven Farm* is a well-crafted tale of witchery, certainly one of the best telefilms created by Spelling/Goldberg Productions, with a super cast. There's wonderful atmosphere created throughout from the bucolic and sinister stillness of the farm to the shadows of branches waving across the bed at night and the evil undercurrents of a beautiful child. It evokes things that go bump in the night.

Curse of the Black Widow (1977) 97 min.; Network: ABC; D: Dan Curtis; Dan Curtis Productions; Release Date: September 16, 1977; Stars: Patty Duke Astin, Tony Franciosa, Donna Mills, June Lockhart, June Allyson, Max Gail, Jeff Corey, Roz Kelly, Sid Caesar, Vic Morrow, Michael DeLano, Robert Burton, Bryan O'Byrne, Tracy Curtis, Irene Forest, Bruce French, Mari Gorman, Elizabeth Grey, H.B. Haggerty, Crofton Hardester, Howard Honig, Rosanna Locke, Robert Nadder.

Valerie Steffan, a mysterious dark-haired woman with a phony European accent, walks into a bar and asks a man, Frank Chadham to help her with her car. He winds up being killed in the deserted parking lot as she morphs into something monstrous. Pretty blonde Leigh Lockwood (Donna Mills with "Farrah Fawcett" feathered hair) then shows up in the office of private eye Mark Higbie (Tony Franciosa) and hires him to find out who killed her fiancé Chadham. Higbie learns that Los Angeles has been plagued by similar killings the past few years which all had gruesome features in common: the victims, mostly men, had their bodily fluids sucked out of them and were found encased in a silken cocoon. What's more they all had connections to Leigh Lockwood. These details were covered up because the investigating officer didn't want word on the street that the city was being terrorized by a giant spider. *Curse of the Black Widow* is a cross between a silly B-movie creature feature and a traditional detective series and is quite entertaining with good production values. It's set in Los Angeles, but many of the bit players are doing "Guys and Dolls" accents. Leigh has a fraternal twin Laura played by the late, great Patty Duke. Bespectacled and wearing a tight bun, Duke is the opposite of her blonde, blue-eyed sister. She is restrained and bookish like Bette Davis in the beginning of *Now Voyager*, but she pulls out all the camp stops later when she metamorphoses into her alter identity Valerie Steffan (and we wouldn't have it any other way). It's not a spoiler to reveal that she is Valerie Steffan, since anyone can recognize Duke's features through the get up from the word go, except apparently her own family members. The same music from *Ellery Queen: Don't Look Behind You* (1971) is used here and gymnasts, tigers, and prostitutes in hot pants all make appearances. Roz Kelly, doing her usual broad tough girl shtick, appears as Flaps, Higbie's secretary. Campy fun.

The Dead Don't Die (1975) 90 min.; Network: NBC: D: Curtis Harrington; Douglas S. Cramer Company; Release Date: January 14, 1975. Stars: George Hamilton, Ray Milland, Reggie Nalder, Jerry Douglas, Linda Cristal, Joan Blondell, Ralph Meeker, James McEachin, William O'Connell, Yvette Vickers, Milton Parsons, Brendon Dillon, Russ Grieves, Bill Smillie.

This is a wonderful and imaginative blend of neo-noir and horror from the same team who collaborated on *The Cat Creature* – director Curtis Harrington and writer Robert Bloch. Set in the 1930's in Illinois and recalling Val Lewton once again, it contains many fine period details from the elegant, splashy titles (reminiscent of 1974's *Chinatown*) and Deco furniture to the Packard cars and cloche hats. A sailor Don Drake (George Hamilton) goes to see his brother Ralph (Jerry Douglas) who is on death row for murdering his wife, convinced Ralph was wrongly convicted. Don's investigation leads him to the eerie Loveland Ballroom in Chicago, the scene of the crime, where Ralph had once danced in one of the grueling marathons run by cheap dance hall promoter Jim Moss (Ray Milland), and further encounters with a mysterious woman in a veiled hat who had been at Ralph's funeral. The woman, Vera LaValle (Linda Cristal) warns him to "leave Chicago now" or risk retribution, adding that trouble will come if "he knows you're here." When Don asks who "he" is, he spies his brother standing in the shadows and takes after him against Vera's objections. He winds up killing a creepy man named Perdido (the fabulous Reggie Nalder) and entrenched in the realm of the occult. This is a delicious macabre entertainment with good cinematography and production values, arguably more fully realized than *The Cat Creature*. Like *The Godfather* (1972), scenes are shot deliberately dark for an "endless night" or nightmare effect. Sometimes it's so dark, it's as if characters are walking through a pitch-black funhouse. Nalder of the strange, pockmarked face (memorable as the assassin in *The Man Who Knew Too Much* (1956)) is used to great effect here as a zombie, possibly inspiring 1979's *Phantasm* and has some truly hair-raising and iconic scenes. Hamilton makes a slightly bland lead, but his matinee good looks befit the Old Hollywood evocation. A mystery in the true sense of the word with great character actors and a nifty ending.

Dear Detective (1979) 120 min.; Network: CBS: D: Dean Hargrove; Roland Kibbee & Dean Hargrove Production in association with Viacom; Release Date: March 28, 1979. Stars: Brenda Vaccaro, Arlen Dean Snyder, Jack Ging, M. Emmet Walsh, Michael MacRae, Jet Yardum, Corinne Conley, Lesley Woods, Ron Silver, John Dennis Johnston.

This pilot for a cozy television series that never came to pass starred the delightful, gravel-voiced Brenda Vaccaro as Kate Hudson, a single mother and divorcee who is also a sergeant with the Los Angeles Police Department. It was based on a 1977 French film *Dear Inspector* starring Annie Giardot which featured a female police inspector who like Kate Hudson, meets her new romance, a professor of Greek, by bumping his bike with her car — thus, a similar meeting in *Dear Detective*'s pilot. Although a female detective was still an anomaly in the 70's, *Dear Detective* didn't go the way of England's *Prime Suspect* in dealing with the sexism Hudson faced, but rather took a witty, light-hearted approach that focused on Vaccaro's charm and likeability and personal life. It also showed her one step ahead of her male colleagues and enjoying a good working relationship with them. Her relationship with her fourth grader daughter Lisa (Jet Yardum) is positive and her collision with Professor Richard Weyland (Arlen Dean Snyder) results in him becoming a promising new boyfriend with his own knack for mystery. The pilot involves a serial killer stabbing local officials in the middle of a crowd with an ice pick without being observed, a feat that remains never properly explained. Not enough focus is given to the mystery; however, Vaccaro is the show and she is feisty, funny, human and imminently watchable, as she always is. It is a pity the show only lasted for three episodes without being picked up.

Death at Love House (1976) 74 min.; Network: ABC; D: E.W. Swack-hamer; Spelling-Goldberg Productions; Release Date: September 3, 1976; Stars: Robert Wagner, Kate Jackson, Sylvia Sidney, Mariana Hill, Joan Blondell, John Carradine, Dorothy Lamour, Bill Macy, Joseph Bernard, John A. Zee, Robert Gibbons, Al Hansen, Crofton Hardester.

This bewitching and intriguing ghost story and mystery was set at Harold Lloyd's Greenacre Estates, one of those palatial and elegant homes from Hollywood's heyday, and recalls both *Sunset Boulevard* (1950) and *Laura* (1944), although it is distinctly made-for-TV fare with the supernatural bend that was a staple in 70's telefilms. Joel and Donna Gregory (Robert Wagner and Kate Jackson) are a married couple who come to Love House, the home of Lorna Love, a silent film goddess, to write a novel about her. Joel's father had been romantically involved with Love and painted a portrait of her that hangs in the house. No sooner have the couple settled in, then strange and disturbing things begin to happen. Joel becomes entranced by Lorna who haunts his dreams, drawn to her portrait, while a malevolent figure seems intent on harming Donna who is pregnant. As they interview those who knew the beautiful Lorna, many describe her as a witch and there are indications in the house, including a black cat, that Lorna was into witchcraft. This is a beguiling and eerie film with fun guest appearances by Joan Blondell, John Carradine and Dorothy Lamour who all enjoy themselves chewing the scenery and lending that touch of Old Hollywood. The beautiful Marianna Hill who plays Lorna Love in flashbacks has an entrancing quality that makes her ability to put a spell on people believable, but the clips that are allegedly Lorna's silent films lose credibility, because they so clearly are filmed in the 70's, not the 20's. Hill looks and is styled more like Sharon Tate than any star from the 20's. Still, this is a fun ghost story and mystery with a wonderful waltz by Laurence Rosenthal that is used very effectively, gothic and decadent Old Hollywood glamour, a fine performance from Jackson, and a few twists along the way. Good popcorn fun.

Death Cruise (1974) 74 min.; Network: ABC; D: Ralph Senensky; Spelling-Goldberg Productions; Release Date: October 30, 1974; Stars: Richard Long, Polly Bergen, Kate Jackson, Edward Albert, Tom Bosley, Celeste Holm, Michael Constantine, Cesare Danova, Amzie Strickland, Alain Patrick, Maurice Sherbanee, West Gale, Marc De Vries.

This fun, lightweight murder mystery is set aboard a cruise liner as three couples win a free Caribbean cruise from "E&M Promotions" without having entered a contest. Shortly they begin to understand that they were lured on board to be murdered one by one. It's Agatha Christie meets *The Love Boat*. The mystery is well-paced and well-done, compact yet taking its time and refreshingly free of quick cuts that have become a staple in contemporary films. Each couple has a fractured marriage despite their initially cheery exteriors. The three couples consist of Jerry and Sylvia Carter (Richard Long and Polly Bergen) whose marriage is troubled by Jerry's philandering; James and Mary Francis Radneys (Edward Albert and Kate Jackson) who aren't on the same page about having a baby; and David and Elizabeth Mason (Tom Bosley and Celeste Holm) whose relationship feels empty now that the nest is. The astute ship doctor, Dr. Burke (Michael Constantine) becomes amateur detective as the body count wracks up. Before disappearing overboard, Jerry sensed that he had met the group before and it was connected to Atlanta in 1970. The twist-upon-a-twist solution might be right out of Dame Christie, but it's orchestrated well. The exteriors of the ship are the Queen Mary, but the spacious interiors look like no cruise cabins I've ever seen. Also skeet shooting, which occurs in this telefilm, is no longer allowed on cruise ships. This pleasant whodunit would be Richard Long's last film before he died several months later at age 46 from multiple heart attacks.

Do Not Fold, Spindle or Mutilate (1971) 73 min.; Network: ABC; D: Ted Post; Samuel Goldwyn Studios; Release Date: November 9, 1971; Stars: Helen Hayes, Vince Edwards, Myrna Loy, Mildred Natwick, Sylvia Sidney, John Beradino, Larry D. Mann, Barbara Davis, Paul Smith, Gary Vinson, Diane Shalet.

Based on a novel by Doris Miles Disney, *Do Not Fold, Spindle or Mutilate* involves an elderly foursome in Pasadena, spearheaded by Sophie Tate Curtis (Helen Hayes), who invent a fictional girl and put an ad in a computer dating service. The problem comes when the ad attracts the dangerously imbalanced Mal Weston (Vince Edwards). An ABC Movie-of-the-Week offering, the telefilm is surprisingly entertaining, due to solid performances by all involved and a good mix of the genuinely frightening with humor in the vein of *Arsenic and Old Lace* (1944). The four leads are all stalwarts and fun to watch: Hayes who received an Emmy nomination; Myrna Loy as her sister Evelyn; Sylvia Sidney as Elizabeth Gibson; and Mildred Natwick as Shelby Saunders. Aside from the computer itself and the stigma then attached to computer dating, the premise of an ad attracting a weirdo certainly hasn't outdated. Edwards is creepy as the murderous date and Beradino of *General Hospital* fame is very good as Detective Hallum, limited as his screen time might be. The four ladies, however, all Hollywood legends, are the show. This well-done comedy mystery was followed by the short-lived TV series *The Snoop Sisters* starring Hayes and Natwick, which unfortunately wasn't as fun as it sounded on paper, in spite of a great cast. The formula of an older female sleuth would be perfected with Angela Lansbury in *Murder She Wrote*.

Dracula (1974) 98 min.; Network: CBS; D: Dan Curtis; Latglen Ltd.; Release Date: February 8, 1974; Stars: Jack Palance, Simon Ward, Nigel Davenport, Pamela Brown, Fiona Lewis, Penelope Horner, Murray Brown, Virginia Wetherell, Barbara Lindley, Sarah Douglas, George Pravda, Hana Maria Pravda.

Filmed in Croatia, England and Yugoslavia, Dan Curtis' adaptation of Bram Stoker's novel, possibly the greatest vampire story ever written, is beautifully mounted and produced, but tells a version more in line with Hammer's 1958 film or Curtis' TV series *Dark Shadows*. The many adaptations of the novel often try to make allegories to the hypnotic nature of love, turning Dracula's exploits into "bad romances," which was not a theme of the original novel. Dracula's past romances were not focused on in the book nor did Sherlock Holmes have a romance with Irene Adler, but most adaptations embellish this aspect. The opening of Curtis' *Dracula* is dynamic and phenomenal, as are the shots of Dracula descending a stone stairway with many archways, capturing a flavor of rural and Medieval Europe. Jack Palance makes his Dracula much more viperlike than many past actors, which is one of the strengths of this production. Like Barnabas Collins and Maggie Evans in *Dark Shadows*, however, Curtis attributes Dracula's obsession with Lucy to her resemblance with one of his past loves. Other touches like music boxes and a vampire pausing with opened mouth to display his fangs before striking are pure Curtis. The scene of the vampire Lucy scratching at the window came from Hammer's 1958 film; this particular scene was also duplicated in the novel *Salem's Lot* by Stephen King and the TV miniseries version of it, but it remains its most shocking in the Hammer film. Also German shepherds were substituted for real wolves here, as they often are, as if viewers can't tell the difference. The classic story involves a solicitor who comes to Transylvania to show Count Dracula some properties, setting off a chain of unspeakable evil. This version penned by Richard Matheson is entertaining with a surprisingly erotic and sensual initial encounter between Dracula and Lucy (sans nudity, of course), but the definitive version remains the superb BBC 1977 version with Louis Jourdan which was meticulously faithful to the book.

Duel (1973) 90 min.; Network: ABC; D: Steven Spielberg; Universal Television; Release Date: November 13, 1971; Stars: Dennis Weaver, Jacqueline Scott, Eddie Firestone, Lou Frizzell, Gene Dynarski, Lucille Benson, Tim Herbert, Charles Seel, Shirley O'Hara, Alexander Lockwood, Amy Douglass, Dick Whittington.

Duel is a made-for-television masterwork and highly influential modern classic penned by Richard Matheson and based on his 1971 short story of the same name which originally appeared in *Playboy*. He considered it to be the ultimate embodiment of his leitmotif "the individual isolated in a threatening world, attempting to survive." The telefilm was also a young Steven Spielberg's first full-length directorial job. The plot is simple and straightforward with numerous allegorical implications. A traveling electronics salesman David Mann (Dennis Weaver) is pursued and terrorized on a lonely stretch of California highway by a malevolent and massive, fume-belching gasoline tanker whose driver is never seen. The unstoppable truck takes on a demonic life of its own and a cat and mouse "duel" of excess road rage ensues, a battle that becomes almost mythic. According to Spielberg, the grimy Peterbilt truck was chosen because it appeared to have a face with the headlights like two big eyes and the grill like teeth. The threatening word "flammable" is written on it. *Duel* is a lean, but powerful expression of man against the unknown; it also has themes of "Mann's" need to prove his masculinity. Although it brings to mind a fabulous *Twilight Zone* episode, it's also reminiscent of the great short stories of the past, such as *Leiningen vs. the Ants* and *Valley of the Beasts.* Above average.

Dying Room Only (1973) 74 min.; Network: ABC; D: Philip Leacock; Lorimar Film Entertainment; Release Date: September 18, 1973; Stars: Cloris Leachman, Ross Martin, Ned Beatty, Dana Elcar, Louise Latham, Dabney Coleman, Ron Feinberg.

On a level with the highly-acclaimed *Duel,* which also had a teleplay by Richard Matheson, *Dying Room Only* is top notch suspense, a cut above many of the television productions of the era. Like *Duel,* the plot is fairly simple and straightforward. While traveling through the Arizona desert and getting off course, Bob and Jean Mitchell (Dabney Coleman and Cloris Leachman) stop to use the rest room at a roadside diner. Bob disappears. What results is nail-biting tension that continues to ratchet as Jean tries to find him. A similar plot would later be used in the terrifying Dutch-French 1988 film *The Vanishing* and in its 1993 American remake of the same name with Jeff Bridges. In *Dying Room Only,* Jean's problems are compounded when the surly locals at the diner and nearby motel don't seem to care and even worse, her car is driven away. The local police also have trouble believing her. What makes this telemovie so effective and frightening is that it's entirely plausible. It taps into the scary reality of the vulnerability of travelers in unknown places. There is also the extraordinary and versatile Cloris Leachman who could carry the film single-handedly if she had to; she never plays dumb and her actions are believable. Above average and at times genuinely hair-raising.

Ellery Queen: Don't Look Behind You (1971) 95 min.; Network: NBC;

D: Barry Shear; P: Leonard J. Ackerman and Edward J. Montagne; Universal Television; Release Date: November 19, 1971; Stars: Peter Lawford, Harry Morgan, E.J. Marshall, Stefanie Powers, Skye Aubrey, Coleen Gray, Morgan Sterne, Bill Zuckert.

This was a precursor to the superb Ellery Queen TV series of the 1970's (see The Television Series). Based on the novel *Cat of Many Tales* by Ellery Queen (pseudonym for Brooklyn cousins Frederic Dannay and Manfred Bennington Lee), the film finds noted criminologist and mystery writer Ellery Queen investigating a serial killer known as the Hydra who is terrorizing New York City. He or she strangles males with blue cords and females with pink ones and seems to be dispatching victims by descending age. The telemovie is greatly enlivened by terrific music by Jerry Fielding and the graphics of cobras sprouting heads as new victims are added. Ellery is played by Peter Lawford as a suave, British, globetrotting swinger (yeah, baby, yeah!) and his uncle Inspector Richard Queen is perfectly portrayed by the wonderful Harry Morgan. The fictional Ellery originally was similar to S.S. Van Dine's dandified (and annoying) gentleman detective Philo Vance and although Jim Hutton became the definitive Ellery on the series, Lawford works fine with his "Rat Pack" swagger and somewhat cheesy smoothness. Shortly the hipster sleuth meets up with lovely Celeste (Stefanie Powers), the sister of one of the victims, a potential suspect and a budding love interest. This is an enjoyable and beautifully edited mystery with lots of good location shots of New York City and plenty of 70's lingo ("The whole town is uptight"; "Ya dig? The Hydra's a cop out!"; "Groovy!"; "Outtasite!"). It also accurately reflects the breakdown of society going on at the time, particularly in New York City, including the dearth of Broadway shows. (Broadway owed its revival to 1977's *A Chorus Line*). Midway Ellery thinks he's got it, but does he?

Escape (1971) 73 min.; Network: ABC; D: John Llewellyn Moxey; Paramount Television Productions; Release Date: April 6, 1971; Stars: Christopher George, William Windom, Marilyn Mason, Avery Schreiber, John Vernon, Gloria Grahame, William Schallert, Huntz Hall, Mark Tapscott, George Clifton, Lucille Benson, Lisa Moore, Chuck Hicks.

This ABC Movie of the Week was a pilot for a television series that was never made starring Christopher George as Cameron Steele, an escape artist and private eye, who gets involved in the kidnapping of a scientist Henry Walding (William Windom) and foils a plot by Walding's mad scientist (what else?) brother (John Vernon) to turn humans into zombies. A blend of sci fi, detection, magic, and supernatural, *Escape* plays like the average TV detective series with a few distinctive quirky aspects, including a welcome guest appearance by Gloria Grahame. The opening credits recall James Bond with montages of girls in silhouette dancing rather cornily, romancing Steele and running. Running and car chases were a staple of 70's television, as was the trope of the character receiving the mysterious phone call to meet someone somewhere they should not (which happens here). After engineering a Houdini-like escape from a death trap set by the kidnappers, Steele delves into the case which brings him into contact with Walding's daughter Susan (Marilyn Mason) who is clad in a screamingly bad "Partridge Family" ensemble meant to be the height of fashion. Think ruffled shirts and shags. It all leads to Susan becoming a damsel in distress and a chance for Steele to engineer some very fun, *Mission: Impossible*-like escapes with Susan and her father in tow. Best are the scenes in an amusement park involving a tunnel of horror and lots of terrific stunt work. The quirkiness works and if they had continued with that and the great guest stars, *Escape* promised to be a fun series. Alas, it was not to be, but Bill Bixby would star two years later as a magician/escape artist/detective in the TV series *The Magician* which ran a single season.

The Eyes of Charles Sand (1972) 74 min.; Network: ABC; D: Reza S.

Badiyi; Warner Brothers Television; Release Date: February 29, 1972; Stars: Peter Haskell, Barbara Rush, Sharon Farrell, Bradford Dillman, Adam West, Joan Bennett, Ivor Francis, Gary Clarke, Owen Bush, Donald Barry, Larry Levine.

Another pilot for a TV series that failed to be picked up, *The Eyes of Charles Sand* begins with stockbroker Charles Sand (Peter Haskell) entering a darkened room with a coffin surrounded by candelabras. He lifts the lid of the coffin and there is the corpse of an elderly man inside who opens eyes that are solid white (a trick that was perhaps popularized by 1963's delicious *Dr. X: The Man with X-Ray Eyes* with Ray Milland), sits up and points an accusing finger at him. He wakes with a cry. At that moment, which is 3 a.m., he receives a call from his Aunt Alexandria Sand (Joan Bennett in her haughty, glamorous *Dark Shadows* period) who informs him that his Uncle Edward has died and he must come immediately. Charles Sand, as it turns out, has inherited a gift called "the sight" as the surviving son of the Sand family and Uncle Edward left him the key to the Sand Legacy, a book with an eye on it. Already Charles is having visions and is approached by pretty Emily Parkhurst (Sharon Farrell), a young woman in a full-length fur and high-heeled boots who begs him to help her; she believes her brother Raymond was murdered by her sister Katherine (Barbara Rush) and Katherine's husband Jeffrey (Bradford Dillman). Charles seeks out the home of this girl who acts ooky spooky and unhinged and begins to find that things don't quite add up. The second half of *Charles Sand* is not as successful as the richly atmospheric and intriguing first half which, aside from everything else, features a fabulous, historic home for Gothic appeal and high production values. Not only does the action become predictable, but the performances of three of the leads (Farrell, Dillman and Rush) cross into overwrought and unbridled territory. If they had been reined in just a bit, *Eyes* would have been quite good; as is, it has much to offer. *Whatever Happened to Baby Jane* author Henry Farrell, king of dysfunctional family fiction, co-adapted this from one of his own stories.

Five Desperate Women (1971) 74 min.; Network: ABC; D: Ted Post; Aaron Spelling Productions; Release Date: September 28, 1971; Stars: Robert Conrad, Anjanette Comer, Stefanie Powers, Joan Hackett, Denise Nicholas, Julie Sommars, Bradford Dillman.

A homicidal maniac (what else?) has escaped from a mental institution just as five lovelies are about to reunite on a private island for their five-year college reunion. To underscore how very nasty the villain is, a radio broadcast reveals he was indicted for slaying his fiancée the night before their wedding. Ouch. The festively-dressed five head out for the deserted island with squirrely boat captain Jim Meeker (Bradford Dillman) and as soon as a friendly dog greets them, one fears that this pooch may become a casualty, given that it's the politically incorrect seventies. Since only the lower half of the killer's body is shown, it's unknown whether he is Meeker or the handsome caretaker Michael Wylie (Robert Conrad). (The not-so-guilty secret surrounding *The Wild, Wild West* is that its star Robert Conrad was considered to have some of the sexiest buns in the business; the extremely tight matador-style pants he wore on the show made him a gay icon. Fortunately, the culprit's pants are not skintight enough to give him instantly away.)

The killer isn't the only unstable one. All of the women have issues. It's *The Group* (1966) meets *See No Evil* (1971) (wherein a blind Mia Farrow is terrorized by a killer whose boots alone are shown). It would've been stronger dramatically if the women were allowed to be more cohesive, both individually and as a group. They don't convince as old schoolmates or friends. They don't even appear to know or like one another much; instead, they come off as strangers thrown together who irritate one another. The lack of a believable bond to pull us in is unfortunate, because a fabulous cast of girl power has been assembled. There's Mary Grace (Julie Sommars), daughter of a tragic-eyed mute shut-in (yes, a shut-in); annoying, alcoholic Lucy (Anjanette Comer) with her Dolly Parton twang; Joy (Denise Nicholas) who decided prostitution was more profitable than any other use of her degree; Dorian (Joan Hackett) who invents a back story to hide her insecurities; and gorgeous, but initially frosty Gloria (Stefanie Powers) who initially comes off as unlikeable, but ultimately proves the strongest and most level-headed character.

Less than it might have been, but still a decent thriller and the strong cast makes it worthwhile.

Teresa Graves as the sassy undercover detective Christie Love.
Photo courtesy of Wolper Productions.

Get Christie Love (1974) 74 min.; Network: ABC; D: William A. Graham; Wolper Productions; Release Date: January 22, 1974; Stars: Teresa Graves, Harry Guardino, Louise Sorel, Paul Stevens, Ron Rifkin, Lynne Holmes, Lee Paul, Tito Vandis, Tracey Roberts, William Hansen, Andy Romano, Davis Roberts.

"We gonna bust you, baby!" This was a pilot for a short-lived blaxploitation TV series starring Teresa Graves as a sassy black female undercover detective, Christie Love (think *Foxy Brown*). Love is sent unwillingly to Miami to find a ledger connected to a drug pin and pulls no punches. She approaches the kingpin's girlfriend Helena Varga (well-played by Louise Sorel) and flat out asks where the ledger is. That's what you call the direct approach. The episode has an occasional nice intimacy and touches on women's issues like the potential abortion of Varga's child where Love shows a certain sisterhood with female characters, although it's fairly routine. Graves (who resembles Whitney Houston) is fine, acting in the broad, badass manner required with occasional softness, but the show apparently lacked the sex and violence that made blaxploitation films popular and was soon canceled. Basically, it follows the format of the average detective series. There are ongoing icky flirtations between Love and her boss Captain Casey Reardon (Harry Guardino), but all is played tongue firmly in cheek. When Love wrestles an assailant disguised as room service in her hotel room and he almost tosses her over the balcony, she tells him, "I guess you know you're not getting a tip." The story is based on Dorothy Uhnak's urban thriller, but the white character was changed to a black one. Sadly, Graves would die at age 54 of burns sustained in a house fire.

The Golden Gate Murders (1979) 104 min.; Network: CBS; D: Walter Grauman; Universal Television; Release Date: October 3, 1979; Stars: David Janssen, Susannah York, Paul Coufos, Tim O'Connor, Lloyd Bochner, Kim Hunter, Alan Fudge, Kenneth Tigar, Regis Cordic, Sandy Ward, Richard O'Brien, Richard Bull, Eric Server, Lee Paul, Jon Lormer.

Superb and thoroughly entertaining mystery, thriller and "something more" concerning a visiting Roman Catholic priest from South Africa who is thrown from the Golden Gate Bridge when he stops there to pay homage to his brother who had died during the bridge's construction. The film brings together not only one of the most charming investigative teams, but also one of the greatest film pairings ever, on par with all the great movie teams in history, such as Bogie and Bacall, Hepburn and Tracy, and Loy and Powell. In this case, it's irascible, crusty Detective Sergeant Paul Silver (David Janssen) of the San Francisco Police Force and the serene, but sharp Sister Benecia (Susannah York) who proves to be his match when she insists on delving further into this case which is being dismissed as a suicide. "Hello, I'm the mad nun," she tells him, to which he responds, "Hello, I'm the mad cop." The film is filled with wonderful choices, such as the believable growing relationship that builds between the two characters, Sol Kaplan's fine music which enhances but does not intrude in the story, the backstory of "The Creeper," and Silver's cat Dirty Harry (named after a famous Clint Eastwood film shot in the city). "Don't get too close," Silver tells Sister Benecia. "The cat is mean. He only drinks boiled milk," but she has already broken the ice with Dirty Harry. With a fine mystery, a terrific romance, good dialogue and a fun interlude where the nun and cop go sightseeing, *The Golden Gate Murders* is a charmer and far above average. Look for Aneta Corsaut (known as Miss Crump on *The Andy Griffith Show*) in a small, uncredited role.

Goodnight, My Love (1972) 73 min.; Network: ABC; D: Peter Hyams; ABC Circle Films; Release Date: October 17, 1972; Stars: Richard Boone, Michael Dunn, Barbara Bain, Victor Buono, Gianni Russo, John Quade, Walter Burke, Lou Wagner, Lou Cutell, John Lawrence, Jan Daley, Luke Andreas, Don Calfa, Vic Vallaro, Bobby Baum.

This was another retro film with a great sense of humor and quirky characters, meticulously recreated in the style of the 1940's and opening with a classic female crooner in a tony nightclub. The very next scene between a surly man and talkative solider on a bus is one of the most shocking bits in the film, coming completely out of left field. Susan Lakely (beautiful Barbara Bain) is the fragile blonde "tomato" who shows up at the Los Angeles office of Francis Hogan (Richard Boone), a gruff down-on-his-luck private eye, and his partner, Arthur Boyle (Michael Dunn), a dwarf, and asks them to find a missing person, her fiancé, Michael Tarlow (Gianni Russo). Since Tarlow hasn't called her for four days, she fears he might have found another woman and wants Hogan to find out for her. "Lady, I'm a private detective. I don't spend my afternoons peeking into some other guy's bedroom window. I don't take jobs like that," Hogan retorts. Lakely tells him she'll pay him $25 a day. He immediately counters, "I'll take a job like that." Needless to say, the investigation leads them to a number of double crosses, beginning with a bump on the head when Hogan goes to Lakely's apartment. The trail also leads to the tony nightclub from the initial scene which is run by corpulent Julius Limeway (Victor Buono, recalling Sydney Greenstreet in *The Maltese Falcon* (1941)) whose signature attire is a white tuxedo. The soldier on the bus, as it turns out, was Lakely's missing fiancé, and to say things aren't as they appear (why would they be?) is an understatement. One wonders if this influenced 1974's *Chinatown*, which took the tongue out of cheek and resulted in a brilliant neo-noir masterpiece. Although not in that league nor the same animal, *Goodnight, My Love* is delicious fun with good characters and a great tribute to the film noir detective mysteries of the 40's. It references many of the era's own masterpieces and keeps its consistent sense of humor without being a satire. One inspired scene involves Hogan with a cop, pumping him for information as they both laugh raucously. The team of Hogan and Boyle is terrific.

Helter Skelter (1976) 194 min.; Network: CBS; D: Tom Gries; Lorimar Productions; Release Date: April 1, 1976; Stars: George DiCenzo, Steve Railsback, Nancy Wolfe, Marilyn Burns, Christina Hart, Cathey Paine, Alan

Oppenheimer, Rudy Ramos, Sondra Blake, George Garro, Vic Werber.

Of a similar caliber as 1967's *In Cold Blood* and adapted from prosecutor Vincent Bugliosi's book, this landmark telefilm captures in chilling detail one of the crimes of the century -- the mass murders orchestrated by pseudo hippie cult figure Charles Manson and his "family" in 1969. *Helter Skelter* is the dark side of the counterculture movement; in fact, documentaries reveal that the Summer of Love in Haight Ashbury was far from loving, but had rapidly morphed into an armed and dangerous free-for-all as social structure was imploding often violently in the country. Charles Manson, a career criminal who spent a great chunk of his life in institutions, managed to assemble his young disciples from mostly middle class families and used drugs and mind games to manipulate them to do his demonic bidding, culminating in the Tate/LaBianca murders in Los Angeles, including the murder of Roman Polanski's 26-year-old pregnant wife Sharon Tate. Steve Railsback's performance as Manson is astonishing and terrifying; watching interviews of the real Manson reveals just how brilliant and on point Railsback is. His realistic portrait anchors the film as it follows the milestones of prosecutor Bugliosi (George DiCenzo) in the formidable task of finding reasons for the serial murders that terrorized Hollywood and remain among the most notorious ever committed. Without Bugliosi, Manson and his family might have walked free. Although at times it does feel as if the wild-eyed girls who followed Manson and behaved like the possessed in the Salem witch trials are being viewed through the lens of Hollywood "squares" (no pun intended), the actresses who portray "Charlie's Angels," as his female accomplices have been called, are actually quite accurate and chilling in their portraits. Nancy Wolfe, in particular, captures the callous detachment and soft-spoken, cold creepiness of Susan Atkins. Family members on that fateful night were instructed to kill rich "pigs" and scrawled the words "Healter Skelter" [sic] and "pig" in their victims' blood, the words "helter skelter" derived from a Beatles song. The story is so horrifying and the roles so well-cast and acted that whatever might be dated fails to diminish the impact of an otherwise powerful production.

Hit Lady (1974) 75 min.; Network: ABC; D: Tracy Keenan Wynn; Spelling-Goldberg Productions; Release Date: October 8, 1974; Stars: Yvette Mimieux, Joseph Campanella, Clu Gulager, Dack Rambo, Keenan Wynn, Roy Jenson, Paul Genge, Del Monroe, Mitzi Hoag, Sam Edwards, Francisco Ortega.

This elegant telefilm almost seems like a foreign film and stars Yvette Mimieux (who also penned the screenplay) as Angela de Vries, a successful artist who moonlights as a syndicate killer. As Bugs Bunny would say, "It's a living!" After killing her mark at a Texas barbecue, de Vries determines that this is going to be her last hit, but the syndicate wants her to kill Jeffrey Baine (Joseph Campanella), head of one of the most powerful unions in the country. It's a risky assignment, but they're willing to pay her $125,000 price and she grudgingly accepts. Meanwhile her love is a struggling photographer and slice of beefcake, Doug Reynolds (Dack Rambo) who doesn't know about his girlfriend's double life. After accepting the assignment, Vries begins to do her homework on the mark and takes steps to get close to him – perhaps too close. The syndicate pressures her to make it quick, but will the assassin face a moral dilemma with her charming target? Is he getting under her skin? Mimieux is sometimes shrouded like a 20's flapper with cloche hats and svelte, fur-lined coats, which gives her the air of the mystery woman she is; she also dons a bikini. There's an old-fashioned 1940's "women's picture" feeling about this and more emphasis on psychology than action. The dialogue includes feminist assertions, such as when "boss" Roarke (Clu Gulager) asks de Vries how many women she supposes make her kind of money and she counters, "How many *men* do you suppose make my kind of money?" This line is given haughtily just before the elevator door closes. Although Mimieux is a decent actress, it is Campanella who really makes a sympathetic impression. With one expression, he reveals much about what Baine's high-profile life cost him. Glossy escapist drama with a twist in the tail.

Home for the Holidays (1972) 75 min.; Network: ABC; D: John Llewellyn Moxey; Spelling-Goldberg Production; Release Date: November 28, 1972; Stars: Eleanor Parker, Sally Field, Julie Harris, Jessica Walter, Jill Haworth, Walter Brennan, John Fink, Med Flory.

Family gatherings can be a bear. Four sisters, three with male names, gather for the holidays at the family manse at the behest of their tyrannical father (Walter Brennan) who believes that he is being slowly poisoned by his new wife Elizabeth (the always ooky spooky Julie Harris). Naturally the homestead is one of those fantastic Gothic houses that were so ubiquitous in these made-for-TV mysteries and it's a stormy night when they arrive. In fact, it continues to be gloomy and stormy, day and night, and the discomfort of the apprehensive sisters increases when their father tells them he wants Elizabeth killed before she finishes the job on him. But instead the sisters begin to die, one by one. Why Elizabeth would remain on the premises when she clearly is under suspicion and the family is fractured is a mystery in itself, but it adds extra tension when she is interacting with the girls and cooking after they've been told she has been slowly poisoning their father. The four sisters consist of motherly, oldest sister Alex (Eleanor Parker), slightly unhinged Freddy (Jessica Walter), promiscuous Jo (Jill Haworth), and the baby of the family, Christine (a very young Sally Field) who still has some innocence intact. Elizabeth had already been on trial for the murder of her prior husband – death by poison, no less, and the girls' mother also may have been driven to kill herself. Conversations are sometimes punctuated by claps of thunder or screams, particularly when the subject of murder is brought up, and all actresses are required to screech at various times. It's not a very festive holiday. Given the small cast, it's not too difficult to figure out who may be behind the serial mayhem, but there's still some old-fashioned fun in going along for the ride. Dig the spit curls on Haworth and Field, one of the fashions of the era.

The House on Greenapple Road (**1970**) 120 min.; Network: ABC; D: Robert Day; Quinn Martin Production; Release Date: January 11, 1970; Stars: Janet Leigh, Christopher George, Keenan Wynn, Tim O'Connor, Julie Harris, Walter Pidgeon, Barry Sullivan, Peter Mark Richman, William Windom, Burr DeBenning, Joanne Linville, Ed Asner, Lawrence Dane, Geoffrey Deuel, Paul Fix, Alice Jubert, Paul Lukather, Ned Romero, Olan Soule, Tina Menard.

This fairly racy (for the time) telemovie spawned the television series *Dan August* with Burt Reynolds, but August is played here by the excellent Christopher George whose sonorous, tough delivery recalls Jack Webb in *Dragnet* and Jack Lord in *Hawaii Five-O*. The plot concerns plainclothes police officer Lieutenant Dan August's investigation into the disappearance of a promiscuous housewife Marion Ord (Janet Leigh) in Los Angeles. The opening is quite graphic with Ord's child Margaret (Eve Plumb of *The Brady Brunch*) arriving home early and finding her mother gone; she leaves before discovering the blood-splattered kitchen, the murder later dubbed "The Red Kitchen Murder." August's path takes him through a variety of men and women who had been in Marion's life, including an amorous minister at the funky Church of Contemplation. The relationship these various characters had with Ord is explored in flashbacks, each scene supplying clues. A few nods to *Psycho* (1960) here: Leigh is named "Marion" and gorgeous Lynda Day (who would become Christopher George's wife) has a cameo as a pot-head receptionist with the last name of "Crane." Leigh played Marion Crane in *Psycho*. A whole host of familiar faces appear in the film, including William Windom, Ed Asner, Julie Harris, and the underrated Joanne Linville. An absorbing and well-crafted mystery where, as can be expected, things are not as they initially appear.

The House that Would Not Die (**1970**) 73 min.; Network: ABC; D: John Llewellyn Moxey; Aaron Spelling Productions; Release Date: October 27, 1970; Stars: Barbara Stanwyck, Richard Egan, Michael Anderson, Jr., Kitty Winn, Doreen Lang, Mabel Albertson.

Séances and spiritualism were very much an agreeable obsession in the mystery genre in the 30's and saw a resurgence again in the 70's in the made-for-TV movie. In this ghost story based on the novel *Ammie, Come Home* by Barbara Michaels, Ruth Bennett (Barbara Stanwyck), an executive secretary at the Department of Agriculture, takes leave to move into a house she inherited from her Aunt Hattie, bringing her niece Sara (Kitty Winn). Although the women love the house, immediately it becomes clear that something unseen and unsettling lies beneath the surface. A neighbor Pat McDougal (Richard Egan), a professor specializing in the black arts, shows up to welcome the ladies and some sort of fearful recognition passes between him and Sara. Ruth meanwhile is plagued by dreams, the sound of footsteps and a voice calling, "Ammie, come home!" They conduct a séance to get to the root of the matter and the disturbances only increase. It seems demonic spirits are fighting for possession of Sara. Interestingly, some of the techniques used here, particularly in the scenes of Sara's possession, were reminiscent of *The Exorcist* (1973) which would create a sensation several years later. Winn, in fact, would appear in *The Exorcist* (1973) and *The Exorcist II: The Heretic* (1977). In spite of the torments both women are enduring, they decide to stay on and determine who the evil spirit is and what her story was. Sara feels she "mustn't" leave, even if she is the one who seems most in danger. This is the sort of thing that fired the imagination of hundreds of watching children who wanted to be ghost hunters and conduct séances themselves and a certain amount of hokeyness (like an old scroll) keeps it harmless, rather than hair raising. *The House that Would Not Die* is old-fashioned fun, a romantic ghost story and mystery with wonderful wind sound effects and decent performances. Although not extraordinary, it is a good time passer and represents Stanwyck's made-for-TV movie debut.

How Awful About Allan (1970) 73 min.; Network: ABC; D: Curtis Harrington; Aaron Spelling Productions; Release Date: September 22, 1970; Stars: Anthony Perkins, Julie Harris, Joan Hackett, Kent Smith, Molly Dodd,

Trent Dolan, William Erwin, Robert H. Harris, Billy Bowles, Jeannette Howe, Kenneth Lawrence.

Based on the novel by Henry Farrell (author of *Whatever Happened to Baby Jane?*), *How Awful About Allan* is a wonderfully spooky thriller wherein a disturbed young man (Perkins) returns home to live with his sister Katherine (Harris) after an eight-month stay in a mental institution. He is plagued by psychosomatic blindness after the house fire that killed his father and disfigured Katherine's face many years ago. Unable to afford the upkeep in the large, Victorian house, Katherine must take in a boarder. Allan shortly becomes convinced that this mysterious boarder is trying to kill him, which is more harrowing since he sees only shadows. (Perkins wore special opaque contact lenses for this film that rendered him partially blind.) This is a delicious, atmospheric tale aided by a great score, moody photography and accomplished stars who hold as much tension in their faces as a sponge does water. Perkins became typecast in off kilter roles after his tour de force performance as Norman Bates in Alfred Hitchcock's *Psycho* (1960), but that doesn't negate his effectiveness and gift for nuance. He is brilliant and matched by Harris who was no stranger to torment and creepfests after starring in the ghost tale *The Haunting* (1963). There are a few improbable moments like chanting voices outside the library that no one but Allan hears, but it only adds to the fun. Lovely Joan Hackett appears as Allan's former love interest, Olive. Note Hackett's Gibson girl do, an early 20th Century hairstyle that saw a resurgence in the 70's.

A Howling in the Woods (1971) 94 min.; Network: NBC; D: Daniel Petrie; Universal Television; Release Date: November 5, 1971; Stars: Barbara Eden, Larry Hagman, Vera Miles, Tyne Daly, Ford Rainey, Lisa Gerritsen, Ruta Lee, Karl Swenson, John Rubinstein, Bill Vint.

I Dream of Jeannie stars Barbara Eden and Larry Hagman are reunited in this thriller and mystery in which fashion illustrator Liza Staines Crocker

(Eden) returns to her childhood town of Stainesville, Nevada where her family once prospered and discovers that something is afoot. For one thing, Liza is in a backwoods town of population 573, but sashays around in fashionable ensembles like a CEO inspecting her plant, lending the production a touch of camp. She has returned to pursue a divorce from her husband Eddie Crocker (Hagman) and plans to stay at the childhood roost for six weeks. Being a small rural town, naturally it's stereotypically populated with squirrely back woods types who beat children, act surly and shoot at dogs who steal chickens. Liza discovers the heart of the mystery lies in the mysterious drowning of a little girl many years ago. Looking incongruously like Alexa Carrington Colby of *Dynasty* in the cast of *Deliverance* (1972), she goes skulking around to get to the root of the town secrets. Both suspenseful and silly enough to be a fun popcorn movie. Lisa Gerritsen who co-starred with William Windom in the short-lived TV series *My World and Welcome to It* appears as an abused child.

I Love a Mystery (1973) 120 min.; Network: NBC; D: Leslie Stevens; Universal Television; Release Date: February 27, 1973; Stars: David Hartman, Les Crane, Hagan Beggs, Ida Lupino, Jack Weston, Deanna Lund, Terry-Thomas, Melodie Johnson, Inger Wegge, Karen Jensen, Peter Mamakos, Andre Philippe, Francine York, Don Knotts.

This is an interminably campy but sprightly revival of Phillip Lord's old radio serial *I Love a Mystery* (which first aired in 1939) featuring three insurance investigators and friends, Jack Packard, Doc Long and Reggie York (Les Crane, David Hartman and Hagan Beggs) who are sent to a remote island mansion to find a missing millionaire. It was originally filmed in 1967, but not released until 1973 and clearly has that kicky sixties feeling about it with screwy humor that brings to mind *The Monkees* or the "Beach Party" movies with Annette Funicello and Frankie Avalon. There also appear to be influences from Matt Helm and other spy movies of the decade. Men wear helmet style haircuts like the Beatles and the music is pure sixties. In spite of datedness, *I Love a Mystery* is still an example of how creative the made-for-TV genre was. The story is allegedly a combination of two original radio episodes. As in so many of the sixties comedies, an Old Hollywood veteran appears alongside a young cast. Ida Lupino plays the eccentric Randolph Cheyne, mistress of the mansion, and mother of three comely daughters, Faith, Hope and Charity (Karen Jensen, Deanna Lund, and Melodie Johnson) and a simpering son Job (Jack Weston). Cheyne is part scientist and has a laboratory filled with moving panels and machines with blinking lights (very sixties). The mansion is beset by spooky unexplainable happenings like a baby crying whenever something dreadful is going to happen to a member of the Cheyne family. Although extremely silly, *I Love a Mystery* is colorful and light in spirit and offers some harmless retro fun. Don Knotts makes a special guest appearance.

Isn't It Shocking? (1973) 73 min.; Network: ABC; D: John Badham; ABC Circle Films; Release Date: October 2, 1973; Stars: Alan Alda, Louise Lasser, Edmond O'Brien, Lloyd Nolan, Will Geer, Ruth Gordon, Dorothy Tristan, Pat Quinn, Liam Dunn, Michael Powell, Jacqueline Allan McClure.

Originally broadcast as an ABC Movie of the Week, *Isn't It Shocking?* concerns a serial killer in the small, aging town of Mount Angel (allegedly Vermont, actually filmed in Oregon) who undresses his 63-year-old victims and uses a shock machine to stop their hearts. The murders are viewed initially as "natural deaths," but local Sheriff Dan Barnes (Alan Alda) isn't convinced. When one of his dear friends and officers Jesse Chapin (Lloyd Nolan) is struck down, he determines to find who is responsible. Although an okay mystery (the motive is the mystery since the killer is shown from the opening), *Isn't It Shocking?* has an unpleasant undercurrent and isn't quite convincing as a portrait of small town life. Barnes is having an affair with a single mom motel owner (Pat Quinn) who is shown in an unfavorable light at every turn as if having children is unforgivable and distasteful. Meanwhile, he has a good rapport with his office manager Blanche (Louise Lasser). Although dressed identical to her "Mary Hartman" character, Lasser is lively and flirtatious here and the chemistry she has with Alda lends a homey warmth to the movie. Ruth Gordon also appears, but is typecast as a dithery eccentric with too many cats. What's shocking, really, is that the victims are only in their early sixties, but the script treats them as if they're ready for pasture. Won Edgar Award for Best Television Feature or Mini-Series.

The Judge and Jake Wyler (1975) 120 min.; Network: NBC; D: David Lowell Rich; Universal Television; Release Date: December 2, 1972; Stars: Bette Davis, Doug McClure, Eric Braeden, Joan Van Ark, Gary Conway, Lou Jacobi, Kent Smith, Barbara Rhoades, John Randolph, Milt Kamen, John Lupton, Michael Fox, Rosanna Huffman, Eddie Quillan, Celeste Yarnall.

This failed pilot for a series was to star the indomitable Bette Davis as a retired lady judge who solves mysteries. In the pilot, Judge Meredith (Bette Davis) hires a parolee Jake Wyler (Doug McClure) to work as her "leg man" when investigating the alleged suicide of a wealthy businessman, the father of their client Alicia Dodd (Joan Van Ark). Alicia Dodd believes her father was murdered. As Davis/Meredith puts it in her clipped tones, "Even in light of the police reports, Miss Dodd wants to hire us at our standard astronomical fees." Naturally the wealthy family is a viper's nest with no love lost between family members and the deceased. Wyler romances Dodd as part of his investigation and runs across people who seem to want the investigation stopped. The clues lead to people in high places like the State Department. It's not surprising that this pilot failed, although another incarnation, *Partners in Crime* with Lee Grant as the judge, was attempted again in 1973 which also failed. It's fun, but hard to imagine as a weekly series. Davis is styled like dowdy Charlotte Vale before her makeover in *Now Voyager* (1942), very schoolmarmish, and seems more caricature than character. She was a formidable actress capable of brilliance, but she could also rely on hammy trademark shtick as she does here. McClure plays his character as too much of a smartass and makes little impression. The secondary characters are the highlights, including Barbara Rhoades as Meredith's secretary Chloe Jones, Joan Van Ark, and John Randolph as James Rockmore, Dodd's former partner. In any case, *The Judge and Jake Wyler* is an okay time passer with a few exciting scenes, but Davis is too mannered and affected for this to have sailed.

The Legend of Lizzie Borden (1975) 96 min.; Network: ABC; D: Paul Wendkos; George LeMaire Productions and Paramount Television; Release Date: February 10, 1975; Stars: Elizabeth Montgomery, Fionnula Flanagan, Ed Flanders, Katherine Helmond, Don Porter, Fritz Weaver, Bonnie Bartlett, John Beal, Helen Craig, Alan Hewitt, Gail Kobe, Hayden Rorke, Amzie Strickland, Robert Symonds, J. Edward McKinley.

Elizabeth Montgomery as axe murderess Lizzie Borden.
Photo courtesy of George LeMaire Productions and
Paramount Television.

This is a spooky and superbly crafted retelling of the infamous turn-of-the-century unsolved murders in Fall River, Massachusetts in which Lizzie Borden was accused of killing her father Andrew Borden and stepmother Abby with an axe. As portrayed by Elizabeth Montgomery, Lizzie Borden is a complex, chilling character who is cold, stubborn, vain and manipulative, mistreating her sister Emma (Katherine Helmond) and servant Bridget (Fionnula Flanagan), yet managing to engender sympathy in some. Emma tells her, "It's just that you're special and special people have always been misunderstood," although she is shown praying to God to forgive her for coddling this potential murderess. Lizzie longs for a more glamorous life and feels suffocated by the frugality of her wealthy father (Fritz Weaver) who won't even use the icebox. He is also inferred to have penchants for necrophilia and incest. The trial is faithful to the actual court transcripts, with the exception of Lizzie's flashbacks, although there are many feminist and other overtones that are undoubtedly 20th Century – specifically 1970's -- projections. For one, prosecuting attorney Hosea Knowlton (Ed Flanders) says of the fevered crowds, "I suppose we can't blame them. They haven't had a good witch hunt in this state since Salem." One suspects this cynical remark so smacking of the cynical 70's was never spoken. Ditto for Knowlton's wife Sylvia (Bonnie Bartlett) saying that hiding behind one's femininity could be a woman's only defense, adding to her husband, "You cast us in this role." *The Legend of Lizzie Borden* deservedly won numerous awards, including the Edgar for Best Television Feature and an Emmy for Montgomery for Best Actress. Production and all performances are first rate. Interestingly, Montgomery was found to be 6th cousins once removed from Lizzie Borden, descending from 17th century Massachusetts resident John Luther.

A Little Game (1971) 73 min.; Network: ABC; D: Paul Wendkos; Universal Television; Release Date: October 30, 1971; Stars: Diane Baker, Ed Nelson, Howard Duff, Katy Jurado, Mark Gruner, Christopher Shea, Helen Kleeb.

The evil child in film came to prominence in 1954's *The Bad Seed* with Patty McCormack as a child murderess and has appeared in various incarnations over time. In this one, which predates 1972's similarly-themed but far superior *The Other,* a little boy Robert Mueller (Mark Gruner) has such hostility towards his stepfather Paul Hamilton (Ed Nelson) that Paul begins to suspect the boy is a sociopath. Naturally the boy with his blond helmet hair, rigid demeanor and German last name recalls Hitler's youth, particularly in his military school uniform; he also has an obsession with guns and was a great admirer of his father who apparently was also rigid and gun-obsessed. When the boy comes home from Hastings Military Academy with his friend Stu Parker (freckled-faced, lisping Christopher Shea), it is clear that Robert is mistreating the other boy, but his overindulgent mother Elaine (Diane Baker) won't hear anything negative about her son, even with the evidence in front of her. Paul then hires Dunlap (Howard Duff), a private detective, to find out if anyone was killed at Hastings. "You've never been to a private detective before, I can tell. It's like going to an abortionist," Duff tells him. Sure enough, there have been some mysterious deaths at Hastings and Paul also finds Robert's diary which logs accounts of murders Robert committed, but when Paul confronts Stu, Stu insists that he and Robert were merely playing a game and none of the deaths actually took place. Paul tries to tell Elaine about his disturbing findings, but she is so horrified that her son would be accused of murder that she demands Paul leave and is prepared to permanently sever their relationship. Even worse, she buys Robert a rifle for Christmas, earning the Stupid Movie Parent Award. *A Little Game* offers nothing new in the way of surprises and has none of the brilliance and sheer terror of *The Other,* even while the relationship between the two boys mirrors that of the identical twins in the Thomas Tryon story. It's abundantly clear that Robert is an evil child from the word go. What *A Little Game* does have, however, is strong performances from the entire cast, some well-played themes and a creepy twist ending.

Live Again, Die Again (1974) 78 min.; Network: ABC; D: Richard A. Colla; Groverton Productions; Release Date: February 16, 1974; Stars: Cliff Potts, Walter Pidgeon, Donna Mills, Mike Farrell, Geraldine Page, Vera Miles, Lurene Tuttle, Stewart Moss, Irene Tedrow, Peter Bromilow, Walker Edmiston, Florence Lake, Tom Curtis.

Donna Mills plays Caroline Carmichael, a woman who dies from rheumatic fever and is kept frozen at her own request, awakening 34 years later through cryogenics to find her husband Thomas (Walter Pidgeon) now elderly and her daughter Marcia (Vera Miles) unhinged and out to kill her. All the family dynamics are off kilter, including the one with the nanny "Sissy" O'Neill (Geraldine Page). This deliciously cheesy premise of "you can't go home again" promises glossy popcorn fun and delivers, offering the fabulous estate and house with filmy curtains (so ubiquitous in 70's made-for-TV fare); Mills coming out of her freeze in full makeup and with fluffy, coiffed hair; the evil daughter with a vial marked "Poison"; a glamorous wardrobe for Mills; and a secret garden, plus plenty of skeletons in the closet. The difficult transition Mills faces, physically and emotionally, is handled well, revealing the ramifications of cryogenics, and the sinister goings-on are genuinely creepy. The one bugaboo is some of the filming choices where frames are layered over one another, making it difficult to discern what is actually happening. *Live Again, Die Again* is better than it sounds on paper and a quite respectable thriller. Mills was not only beautiful, but a fine, versatile actress and her strong performance keeps things grounded and intriguing. The beautiful setting and effective music does the rest.

The Log of the Black Pearl (1975) 85 min.; Network: NBC; D: Andrew V. McLaglen; Mark VII Ltd. and Universal Television; Release Date: January 4, 1975; Stars: Ralph Bellamy, Kiel Martin, Jack Kruschen, Glenn Corbett, Anne Archer, Henry Wilcoxon, John Alderson, William Kerwin, Edward Faulkner, Pedro Armendáriz Jr., José Ángel Espinosa, Dale Johnson.

No catalogue of mystery would be complete without a little high seafaring adventure and hunting for sunken treasure. Upon the death of his grandfather Alexander Sand (Henry Wilcoxon), a young stockbroker Christopher Sand (Kiel Martin) inherits a ship called the Black Pearl and a medallion which is allegedly the key to a sunken treasure. Little does he know, however, but there are other sinister individuals also after this booty. He assembles a crew, including a crusty old salt Captain Fitzsimmons (Ralph Bellamy) and alcoholic sailor Jocko Roper (Jack Kruschen) and sets sail for Puerta Vallarta. Because his grandfather had considerable debt, Sand also agrees to take along three paying passengers: an American coffee broker from Rio Michael Devlin (Glenn Corbett), his associate Eric Kort (John Alderson), and their gorgeous secretary Lila Bristol (Anne Archer). Needless to say, the agreeable trio are not who they say they are and signs of sabotage and sinister doings begin to manifest. *The Log of the Black Pearl* is a fine tale of adventure on the high seas with plenty of intrigue, romance (that happens all too quickly, of course), deep sea diving, and murder. Anne Archer had one of the great faces of cinema (or television), equal to Ava Gardner and Elizabeth Taylor, and is a fine femme fatale/heroine. In films like this, one expects the villains will carry knives, not guns, and they do. Good, old-fashioned fun with on-location scenery in Mexico.

Longstreet (1971) 90 min.; Network: ABC; D: Joseph Sargent; Paramount Television; Release Date: February 23, 1971; Stars: James Franciscus, Martine Beswick, Bradford Dillman, John McIntire, Jeanette Nolan, Barry Russo, Judy Jones, Barney Phillips, Martin Kosleck, Lincoln Demyan, Lisabeth Field, James De Closs, Frances Spanier.

This was a pilot for a television series of the same name which ran 1971-1972 and starred James Franciscus as Mike Longstreet, an insurance investigator in New Orleans who loses his sight and his wife in an explosion and tries to track down his wife's killers. Ever creative gimmicks were used to distinguish television detectives and the blind detective was an interesting twist. The pilot opens with a robbery and cuts to Longstreet and his pretty wife Ingrid (Judy Jones) who are enjoying a night on the town and come home to a bottle of wine festooned with a ribbon that has been mysteriously left for them. As Longstreet goes to get glasses, the bottle explodes, killing Ingrid and blinding him. Longstreet is then sent to an expensive sanitarium where he is given a spacious apartment and put under watch, given that the bomb is assumed to have been for him. He begins working with Dr. Dan Stockton (John McIntire) to learn to rely on his senses. Meanwhile when he learns that more robberies have taken place in New Orleans, he suspects a connection between the crimes and what happened to him and has the police reports transcribed into braille. As Longstreet tracks down the criminals responsible for the robberies and his wife's death, he also makes the journey of acceptance with his loss, finally adding a cane and seeing eye dog to his arsenal. This is a strong, well-paced and well-acted pilot which allows viewers to hear the world from Longwood's perspective and inspires interest in further adventures of the character. The one problem is an ending which feels rushed in contrast to the dynamic opening.

Maneater (1973) 69 min.; Network: ABC; D: Vince Edwards; Universal Television; Release Date: December 8, 1973; Stars: Sheree North, Ben Gazzara, Kip Niven, Laurette Sprang, Richard Basehart, Claire Brennan, Stewart Raffill, Lou Ferragher, Jerry Fitzpatrick.

There have been many variations of the classic hunter-becomes-the-hunted scenario in Richard Connell's story *The Most Dangerous Game* and this exciting version has the protagonists facing off against those most magnificent of big cats, tigers. The footage of the tigers alone is worth the price of admission. Two couples on a vacation are traveling across the desert (where else?) when their motorhome breaks down close to a roadside attraction called "1 Million B.C." The site features two "man-eating" tigers and is run by an unbalanced ex-circus animal trainer, Brenner the Great (Richard Base-hart). Brenner was fired from the circus when his cats killed someone and has been relegated to this motheaten roadside fare where he longs for his cats to be free. When the vulnerable quartet run up against him, he decides to pit them against the cats for the thrill of the sport and soon the couples are running for their lives against two great predators at night. It forces them to use survival skills they never dreamed they had. The high point of this telefilm is the thrilling footage of the beautiful beasts, dark as much of it may be, who are shown swimming in swampy waters as, in one instance, their potential prey, Nick and Gloria Baron (Ben Gazzara and sexy Sheree North) are submerged underwater and breathing through bamboo straws. The other couple, Shep and Polly are played by Kip Niven and Laurette Sprang. Gazzara makes a good centered protagonist who also has some insight into tiger behavior to aid them in their survival strategies and Basehart is a fine lunatic. *Maneater* is a fun popcorn adventure.

Mind Over Murder (1979) 100 min.; Network: CBS; D: Ivan Nagy; Paramount Television; Release Date: October 23, 1979; Stars: Deborah Raffin, David Ackroyd, Bruce Davison, Andrew Prine, Christopher Cary, Robert Englund, Penelope Willis, Wayne Heffley, Carl Anderson, Jan Burrell, Paul Reid Roman, Paul Lukather, Lanny Duncan, Rex Riley, Jack Griffin, Clint Young, Don Ray Hall, Michael Horsley, Linda Ryan.

Suzy (lovely Deborah Raffin), a dancing hamburger by profession, is plagued by nightmares and visions involving time standing still and a malevolent bald man (Andrew Prine). The man appears not only in her dreams, but even in her bed and on the streets as everyone around them freezes. When she drops an egg in the kitchen one day, suddenly the egg falls in slow motion and she hears voices inside a cockpit as if over a receiver. When the egg hits the ground, the plane crashes and she screams. Her jackass boyfriend Jason (Bruce Davison) doesn't believe her and won't listen to her, so she seeks the help of an FBI agent, Ben (David Ackroyd). She is even more convinced that she is experiencing the paranormal when she sees a headline in the paper about the plane crash that she heard in her mind. Ben feels Suzy's premonitions about the bald man might place her in danger and he is right. *Mind Over Murder* has been compared to *Eyes of Laura Mars* which came out the year earlier, because both involve female protagonists with visions of mayhem, but while *Laura Mars* was flamboyant, campy and unintentionally funny ("Donaaaalllldd!!"), *Mind Over Murder* is dark, genuinely frightening and in parts sadistic. The technique of slowing or freezing a scene in which only Raffin and the terrifying bald man are animated is terrific and effective. There is also wonderful imagery and unsettling music by Paul Chihara throughout and Deborah Raffin gives a solid performance that holds the whole thing together. Weaker are the supporting male characters, aside from Ackroyd, who all show one-note signs of sexism or latent misogyny (in the case of the bald man). A strong and artistically done exercise in terror.

Murder by Natural Causes (1979) 100 min.; Network: NBC; D: Robert Day; CBS Entertainment Production; Richard Levinson/William Link Productions; Release Date: February 17, 1979; Stars: Hal Holbrook, Katharine Ross, Richard Anderson, Barry Bostwick, Bill Fiore, Phil Leeds, Eve McVeagh.

This clever, well-regarded mystery is in the vein of *Sleuth* (1972) and *The Last of Sheila* (1973) and also plays very much like a good *Columbo* story, which isn't surprising since it was written by the creators of *Columbo*, Richard Levinson and William Link. Arthur Sinclair (Hal Holbrook) is a renowned mentalist who preys upon the wealthy and gullible, even though he himself has a pacemaker. His younger, greedy and icy wife Allison (Katharine Ross) is having an affair with a young and equally greedy actor Gil (Barry Bostwick of *Rocky Horror* fame) and the two of them are plotting to scare Arthur to death. Their plan is to have Gil use his acting skills and break into the house. He will hold Arthur at gunpoint and cause another heart attack, this one fatal. Naturally the best laid plans are bound to go wrong and as one might imagine, these plans do. Masterfully written and acted, *Murder by Natural Causes* is a wonderful actor's film with characters who all are phonies in one way or another. But can Arthur Sinclair really read people's minds? Although the twists and turns are to be expected in this sort of mystery, it is the intensity of the scenes between actors that is particularly exceptional here. There is also an "in" joke when Gil is playing in *Prescription Murder*, the name of the first *Columbo* episode.

Murder on Flight 502 (1975) 97 min.; Network: ABC; D: George Mc-Cowan; Spelling-Goldberg Productions; Release Date: November 21, 1975; Stars: Ralph Bellamy, Polly Bergen, Theodore Bikel, Sonny Bono, Dane Clark, Laraine Day, Fernando Lamas, George Maharis, Farrah Fawcett-Majors, Hugh O'Brian, Molly Picon, Walter Pidgeon, Robert Stack, Brooke Adams, Danny Bonaduce, Vincent Baggetta.

Murder on Flight 502 is sub-par but typical made-for-TV fare with cardboard characters, each with potboiler backstory (including the requisite alcoholic), sometimes silly dialogue and cheap sets. The all-star cast is almost as much an eccentric hodgepodge as Liza Minnelli and David Gest's wedding party. It was put out at the same time as the superior, but also open-to-parody campfest *Airport 1975* which had stewardess Karen Black forced to fly the plane and included a singing nun (Helen Reddy) and a child in need of an organ transplant (Linda Blair) among its passengers. These films were followed by Leslie Nielsen's hilarious 1980 spoof *Airplane!* A murderer is aboard Flight 502 and airline security receives his threatening note as the plane is underway from New York to London. Can they prevent the murders midflight? Apparently not, because the first body falls and the passengers are thrown into a state of chaos. The curio cast is the fun here, although some of the acting is dire. Among the huge ensemble are Farrah Fawcett (before her trademark feathered hair) and Brooke Adams as stewardesses, sporting genuine TWA uniforms; Sonny Bono as – what else? – a singer whose manager tells him, "When you're on top, you can rape Whistler's mother … and get away with it" (ain't that the truth!); Polly Bergen as an alcoholic murder mystery writer; and Fernando Lamas as a thief. Several of the passengers actually have had bitter dealings with one another in the past and amazingly find themselves on the same flight. Meanwhile, tensions are high as no one knows who the killer is and who may be next. Typical, though lesser TV suspense-on-a-shoestring with a few surprise twists and some groaners (Bono actually utters the phrase "The beat goes on.").

Murder Once Removed (1971) 74 min.; Network: CBS; D: Charles Dubin; Bob Markell Productions and Metromedia Productions; Release Date: October 29, 1971; Stars: John Forsythe, Barbara Bain, Richard Kiley, Reta Shaw, Wendell Burton, Joseph Campanella.

Stunning Lisa Manning (special guest star Barbara Bain of *Mission: Impossible* fame) is having an adulterous affair with the handsome local doctor Ron Wellesley (John Forsythe), but her husband Frank Manning (Richard Kiley) is not only onto them, but has had the doctor investigated. Frank discovered that Ron fled his prior town of Yeagerstown after being suspected of various suspicious deaths and confronts him with his findings, asking that Ron not conspire to kill him as well. Meanwhile one of Ron's regular patients is Fred Kramer (Wendell Burton), a young man recently back from "Nam." The set up here is reminiscent of *Murder by Natural Causes*, a twisty murder mystery set among the upper crust. "I never quite got used to losing a patient," Dr. Wellesley says at one point to his friend Lieutenant Phil Proctor (Joseph Campanella). In the tradition of Alfred Hitchcock, the two men show a ghoulish fascination with murder, discussing doctors who have also been murderers. When Frank winds up dead, needless to say, the loopy Vietnam Vet is framed for the murder. One of the things that distinguishes this telefilm – which is characteristic of 70's made-for-TV mysteries, in general – is a sense of humor and light touch. When a dog howls as Frank is going for a treatment at Ron's practice, Ron's feisty nurse Regis (Reta Shaw) remarks, "Another patient. He howls every time we lose one." The preposterousness of this exchange is what keeps such films entertaining. *Murder Once Removed* is intriguing, because all of the characters, as it turns out, grew up together and Nurse Regis is nosy and unpredictable. We all know the murderous scheme won't go as smoothly as expected and the twists keep coming until the last frame.

Nero Wolfe (1979) 120 min.; Network: ABC; D: Frank D. Gilroy; Paramount Television; Release Date: December 19, 1979; Stars: Thayer David, Tom Mason, Brooke Adams, Anne Baxter, Biff McGuire, John Randolph, David Hurst, John O'Leary, Sarah Cunningham, Lew Charles, Frank Campanella, John Gerstad, John Hoyt, Ivor Francis, Allen Case.

This is a top-drawer adaptation and production of Rex Stout's *The Doorbell Rang* featuring his corpulent armchair detective Nero Wolfe and Wolfe's confidential assistant Archie Goodwin. Purists have considered Thayer David a definitive Wolfe while Tom Mason is equally fine as Archie and David Hurst impeccable as Fritz, Wolfe's temperamental gourmet chef ("Five berries or I cook something else!"). With Brooke Adams and the divine Anne Baxter in the cast, what more could one ask for? Like P.G. Wodehouse's Bertie Wooster and his butler Jeeves, Wolfe lives in an all-male household. Wolfe's luxurious brownstone on West 35th Street with its rooftop greenhouse devoted to orchids and one-way pane of glass on the front door which enables Archie to see visitors is beautifully captured here. It's also fun to see some wonderful New York City institutions, now bygone, like the Empire Diner and Epicure's Kitchen. Baxter is Rachael Bruner, a wealthy realtor who distributed a book exposing the FBI to "all the important people" in New York City and is now being followed by FBI operators. She offers Wolfe $100,000 to get them off her back and more if he succeeds. Goodwin and Wolfe suspect there's more to it and they're right.

With high production values and a seamless cast, *Nero Wolfe* is a joy for mystery lovers and literate in a way that most television is not. It includes secret panels, passwords ("a cat may look at a king") and great Wolfesian dialogue ("My orchids are my concubines – insipid, expensive, parasitical and temperamental" and "Two brilliant minds under one roof would be intolerable."). Originally slated as the pilot for a series, it is a pity it never materialized and that Thayer David passed away before getting an opportunity to embody Wolfe again.

Night Slaves (1970) 71 min.; Network: ABC; D: Ted Post; Bing Crosby Productions; Release Date: September 29, 1970; Stars: James Franciscus, Lee Grant, Scott Marlowe, Andrew Prine, Tisha Sterling, Leslie Nielsen, Morris Buchanan, John Kellogg, Virginia Vincent, Cliff Carnell, Victor Izay, Raymond Mayo, Russell Thorson, Nancy Valentine.

Clay Howard (James Franciscus) decides to drop out from his high-pressured job and immediately has an accident which requires him to have a metal plate installed in his head; the accident also kills two people, the Robertsons. He and his stunning wife Marjorie (Lee Grant) are advised to pull up stakes and take a rest, so they drive down to a small town, Eldrid, California, dubbed "A Bit of the Old West," which is overseen by a sinister sheriff Henshaw (Leslie Nielsen). Marjorie is charmed and wants to stay there to shop for antiques. Meanwhile she has been romantically involved with Clay's partner Matt Russell (Scott Marlowe), but hasn't told her husband. The Howards take rooms in a local inn and when they go to sleep that night, Clay is plagued by nightmares about the accident. He wakes and goes to the open window where he discovers something strange going on. All the locals are gathering and unloading things from trucks, a scene reminiscent of *Invasion of the Body Snatchers* (1978). Meanwhile a strange woman Naillil (Tisha Sterling) appears in his room and tells him Marjorie is "down there" with the people. He runs down in time to see Marjorie drive off on one of the trucks.

The entire town is now deserted. When he wakes up the next day, Marjorie and he laugh about what must have been a dream, but meanwhile he finds disturbing evidence, such as burrs on Marjorie's dress, that indicate it might not have been one. Something weird is going on, but what? This sci fi mystery holds the interest and has an unreal ambience, given that it was filmed on two backlots. There are some anomalies, such as the fact that Clay has a plate put in his head without having to have his head shaved, but the story is eerie and intriguing. Is it a dream and has Clay killed someone or is there really an alien master who holds sway over the population and the beautiful Naillil? Ambiguity and dreamlike ambience help *Night Slaves* along.

The Night Stalker (**1972**) 75 min.; Network: ABC; D: John Llewellyn Moxey; American Broadcasting Company; Release Date: January 11, 1972; Stars: Darren McGavin, Carol Lynley, Simon Oakland, Ralph Meeker, Claude Akins, Charles McGraw, Kent Smith, Barry Atwater, Larry Linville, Jordan Rhodes, Elisha Cook, Jr., Stanley Adams.

From the producer of *Dark Shadows,* Dan Curtis, this telefilm became ABC's highest-rated television movie and eventually became a terrific series *Kolchak: The Night Stalker* starring Darren McGavin. It concerns newspaper reporter Carl Kolchak (Darren McGavin) who has been fired from various papers because of his difficult personality and finds the scoop of a lifetime when a serial killer in Las Vegas proves to be a vampire. He goes on his own crusade to try to stop the monster (played by Barry Atwater), encouraged by his girlfriend Gail (Carol Lynley who has her usual spacy line readings). Kolchak also narrates the film. Although highly-regarded and even considered iconic, *The Night Stalker* is not on a par with some of the other truly exceptional productions of the time, such as *Reflections of Murder* (1974), and would be bested, to my mind, with *The Norliss Tapes* (1976) which had better location scenery, a more interesting and literate narrative and the stronger female lead of Angie Dickinson. The technique of highlighting the monster's red-rimmed eyes had already been used in Hammer's *Dracula* (1958) and the use of a stunt man is occasionally obvious. However, there is no question the movie hit a nerve with audiences and became a sensation and the series that followed was unique and exceptional. McGavin's world-weary, monster-hunting reporter and his abrasive, rumpled persona also won high marks with fans. *Kolchak: The Night Stalker* lasted a single season and was said to have inspired *The X-Files*.

Darren McGavin investigates a serial vampire in *The Night Stalker* (1972). Photo courtesy of ABC.

The Norliss Tapes (1973) 72 min.; Network: NBC; D: Dan Curtis; Metromedia Productions; Release Date: February 21, 1973; Stars: Roy Thinnes, Angie Dickinson, Claude Akins, Michele Carey, Vonetta McGee, Hurd Hatfield, Bryan O'Byrne, Robert Mandan, Edmund Gilbert, Jane Dulo, Stanley Adams, Bob Schott, George DiCenzo, Patrick Wright, Nick Dimitri.

This delicious telefilm, one of my personal favorites, is from *Dark Shadows* producer Dan Curtis and based on a short story by Fred Mustard Stewart. Set in San Francisco, it opens with writer David Norliss (Roy Thinnes) telling his publisher Sanford T. Evans (Don Porter) he is unable to complete his new book debunking the supernatural. Evans senses something is very wrong and drives to Norliss' apartment, which he finds in complete disarray, with only a tape as a last clue. As the tape plays, Norliss tells his fantastic tale which becomes the narration for the flashback. He was originally intending on exposing the phonies in spiritualism, the trick mediums and fortunetellers, until meeting Ellen Sterns Cort (Angie Dickinson), the wealthy widow of a sculptor James Raymond Cort (Nick Dimitri) who claims her husband is now a malevolent being come back from the dead. After witnessing unexplainable things first hand at her Carmel estate, Norliss teams with her to help. This telefilm is extremely entertaining, old-fashioned fun almost like a good Nancy Drew mystery or campfire story. It's a wonderful blend of mystery and supernatural with a terrific monster and investigative team (Thinnes and Dickinson) who refreshingly don't get romantically involved, however attractive they both are. There are gorgeous shots of the Pacific coast, including the 17-mile drive and a good sense of literature pervading everything ("acres of lush cypress and tall pines looming over me"). Dickinson lends her special blend of class, once again exuding the aura of a great gal and Vonetta McGee has a delicious and colorful turn as Madame Jeckiel, a spiritualist.

The Old Man Who Cried Wolf (1970) 73 min.; Network: ABC; D: Walter Grauman; Aaron Spelling Productions; Release Date: October 13, 1970; Stars: Edward G. Robinson, Martin Balsam, Diane Baker, Ruth Roman, Percy Rodrigues, Sam Jaffe, Edward Asner, Martin E. Brooks, Paul Picerni, Robert Yuro, William Elliott, James A. Watson Jr., Naomi Stevens, Virginia Christine, Jay C. Flippen.

Elderly Emile Pulska (Edward G. Robinson) is visiting his old friend

Abe Stillman (Sam Jaffe) at Abe's candy store when a man (Percy Rodrigues) enters and attacks Abe with a rubber hose, stealing his money. Emile comes to investigate and is knocked senseless. When Emile wakes up, he is surrounded by cops and local people and is told Abe died of a heart attack. No one will believe him when he tells them Abe was murdered. There is even a woman, Mrs. Raspili (Naomi Stevens) who claims to have witnessed Abe having a heart attack, although Emile knows she wasn't there and rightfully suspects she is in cahoots with someone. Sadly, this telefilm mirrors the all-too-common dangers of elderly people who live in urban environments or neighborhoods that have gone bad and the condescending attitudes towards the elderly. Emile is perfectly cognizant but others around him try to convince him he is losing it and his family puts him under medical observation. The cops are sarcastic towards him and even try to accuse him of racism, since the perpetrator was black. Emile knows the truth of what he has seen and decides to investigate on his own, but he is being observed and is indeed facing a conspiracy. This is one of those dramas of the lone wolf seeking justice where no one can be trusted, including officials, a theme that played frequently in the cynical 70's. Robinson is excellent in the title role and generates much sympathy toward his character, while Rodrigues makes a great icy villain. The always-reliable Martin Balsam plays Abe's son Stanley who is unwittingly drawn into the plot against his father.

One of My Wives is Missing (1976) 94 min.; Network: ABC; D: Glenn Jordan; Spelling-Goldberg Productions; Release Date: March 5, 1976; Stars: Jack Klugman, Elizabeth Ashley, James Franciscus, Joel Fabiani, Milton Selzer, Ruth McDevitt, Bryon Webster, Garry Walberg, Tony Costello.

This excellent mystery in the vein of *Sleuth* (1972) has numerous twists and turns where nothing is the way it seems. Set in the bucolic waterfront resort of Skuylkill Village in upstate New York, it opens with Inspector Murray Levine (Jack Klugman) and the manager of the Village Theater at a production of *Dial M for Murder*. They discuss the case like the two loveable codgers in *Shadow of a Doubt* (1943). Daniel Corban (James Franciscus) who is honeymooning with his new wife meanwhile reports her missing to Levine. The inspector seems maddeningly unconcerned and unwilling to investigate, citing that Corban's wife left willingly after an argument, so isn't a missing person. The plot thickens when a woman (Elizabeth Ashley) shows up, claiming to be Corban's wife, but Corban has never seen her before in his life. He can't find anyone to believe him and in fact, witnesses show up who make him feel he's losing his mind. Based on a Robert Thomas play *Trap for a Single Man* which was made into the also excellent 1969 telefilm *Honeymoon with a Stranger* with Janet Leigh, the film keeps viewers guessing and succeeds on the strength of three marvelous leads. Like *Dial M for Murder*, its roots in the stage are discernible, as most of it takes place inside. Wonderful character actress Ruth McDevitt also makes her final film appearance here.

Paper Man (1971) 90 min.; Network: CBS; D: Walter Grauman; 20th Century Fox Television; Release Date: November 12, 1971; Stars: Dean Stockwell, Stefanie Powers, James Stacy, Tina Chen, Elliott Street, James Olson, Jason Wingreen, Dan Barton, Sue Taylor, Johnny Scott Lee, Marcy Lafferty, Ross Elliott, Robert Patten, Len Wayland, Dean Harens, Bob Golden.

When a college student Joel Fisher (Elliott Street) gets a credit card in the mail that doesn't belong to him, he begins a prank with three fellow students to use the card under a fake identity which is created with bogus files inserted into computer databases. They will pay the bills themselves when their families send money, so they assume there will be no serious repercussions and they will get the credit so difficult (then) for students to obtain. However, the prank turns deadly when one of them (or possibly the computer itself) begins murdering them, one by one. Has the computer taken on a life of its own or is there a real human behind the murders? In some ways, *Paper Man* is ahead of its time, because it deals with identity theft, although the computers are shown to be big boxes with lots of blinking lights, which was the fashion in the sixties and early seventies. Amusing is when med student Jerry (James Stacy) decides they should give their fictitious "paper man," Henry Norman, a $25-grand annual salary as if that is formidable. Tension is nicely created with a triangle between sexy psych student Karen McMillan (Stefanie Powers), Jerry and the computer nerd Avery Jensen (Dean Stockwell) who helps them program the system initially until he gets cold feet. As each of them are shown to have some capability with the computer and Karen protests her ignorance seemingly too much, that angle presents itself as a red herring as well. There is also a robot of sorts that is used for the medical students, which begins to become spookily animated and human. The film retains its tension, even when the cast is thinned out enough to present very few suspects and a somewhat obvious conclusion. The suspense then becomes focused on how it will all resolve. The one drawback is a certain character's stupidity and gullibility which serves to advance the plot, but defies belief. A fairly solid cyber mystery.

The President's Plane is Missing (1973) 96 min.; Network: ABC; D: Daryl Duke; ABC Circle Films; Release Date: October 23, 1973; Stars: Buddy Ebsen, Peter Graves, Arthur Kennedy, Raymond Massey, Mercedes McCambridge, Rip Torn, Louise Sorel, James Wainwright, Dabney Coleman, Joseph Campanella, Richard Eastham, James B. Smith, Maida Severn, Ivan Bonar, Gary Haynes, Patty Bodeen, Barbara Leigh.

This tense and nail-biting thriller concerns the disappearance over Arizona of Air Force One, the flight carrying President of the United States Jeremy Haines (Tod Andrews) who had been en route to Palm Springs for a holiday. When the wreckage is discovered, pathologists are unable to confirm identification of the president's body among the dead and his parachute is found unopened. Meanwhile the United States is on the brink of a nuclear war and the Vice President Kermit Madigan (Buddy Ebsen), who has been ill-informed by the President, must take the helm. He is forced to rely on his advisers who are at odds and try to manipulate him to follow their own hidden agenda, which, for one, involves a first strike against a foreign country without due cause. Meanwhile reporter Mark Jones (Peter Graves) is intent on investigating the President's disappearance. As he puts it, "We are on the brink of nuclear war and they're hiding and evading and no commenting and I want to know. I don't care if Haynes went crazy or was abducted or defected or ran off with someone's wife. I want to know." The film stays tense and exciting until the conclusion with fascinating insights into the working of government and excellent performances all around. This above average telefilm is based on the novel of the same name by Robert J. Serling (Rod's brother).

Reflections of Murder (1974) 98 min.; Network: ABC; D: John Badham; ABC Circle Films; Release Date: November 24, 1974; Stars: Tuesday Weld, Joan Hackett, Sam Waterston, Michael Lerner, Lucille Benson, Lance Kerwin, James Newcombe, Sandra Coburn, John Levin, Jesse Vint, William Turner, Don Sparks.

A remake of Henri-George Clouzot's 1955 French classic *Les Diaboloques*, *Reflections of Murder* is a superbly crafted and eerie suspense tale of two women, a wife and a mistress, who conspire to commit murder. Headmistress of the Island School, a private school for boys, delicate Claire Elliott (Joan Hackett) is being pressured by her abusive husband Michael (Sam Waterston) to sell the school as he ramps up his humiliation and maltreatment of her even in public. She forms a secret alliance with his equally mistreated mistress Vicky (Tuesday Weld). They will murder Michael and hide his body in the murky pool in front of the school. The problem is the body vanishes and it appears Michael or someone is taunting them for the deed.

One of the many strengths of this topnotch production is the wonderful attention to characterization and relationships, almost European in feel, as well as the rich atmospheric setting. Filmed at Rosary Heights in Woodway,

Washington, there is a sense of decay and malignancy about the grounds and a shadowiness that suggests foreboding and ghosts. Hackett and Weld are superb, Hackett's vulnerability and fragility a wonderful contrast to the flinty Weld. They have an intensity and electricity together in their Faustian bond, both pixie-haired like two halves of the same soul. Waterston matches them all the way with his arrogance and sadism, while the delicious touches like a nosy landlady (Lucille Benson) who has seven dwarves display Hitchcockian humor and irony. Lance Kerwin is also superb as a student at the school who like the children in *The Innocents* (1961) senses what's going on. Under less capable hands, this adaptation of the Pierre Boileau and Thomas Narcejac novel might have become hokey; instead we have an extremely accomplished telefilm with the depth and texture of great literature.

The Return of Charlie Chan (1973) 91 min.; Network: ABC; D: Daryl Duke; The Charlie Chan Company in association with Universal Television; Release Date: July 17, 1979; Stars: Ross Martin, Richard Haydn, Louise Sorel, Joseph Hindy, Kathleen Widdoes, Don Gordon, Peter Donat, Leslie Nielsen, Rocky Gunn, Virginia Ann Lee, Ernest Harada, Soon-Tek Oh, Patricia Gage, Ted Greenhalgh, Graeme Campbell, Neil Dainard, Otto Lowy, Pearl Huang, Adele Yoshioka.

This is a loving tribute and sequel to the Fox and Mongram Charlie Chan series based on Earl Derr Biggers' benevolent and wise Honolulu detective. Warner Oland and Sidney Toler were both terrific as Chan in those films from the 30's and 40's and Ross Martin makes a respectable Chan, allegedly retired and enjoying his grandchildren from his huge brood until lulled out of retirement. The case that draws him out is that of murder and intrigue aboard the yacht of a Greek shipping tycoon Alexander Hadrachi (Leslie Nielsen). Nielsen plays the Greek with dark contact lenses, a phony accent and ridiculous eyebrows glued onto his own, but the fact that numerous people look like they're in disguise suits the whodunnit ambience. Martin carries on the tradition of having a white actor portray the Asian sleuth while Asian actors play his large brood. The fun and irony is that the Asian actors play completely Americanized youngsters, while Chan is steeped in ways and proverbs of the East. It's terrific to get glimpses of the whole Chan family and to have Chan's daughter Doreen (Virginia Ann Lee) a somewhat active member of the plot. Chan is shown as part Sherlock Holmes, deducing things from trifles and passing the skill onto his grandkids, while the film carries on staples and traditions from the original films like the shadowy shipboard cloak-and-dagger, the Chan son ("no. 8 son") who sneaks onboard in disguise when he is supposed to be at college, and Chan's proverbs ("Grandchildren are like summer rain – disconcerting, but very necessary."). This is a fun film with good production values and great color (color never looks so good anymore), but the one drawback is the overly convoluted denouement. By the end, viewers are still left scratching their heads. Still, *The Return of Charlie Chan* is fine, old-fashioned entertainment and extra fun can be had with the vintage décor and wild beehive hairstyles.

Revenge (1971) 74 min.; Network: ABC; D: Jud Taylor; Mark Carliner Productions; Release Date: November 6, 1971; Stars: Shelley Winters, Bradford Dillman, Carol Rossen, Stuart Whitman, Roger Perry, Leslie Charleson, Gary Clarke, Johnny Scott Lee, George Burrafato, Pelly Sutton.

A strange woman Amanda Hilton (Shelley Winters) switches briefcases with San Francisco businessman Frank Klaner (Bradford Dillman) and when she invites him to retrieve it at her Victorian house (a relic that survived the great earthquake and built, as she explains to him, by her husband's grandfather to "keep his mad wife off the streets"), she hits him with a poker and keeps him ensconced in her basement. Madness indeed. Hilton believes him to be the man responsible for her daughter's suicide, something that the script never proves or disproves. Meanwhile Klaner's wife, Dianne (Carol Rossen), alarmed when her husband doesn't come home, begins to have vague feelings and vibrations about his whereabouts, sensing he is "underground." She consults quack psychic Mark Hembric (Stuart Whitman), who agrees to undertake an investigation with her, even though he admits he uses tricks. Dianne's vibrations grow stronger and lead them to Hilton's house of horror. The psychic and paranormal themes cropped up frequently in the 70's, as evidenced by a number of the films reviewed for this book. Either writers were borrowing from one another or one popular work with a paranormal theme initiated the craze. This is an above average chiller, based on a novel by Elizabeth Davis, with a carefully modulated and frightening performance from Winters and an unnerving electronic score by Dominic Frontiere.

Ritual of Evil (1970) 100 min; Network: NBC: D: Robert Day: Universal Pictures; Release Date: February 23, 1970; Stars: Louis Jourdan, Anne Baxter, Diana Hyland, John McMartin, Wilfrid Hyde-White, Belinda Montgomery, Carla Borelli, Georg Stanford Brown, Regis Cordic, Dehl Berti, Richard Alan Knox, Johnny Williams, Jimmy Joyce.

Although dated, *Ritual of Evil* is also deeply disturbing and genuinely frightening, capturing the sheer evil that went on beneath the flower children and beautiful Hollywood people in the 60's. *Rosemary's Baby* (1968) may have inspired it, but it also had its roots in the real-life Manson murders which rocked California and the nation in December of 1969. It opens eerily with a stormy night and chanting where a beautiful woman in a sexy nightgown is walking through the storm to the cliff. It's as unsettling as it possibly could be, recalling the nightmarish visuals of *Spirits of the Dead* (1968). This woman Aline Wiley (Carla Borelli) is then found dead on Morning Glory Lane by a black folk singer and ex-druggie Larry Richmond (Georg Stanford Brown) who lives on the beach of the estate. She was the 24-year-old heiress to the immense Wiley fortune, known for throwing wild parties with the idle beautiful people, and her aunt is an alcoholic movie star Jolene Wiley (Anne

Baxter). Psychiatrist David Sorell (handsome Louis Jourdan) who treats Aline's younger sister Loey (Belinda Montgomery) comes to investigate, not believing the verdict of suicide. His suspicions are confirmed by Richmond who tells him about Aline's parties where she "got all those beautiful people together and made them swing." Like Loey, Richmond has been experiencing nightmares about strange rituals that he can't distinguish from reality. He adds, "There are things inside all of us, things we don't know about – demons. She could call out demons . . . I didn't want to fall into that bag anymore." Then Richmond winds up dead. *Ritual of Evil* came after *Fear No Evil* as the second pilot for an unrealized series called *Bedeviled* starring Jourdan as Sorell, a psychiatrist/occult detective. The occult was an obsession in the 70's, following the success of the aforementioned *Rosemary's Baby* and the hit horror daytime soap *Dark Shadows*. The film is populated by beautiful people, including Diana Hyland of the shockingly lemon-blonde hair as Leila Barton, Sorell's love interest. *Ritual of Evil* is one of the most terrifying and deeply unsettling of the horror telefilms. It looks at the world of Satanic cults, orgies and uninhibited, privileged hippies, the idle rich who have opened Pandora's box. It convincingly mirrors the dark side that existed in sunny California and came to light with the Tate-LaBianca murders. (See *Helter Skelter*).

The child-vampire Danny Glick (Brad Savage) begs to be let inside in *Salem's Lot* (1979).
Photo courtesy of Warner Brothers Television.]

Salem's Lot (1979) 184 min.; Network: CBS; D: Tobe Hooper; Warner Brothers Television; Release Date: November 17, 1979; Stars: David Soul, James Mason, Lance Kerwin, Bonnie Bedelia, Lew Ayres, Julie Cobb, Elisha Cook Jr., George Dzundza, Ed Flanders, Clarissa Kaye-Mason, Geoffrey Lewis, Barney McFadden, Kenneth McMillan, Fred Willard, Marie Windsor.

Although I'm not a fan of Stephen King's writing (which often features scenes of spousal and child abuse), this top-notch adaptation of King's lengthy second novel into a miniseries is a work of epic horror entertainment. The story involves a writer Ben Mears (David Soul) returning to Jerusalem's ("Salem's") Lot, a small town in Maine where he'd lived as a child, only to discover it is being plagued by vampirism. Director Hooper carefully crafted the visuals, paying homage to a slew of horror movies, including *Psycho* (1960), *Dracula: Prince of Darkness* (1966), *Nosferatu* (1972), *The Exorcist* (1973) and *The Night Stalker* (1972). The score by Harry Sukman lends much to the film's success in the way Bernard Herrmann's music contributed immeasurably to Hitchcock movies. Aside from that, any film with James Mason has an ace in the hole and here he effectively steals every scene as Richard K. Straker, the sophisticated, sinister and sibilant antiques dealer who takes over the Marsten House, a decaying Victorian on a hill that has a history of horrific happenings attached to it. In one chilling scene, cultured Straker carries in a bundle wrapped in black plastic, lays it on a table in the basement, and unwraps it to reveal the missing Glick boy. Straker is the mysterious bodyguard and watch dog for the "Master," the vampire Kurt Barlow (played by an uncredited Reggie Nalder who is made up like a blue Count Orlok from the 1922 vampire classic *Nosferatu*). (Nadler never speaks in the movie, by the way.) In another delicious scene, Constable Parkins Gillespie (the terrific Kenneth McMillan) visits Straker to investigate the missing Glick boy and tells him he's always on duty. Displaying a streak of dark humor, Straker replies, "Hmm. That makes me feel safe and snug." The film has many classic, old-fashioned elements like the "oh-so-cold" oblong box that two characters must deliver to the Marsten House and the young boy with a fascination with monsters who becomes one of the main protagonists, Mark Petrie (played by the superb Lance Kerwin). There are also many fine stalwarts in the cast, such as Marie Windsor, Elisha Cook Jr. (who plays the resident small-town kook) and Lew Ayres. Like a sprawling vampire Peyton Place, *Salem's Lot* remains a very influential and creepy telefilm that is considered by many ardent fans to be one of the best vampire films ever.

Satan's School for Girls (1973) 74 min.; Network: ABC; D: David Lowell Rich; Spelling-Goldberg Productions; Release Date: September 19, 1973; Stars: Kate Jackson, Pamela Franklin, Lloyd Bochner, Roy Thinnes, Jamie Smith-Jackson, Jo Van Fleet, Cheryl Stoppelmoor (Ladd), Frank Marth, Terry Lumley, Gwynne Gilford, Bill Quinn, Ann Noland, Bing Russell.

Catholic schoolgirls such as myself could identify with this supernatural thriller set in a private girls' school, the 300-year-old Salem Academy for Women in Massachusetts, if only because it focuses on schoolgirls, albeit college-age girls. When her sister Martha (Terry Lumley) is found hanging in her living room, Elizabeth Sayers (Pamela Franklin) won't accept the verdict of suicide and decides to investigate by enrolling in the school herself. She is greeted by a trio of long-haired students, two of whom would go on to star in *Charlie's Angels*, Kate Jackson and Cheryl Ladd, and meets the ingratiating headmistress Jessica Williams (Jo Van Fleet). The headmistress hands her an oil lamp, explaining that the school sometimes suffers from erratic blackouts, due to its being so far from the main power lines, setting the stage for things that go bump in the night. In spite of the Victorian trappings at the school, the seventies are everywhere from the stringy hairstyles and bellbottoms of some of the students to the indications of charismatic cult leadership. But much of the action is Gothic mystery with girls in nightgowns carrying old-fashioned oil lamps through dark corridors on stormy nights like something out of a Mary Roberts Rinehart novel. A painting done by Debbie (Jamie Smith Jackson) appears to be a portrait of her frightened sister, so Elizabeth sets out to find what she can that night. In the cellar of the school, she recognizes the room in the painting which she later learns was the setting for several murders long ago. The menace begins to increase as more deaths occur and soon the true sinister nature of the school is revealed. Delicious fun in the manner of *Crowhaven Farm*.

Kim Novak and Doug McClure are eerie shipmates in
Satan's Triangle (1975). Photo courtesy of ABC and
Danny Thomas Productions.

Satan's Triangle (1975) 75 min.; Network: ABC; D: Sutton Roley; American Broadcasting Company and Danny Thomas Productions; Release Date: January 14, 1975; Stars: Doug McClure, Michael Conrad, Kim Novak, Alejandro Rey, Jim Davis, Ed Lauter, Titos Vandis, Zitto Kazann, Peter Bourne, Hank Stohl.

This spooky thriller set in the Devil's Triangle a.k.a. Bermuda Triangle involves two U.S. Coast Guard pilots Pagnolini (Michael Conrad) and Haig (Doug McClure) who respond to an SOS and find a derelict yacht called the Requoit with dead people on board. Their joshing about spirituality as they fly to the Triangle recalls the horseplay among men that gave *The Thing From Another Planet* (1951) a wonderful believable looseness. Haig lowers himself down to investigate and in the darkened cabin, discovers one survivor, Eva played by beautiful, blonde, smoky-voiced Kim Novak. When the attempt to airlift them fails, Haig spends the night with Eva on board the Ship of Horrors and she recounts a story of what happened which involved a priest discovered afloat in the ocean that her party rescued. The concept of people at sea who stumble on a ship full of dead people has been used numerous times, including in *Dead Calm* (1989) with Nicole Kidman, but rarely as effectively as here. The dead priest hanging from the mast and the sailor lashed to the wheel are chilling images, reminiscent of Bram Stoker's *Dracula*. There are some allusions to *Moby Dick* as well when two sailors were after a giant marlin. Novak is a great choice with her haunting quality and the film lightly pushes the envelope by showing her bare-backed with the illusion of nudity, all the more alluring because it is kept subtle. The ABC Movie of the Week, of which this is a sample, was one of the most exciting and inventive programs on television in the 70's, offering an array of telefims, often in the suspense or supernatural vein, with great locations and production values. Without the technology or big budget, TV films like *Satan's Triangle* managed to terrify and create movie magic. The killer ending here deserves its reputation.

Savages (1974) 75 min.; Network: ABC; D: Lee H. Katzin; Spelling-Goldberg Productions; Release Date: September 11, 1974; Stars: Andy Griffith, Sam Bottoms, Noah Beery, Jr., James Best, Randy Boone, Jim Antonio, Jim Chandler.

Based on the novel *Deathwatch* by Robb White, this telefilm features lovable TV icon Andy Griffith in a villainous role. Griffith plays hot shot lawyer Horton Maddock who convinces Ben Campbell (Sam Bottoms) to be his guide in a hunting expedition for big horn sheep in the desert. Ironically, Griffith would later play a hotshot lawyer named Ben Matlock in the courtroom detective series *Matlock*. Campbell has a sense of foreboding from the start and his fears prove justified, not only because Maddock exudes a palpable air of menace, but because the trigger-happy sadist shoots a man accidentally and then tries to pin the crime on Campbell. After unsuccessfully trying to buy Campbell off and forcing him to bury the corpse, Maddock then strands him in the desert with the intention of killing him. "It's part of my business to be a measurer of men," he tells his unfortunate victim. "In my opinion, you have every intention of reporting this accident." Campbell, however, has the expertise of the desert that Maddock lacks and determines to outwit the psychotic attorney. At one point, Campbell remembers that the murdered man used to say animals were just like men, in that they couldn't live in the desert without water. "You've got to follow the tracks," he murmurs to himself. The suspense is in seeing who will come out the winner in this battle of wits. Campbell is at the mercy of the elements and on foot, whereas Maddock has a rifle, ample supplies and a jeep and dogs his victim at every turn. *Savages* is distinguished by a superb, chilling performance by Griffith who is a far cry from his benevolent, homespun sheriff Andy Taylor on *The Andy Griffith Show*. Viewers will want to see him get his comeuppance and be kept on the edges of their seats as the struggle plays out.

Scream, Pretty Peggy (1973) 74 min.; Network: ABC; D: Gordon Hessler; Universal Television; Release Date: November 24, 1973; Stars: Sian Barbara Allen, Bette Davis, Ted Bessell, Charles Drake, Allan Arbus, Jessica Rains, Christiane Schmidtmer, Johnnie Collins III, Tovah Feldshuh.

The film opens with a girl Agnes Thornton (Tovah Feldshuh) trying to escape a great Gothic house in the dead of night as the wind blows furiously. Her car won't start. She sees a creepy figure in a nightgown who remains in the shadows. She attempts to get into another car when she is brutally stabbed by the mysterious figure. Flash forward to art major Peggy Johns (Sian Barbara

Allen) forcefully nabbing the housekeeping job for 75 cents an hour that is advertised on her college campus. It is at the home of sculptor Jeffrey Elliot (Ted Bessell) and his alcoholic mother (Bette Davis) and Peggy drools at the chance to work for the famous sculptor. When Mrs. Elliot is incapacitated in a fall, Peggy insists on moving in. She is told she should never go into the room above the garage and she soon learns that like Rochester's wife, someone is being kept in that attic. The trope of the oddball doings in a Gothic house is always fun and this telefilm isn't short on atmosphere. What it is short on is subtle acting and an even marginally subtle script. Sian Barbara Allen is annoyingly eager and pushy and has a very 70's appearance with long, stringy hair; denim jacket; and jeans with wide bell bottoms. She practically forces herself on the family and insists on plunging into everything, in spite of being warned off. When she is told reluctantly she can stay temporarily in the room next to Mrs. Elliot, she announces she will get flowers and plants and "change the whole room." Everything is telegraphed too obviously, such as Mrs. Elliot trying to dissuade Peggy from taking the job or poking her nose into the room above the attic ("You mustn't go up there. Nevah...NEVAH!"). Davis shuffles as she did in *Whatever Happened to Baby Jane* (1962), using her trademark halting speech and sense of ennui as if she is fresh from a nap. There are some scares, such as when Peggy goes out in the night to fix a flapping garage door and sees the figure in the nightgown closing the door. For the most part, however, Allen is so irritating, one wants to see her get the axe, shears or whatever the murderer in the nightgown is wielding. *Scream, Pretty Peggy* is similar to William Castle's *Strait-Jacket* (1964), although *Strait-Jacket*, however campy, had far superior acting and was far more fun.

The Screaming Woman (1972) 73 min.; Network: ABC; D: Jack Smight; Universal Television; Release Date: January 29, 1972; Stars: Olivia de Havilland, Ed Nelson, Joseph Cotten, Laraine Stephens, Charles Knox Robinson, Walter Pidgeon, Alexander Hay, Lonny Chapman, Charles Drake, Russell

Wiggins, Gene Andrusco, Russell Thorson, Kay Stewart, Joyce Cunning, John Alderman, Ray Montgomery, Dee Carroll, Jan Arvan, Jackie Russell, Glen Vernon, Shannon Terhune.

Olivia de Havilland plays Laura Wynant, a wealthy older woman fresh from a sanitarium who takes a carriage ride on her estate one morning and sees a dog digging at the ground. She alights from the carriage to stop the dog from digging and hears a moan and faint voice. This disturbs her and she isn't sure if it's her imagination at first until a face makes itself visible from beneath the dirt. Wynant runs shrieking into the woods – an overwrought scream that goes on endlessly and melodramatically yet is deeply unsettling. This is the titular Screaming Woman. Needless to say, Wynant is living in a hotbed of money-grubbing treachery and no one believes her claim that a woman is buried at the old smokehouse. Her son Howard (Charles Knox Robinson) is hesitant to have his mother declared incompetent but is desperate for money, while his shrewish, greedy wife Caroline (Laraine Stephens) can't wait to have the old woman re-committed and sees this as an opportunity. Family attorney and friend George Tresvant (Joseph Cotten) doesn't take seriously Wynant's claims either, although he shrewdly tells Howard who snaps about his need to have his mother declared incompetent, "Do you realize what that would entail?" Meanwhile a neighbor Carl Nesbitt (Ed Nelson) has just accidentally killed his wife after an argument and buried her at the smokehouse. As Wynant is treated patronizingly and further humiliated at home, a plight all too common with elders, she decides to take matters in her own hands to rescue the buried woman and herself before it is too late. This is a solid old-fashioned chiller based on a short story by Ray Bradbury. De Havilland's Old Hollywood style acting elevates the proceedings because besides lending an element of class and regality, the likes of which are never seen anymore with the demise of the studio system, it is skilled and powerful beneath the affectations. Nelson also is terrific as the befuddled murderer. The "woman in peril" or "woman of a certain age in peril" was a staple in Hollywood for a number of years and a chance for Old

Hollywood stars like de Havilland to work. *The Screaming Woman* reunites her with *Hush, Hush Sweet Charlotte* (1964) former co-star Joseph Cotten. Good fun and dig that sky blue Princess phone!

She Cried Murder (1973) 74 min.; Network: CBS; D: Herschel Daugherty; Universal Television; Release Date: September 25, 1973; Stars: Lynda Day George, Telly Savalas, Mike Farrell, Kate Reid, Len Birman, Jeff Toner, Murray Westgate, Robert Goodier, Richard Alden, Aileen Seaton, B. Hope Garber, Stu Gillard.

A beautiful blonde model Sarah Cornell (Lynda Day George) enters a subway car and witnesses a man in a low brim hat throw a woman onto the track. The victim is in a red dress which makes her stand out in the scene. When Cornell exits the car, the man in the low brim hat passes her on the platform and they eyeball one another knowingly. The next day at her shoot, Cornell decides she must report what she witnessed to the police. When the police arrive, however, one of them, Inspector Joe Brody (Telly Savalas) is the man who committed the murder and she immediately pretends she can't remember too much. Rather than letting it go, Brody then proceeds to stalk her and even kidnaps her son and holds him at a theater, although she manages to retrieve the boy. The police initially laugh at her statement that Brody is the killer and is threatening her life, but Brody's partner Walter Stepanic (Mike Farrell) finds evidence at the home of the victim to implicate him. Then Stepanic, Brody and Cornell begin a cat-and-mouse chase with Stepanic trying to get Brody before he can get Cornell. Although spread out to 73 minutes, *She Cried Murder* is set up and plays like a typical television detective show episode. The "cop show" music by John Cacavas furthers the impression. Like so many television shows and films, the characters behave stupidly and irrationally. Brody inexplicably digs himself deeper by going after this woman, even using his own name in his pursuit, while Cornell, although being menaced, drives an open red convertible and has to be told to lock the door when she hides out in the apartment of her friend and fashion colleague Maggie Knowlton (Kate Reid). One would think simply having her son testify that he was kidnapped might do it. Lynda Day George could have easily been one of *Charlie's Angels* and her acting is on that kind of serviceable, but superficial level. Savalas and Farrell don't make strong impressions either, although they would go on to better things, the great *Kojak* and *MASH,* respectively. Average, but enjoyable time passer.

She Waits (1972) 74 min.; Network: CBS; D: Delbert Mann; Metromedia Productions; Release Date: January 28, 1972; Stars: Patty Duke, David McCallum, Dorothy McGuire, Beulah Bondi, James Callahan, Nelson Olmstead, Lew Ayres.

This is another above average ghost story and mystery on the lines of *Rebecca* or *Gaslight* where a young bride enters her new husband's household which seems to be haunted by the malevolent presence of his former wife. No sooner has Mark Wilson (helmet-haired David McCallum) brought his new wife Laura (Patty Duke) home to meet his ailing mother Sarah (Dorothy McGuire), then strange and foreboding things begin to occur to Laura, such as the bewitching waltz she hears everywhere. Possessive (no pun intended) mother Sarah then warns Laura that she should leave the house immediately, claiming the "barrier between life and death is impregnable," Mark's former wife Elaine is still in the house and "she waits." This naturally upends Laura. Mark seemed reluctant to tell Laura exactly what happened to Elaine who died in the house and everyone around Laura is clearly ill at ease as well. Although nothing is particularly surprising here, *She Waits* is a fine, spooky production with moody cinematography and a Gothic set up that also recalls *The Spiral Staircase* (1946), which starred Dorothy McGuire as the innocent. Morton Stevens (who scored the phenomenal theme for *Hawaii Five-O*) composed the haunting waltz that adds much elegance and eeriness to the proceedings and an added bonus is Patty Duke, a cult favorite who was capable of being an extremely fine actress and deliciously histrionic and hammy when the occasion arose. Her cult status resulted more from the latter than the former. Beulah Bondi gives her usual sonorous and stony readings, lending a foreboding presence as a servant.

She's Dressed to Kill (1979) 100 min.; Network: NBC; D: Gus Trikonis; Barry Weitz Films; Release Date: December 10, 1979; Stars: Connie Sellecca, Jessica Walter, John Rubinstein, Jim McMullan, Clive Revill, Gretchen Corbett, Barbara Cason, Cathie Shirriff, Corinne Calvet, Eleanor Parker, Peter Horton, Jonathan Banks, Marianne McAndrew.

This is one of my favorite made-for-TV whodunits, a flamboyant version of *And Then There Were None* set in the fashion world, coming on the heels of another flamboyant, but big screen fashion-world whodunit, *The Eyes of Laura Mars* (1978) with Faye Dunaway. Once-reigning couturier Regine Danton (Eleanor Parker) invites a group of her top models, a fashion editor, fashion critic, photographer and others to a private showing of her new collection atop a remote mountain accessible only by cable car (Palm Springs Aerial Tramway). It's a party filled with bitchy queens, divas, models harboring secrets or vices, and sweet, gorgeous Alix Goldman (Connie Sellecca), an aspiring model and the innocent entering without reservation this cutthroat world. Sure enough a stormy night causes a generator to short (what else?) and they not only lose electricity, but the cable car goes out of commission, stranding them all. One by one, the models then begin to be murdered. *She's Dressed to Kill* pulls out all the stops in classic whodunit style, using nearly every trope in the book, including the group of colorful suspects being gathered in the living room to determine their whereabouts. It is a colorful group indeed. As Regine Danton, Parker chews scenery shamelessly with a Tallulah Bankhead imitation replete with alcoholic venom, cigarettes in long holders, furs and "darlings!" Jessica Walter as Irene Barton, the owner of the modeling agency, gives her usual solid performance, channeling Sue

Mengers, the legendary hard-nosed Hollywood talent agent while the models include a big game hunter with a pet leopard and a former Miss America. There's a disgruntled pretty boy assistant Tony Smith (Peter Horton) whose designs are being stolen wholesale by Danton and mousy Laura Gooch (Gretchen Corbett) who is being romanced by the photographer Alan Lenz (John Rubinstein). All of them are given enough shade to be suspects or potential victims. Then Sheriff Halsey (Jim McMullan) shows up over the side of the mountain to poke his nose into the investigation. It's all played right, fairly cheezy but fun and the twisty solution would be seen in other whodunits that followed.

Sherlock Holmes in New York (1976) 99 min.; Network: NBC; D: Boris Sagal; 20th Century Fox Television; Release Date: October 18, 1976; Stars: Roger Moore, John Huston, Patrick Macnee, Charlotte Rampling, David Huddleston, Signe Hasso, Gig Young, Leon Ames, John Abbott, Jackie Coogan, Maria Grimm, Marjorie Bennett, William Benedict.

In spite of impeccable production values, this is one of the weaker takes on the great detective Sherlock Holmes, almost making a spoof of the character, although it does provide some fun and incorporates a number of the classic elements (with which it takes great liberties). This same habit of distorting and taking liberties with the original creation also happens frequently with *Dracula* where, as example, the characters of Mina and Lucy are often inexplicably interchanged. Sir Arthur Conan Doyle's brilliant creation occasionally donned disguises, which was a treat in the books, but here, Holmes' penchant for disguise is given sledgehammer effect by happening right at the outset. All that aside, an entertaining and decent plot is concocted for He of the deerstalker cap, pitting him against his arch enemy Moriarity (John Huston) and "The Woman" Irene Adler (Charlotte Rampling). Holmes (Roger Moore) is informed by Moriarity that "the crime of the century, for the past century and all centuries to come, is now in preparation" (what else?) and sets out to prevent it with his trusty co-hort, Dr. Watson (Patrick Macnee whose witty characterization is in keeping with the classic Dr. Watson, Nigel Bruce). It leads Holmes to New York back to the only woman who ever stirred him romantically, Irene Adler, whose son Scott has been kidnapped. At the same time, he learns the entire New York Gold Depository has been robbed. Moore, Macnee and Huston may not be considered the definitive Holmes, Watson and Moriarity, and may indeed be jarring for some, but they still do credible and enjoyable work and the sights and sounds of old New York and London are nicely recreated (all but one done in a studio). The script also makes a few major and minor leaps about Holmes that are not found in the books. Although not the definitive Sherlockian entertainment, *Sherlock Holmes in New York* still offers escapist fun for those who want the game to be afoot! (The phrase "the game is afoot" actually first came from Shakespeare's 1597 *King Henry IV Part I* and was used in the 1904 Holmes story "The Adventure of the Abbey Grange").

Skyway to Death (1974) 74 min.; Network: ABC; D: Gordon Hessler; Universal Television; Release Date: January 19, 1974; Stars: Ross Martin, Stefanie Powers, Bobby Sherman, Tige Andrews, Nancy Malone, David Sheiner, John Astin, Joseph Campanella, Ruth McDevitt, Severn Darden, Billy Green Bush, Lissa Morrow.

This is a terror-on-the-tramway thriller and once again, it's the Palm Springs Aerial Tramway in Palm Springs, California that is the setting. A disgruntled former employee, mechanic Walter Benson (Billy Green Bush) sabotages the power room at the base when his boss Sam Nichols (Tige Andrews of *Mod Squad* fame) won't rehire him. This causes the car to stall mid-air in its descent as powerful Santa Ana winds are picking up. Naturally the car holds a smorgasbord of passengers with soap opera backstories, all of which have 74 minutes to be resolved. Passengers include beautiful Nancy Sorenson (Stefanie Powers) and her lover engineer Bob Parsons (Joseph Campanella). In deference to the burgeoning women's movement, he wants marriage, she doesn't. Nancy is part of the Friendship Society that takes out seniors regularly and has brought her "aunt" Louise (the adorable Ruth McDevitt) from the home for this day trip. McDevitt lends a lot of life and color to the production. Also trapped are Martin Leonard (Ross Martin) and his wife Ann (Nancy Malone) who are having marital difficulties which are aired out in full earshot of the other passengers in the claustrophobic car. When her husband grouses that the delay is impacting his business trip to San Francisco, Ann yells, "Stop lying! I know there's no business trip and I know about that girl in San Francisco!" Not exactly an ice breaker, but perhaps free entertainment for the other passengers. Lastly, there are pickpocket Steve Kramer (Severn Darden), a sheepish acrophobic Andrew Tustin (John Astin) and blue-eyed seventies heartthrob Bobbie Sherman as car operator Barney Taylor. It will be up to Taylor with the aid of several other passengers to save the day, resulting in even the acrophobe having to climb outside the tramway car thousands of feet above the canyon to assist. This is a fairly entertaining disaster popcorn flick with some good stunt work, a fun cast and amusing interpersonal hokum.

Someone's Watching Me (1978) 97 min.; Network: NBC; D: John Carpenter; Warner Brothers Television; Release Date: November 29, 1978; Stars: Lauren Hutton, David Birney, Adrienne Barbeau, Charles Cyphers, Grainger Hines, Len Lesser, John Mahon, James Murtaugh, J. Jay Saunders, Michael Laurence, George Skaff, Robert Phalen, Robert Snively, Jean Le Bouvier, James McAlpine, Edgar Justice, John Fox.

In the 70's, the age of the Watergate scandal, there was an obsession with tapes and surveillance, as evidenced by such films as *Klute* (1971) and *The Conversation* (1974). *Someone's Watching Me*, a stalker thriller, falls into this vein. Gap-toothed former Revlon model Lauren Hutton plays Leigh Michaels, a woman who has fled a bad love affair to begin a new life in Los Angeles where she gets a job in live television and moves into a tony Los Angeles high rise with a balcony. No sooner has she moved in, then she becomes the obsession of a stalker who has her apartment wired and is also observing her through her window with a telescope. One of the first things he does is anonymously send her a telescope, in fact. It's a classic set up for a thriller and Carpenter's directorial touches are strong, but there are some weaknesses. For one, Michaels is uncomfortably weird, one of those people who like to say they're crazy as if it makes them amusing when it actually makes them irritating. Her sense of humor includes telling Paul Winkless (David Birney), a man she picks up in a bar and begins dating, that she has a fear of being raped by dwarves and wants to make sure he isn't one or when her landlord assures her he locked her door after he left, she says, "A little early to be drinking, isn't it?" She also talks out loud to herself in a way that doesn't feel natural and does stupid things like walking around in front of the window in scant clothing or going to meet her tormenter in the basement alone, armed only with a knife. Decades later a similar theme would be explored in Ira Levin's *Sliver* which was made into a 1993 film with Sharon Stone, but this often recalls *Klute* and ultimately becomes an obvious homage to *Rear Window* (1954). Attractive Adrienne Barbeau, who would marry director John Carpenter, appears as Sophie, Michaels' lesbian co-worker, her presence welcome but insufficient. In spite of characters that are thin and sometimes plastic dialogue ("It's why we insulate our lives with locks and change our phone numbers and guard our space with television cameras and guns") (who talks that way?), *Someone's Watching Me* is an entertaining woman-in-peril thriller with an intrepid and insufferably foolish heroine. Like a ride through a dark funhouse, it offers escapist fun and chills and its oft-used tropes work every time.

Stonestreet: Who Killed the Centerfold Model? (1977) 73 min.; Network: NBC; D: Russ Mayberry; Universal Television; Release Date: January 16, 1977; Stars: Barbara Eden, Joseph Mascolo, Joan Hackett, Richard

Basehart, Louise Latham, Elaine Giftos, James Ingersoll, Val Avery, Sally Kirkland, Gino Conforti, Ryan MacDonald, LaWanda Page, Len Wayland, Ann Dusenberry.

This fun, ultra-seventies and deliciously cheesy pilot for a series that was never picked up stars Barbara Eden as Liz Stonestreet, a Los Angeles private detective whose late husband, a police detective, was killed in the line of duty; she is now continuing familiar work. When Mrs. Shroeder (Louise Latham) hires her to find her son Eddie (James Ingersoll), a young hoodlum, Liz goes undercover as a gum-chewing saucepot at "Eve's Art," an eclectic porn palace where he worked. Girls there are required to wear cheap, ill-fitting costumes and hot pants and it's a wonderful excuse for Eden to stride down the street in a transparent crocheted blouse with bra visible underneath (before Madonna made this look popular in the 80's). She shortly discovers items in Eddie's locker that link him to a missing heiress, Amory Osborn (Ann Dusenberry) who apparently was dabbling in porn under an alias. Against the advice of her boss Max Pierce (Joseph Mascolo), Stonestreet insists on delving further into the connection between the heiress and the hood. Although the titles are on the silly side with Eden (in spit curls) taking the two-fisted stance with a gun common to crime shows, *Stonestreet* provides plenty of 70's fun from the strong cast of supporting characters (including the great Joan Hackett, Elaine Giftos and Val Avery) to the *Shaft*-like music by Patrick Williams and the always-delightful and beautiful Eden. The series was never picked up, but Eden would go on to star as a psychic psychiatrist who investigates crime in several entertaining made-for-TV movies in the 90's.

Sweet, Sweet Rachel (1971) 72 min.; Network: ABC; D: Sutton Roley; American Broadcasting Company; Release Date: October 2, 1971; Stars: Alex Dreier, Stefanie Powers, Pat Hingle, Louise Latham, Steve Ihnat, Brenda Scott, Chris Robinson, Richard Bull, John Hillerman, Rod McCarey, William Bryant.

Above average, eerie and fascinating pilot film for *The Sixth Sense* with Alex Dreier as paranormal expert Dr. Lucas Darrow. The 1972 series which ran for 24 episodes starred Gary Collins as Dr. Michael Rhodes. In the compelling pilot, wealthy Paul Stanton (Rod McCarey) sees a vision of his wife Rachel (Stefanie Powers) beckoning to him from behind a gate and imploring him to help her. When he runs forward to her aid, he crashes through a plate glass window to his death in the courtyard below. Rachel meanwhile gets a call from a mysterious voice who repeats the words, "eye, knife, raven, doll, coffin." The distraught Rachel seeks the help of Dr. Darrow who determines to learn the identity of the person with telepathic powers who may be inducing this psychic malevolence. Meanwhile Rachel's slippery Aunt Lillian and Uncle Arthur (Louise Latham and Pat Hingle) come to her aid, the dowdy and unassuming couple radiating something sinister. Dr. Darrow must find out who is trying to drive Rachel mad, even if Rachel herself might be culpable, and has a blind assistant Carey (Chris Robinson) with psychic powers to help him. As in a number of made-for-TV films of this era, the setting features a fabulous palatial house and estate with a sumptuous winding staircase and an ornate balcony overlooking the ocean. A feeling of the supernatural and metaphysical pervades it; it is often shot in the dark with funereal music, although even the daytime feels bewitched. At its heart is a good mystery with plenty of red herrings and a little bit about eyeglasses as a motif for the second sight theme. The acting is uniformly excellent and believable with particularly fine work from Stefanie Powers who is listed as a guest star and still has a bit of her *Girl From U.N.C.L.E.* look here. Aside from a few 70's moments involving "kids" freaking out on a houseboat, *Sweet, Sweet Rachel* is not a bit dated. The great John Hillerman also makes a brief appearance as a doctor.

A Taste of Evil (**1971**) 71 min.; Network: ABC; D: John Llewellyn Moxey; Aaron Spelling Productions; Release Date: October 12, 1971; Stars: Barbara Stanwyck, Barbara Parkins, Roddy McDowall, William Windom, Arthur O'Connell, Dawn Frame, Bing Russell.

This ABC Movie of the Week offering is a retelling of Hammer's 1961 chiller *Scream of Fear* (British title: *Taste of Fear*) by the same author Jimmy Sangster. Set on a San Francisco estate, it drips with atmosphere, owing to the fabulous house and grounds and rich production values. The creative use of a bit of forest, mood and a grand house are very reminiscent of Hammer, in fact, as is the heroine's penchant for flowing white nightgowns. Susan Wilcox (beautiful Barbara Parkins) returns home from a Swiss sanitarium seven years after being raped in her playhouse at age 13. Her mother Miriam (Barbara Stanwyck) is now married to a longtime friend and hard drinker Harold Jennings (William Windom). Although she can't remember her attacker, Susan believes it was Harold. When Harold goes off on a sudden business trip, she keeps seeing his dead body on the estate and one windy night through the filmy white curtains of her bedrooms, she sees him standing motionless on the lawn below her. Is she unraveling or is someone trying to drive her mad? Roddy McDowall (with a 70's helmet haircut) plays her sympathetic psychiatrist and Arthur O'Connell is the dim-witted handyman John, in line with *Dracula*'s Renfield. The first half of the film is terrific with Parkins plagued by apparitions, but midway there is a dramatic twist. Although the plot takes on new steam and intensity with this unexpected turn, it also relies on incredulous coincidence. All in all, a fun, old-fashioned thriller with lots of atmosphere, a good cast and a fine story, if somewhat preposterous.

They Call It Murder (**1971**) 95 min.; Network: NBC; D: Walter Grauman; Paisano Productions in association with 20th Century Fox Television; Release Date: December 17, 1971; Stars: Jim Hutton, Lloyd Bochner, Jessica Walter, Jo Ann Pflug, Robert J. Wilke, Miriam Colon, Edward Asner, Leslie

Nielsen, Carmen Mathews, Nita Talbot, Vaughn Taylor, Vic Tayback, Harry Townes, Michael Pataki.

Above average, twisty whodunit set in the small California town of Madison City and based on *The D.A. Draws a Circle*, the first of nine Erle Stanley Gardner mysteries featuring his protagonist D.A. Doug Shelby; it is the only one that was filmed. Gardner, who was best known for *Perry Mason*, is credited as executive story consultant and his literary agent Cornwell Jackson was executive producer on the telemovie. An ex-convict Morton Rome is found floating in the Antrim family's pool. D.A. Doug Shelby (Jim Hutton) wants to find out whodunit and shortly discovers the victim didn't die in the pool but was shot elsewhere, twice, with two different guns, using the same entrance hole. Jane Antrim (Jessica Walter) and her mother Doris (Carmen Mathews) aren't giving any answers and neither is Jane's father-in-law Frank (Leslie Nielsen doing an Irish brogue) who lives with them and is paralyzed from a car accident that killed Jane's husband Brian. Then private eye Jeff Poland (Vic Tayback) shows up investigating insurance fraud. Jane Antrim gets $500,000 if her husband's death is proven to be legitimate. But there were no skid marks when Brian's car crashed. As Poland puts it, "There's a word for that. They call it murder." Hutton essentially plays the same as he would Ellery Queen and makes a straight, enjoyable lead, reminiscent of Dean Jones. The talented Nielsen is a bit over the top and Nita Talbot makes her usual delicious appearance as aging horror queen Rona Corbin who was at the same sanitarium as the victim. Talbot's delivery is always priceless. The denouement, explained in picture boxes and split screens as in *It Takes a Thief*, is a doozy and should comfort mystery writers that no solution is too convoluted or far-fetched.

Trilogy of Terror (1975) 73 min.; Network: ABC; D: Dan Curtis; Dan Curtis Productions; Release Date: March 4, 1975; Stars: Karen Black, Robert Burton, John Karlen, George Gaynes, James Storm, Kathryn Reynolds, Orin Cannon, Gregory Harrison, Tracy Curtis.

Trilogy of Terror is deservedly a favorite among horror fans and consists of three stories featuring the late and great cult icon Karen Black. Its fame, like 1945's British horror anthology *Dead of Night,* rests chiefly on the third segment which is a mini-masterwork and possibly one of the best-remembered made-for-TV stories in the history of television. Director Dan Curtis (of *Dark Shadows* fame) made his mark in the genre like Hammer Studio's Terrence Fisher, and the three stories, although overshadowed by the third, are all quite good with twists at the end, even though the second segment has an overplayed and obvious storyline. Black has a field day and is fabulous as each deeply twisted personality for which each segment is named. Like Patty Duke, she has cult status for being over-the-top, but in point of fact was a first-rate actress whose A-list career was derailed into horror. In the first segment, "Julie," Black is a mousy schoolteacher whose student Chad (Robert Burton) schemes to take advantage of her sexually, but he doesn't know what he's dealing with. There's an "in" joke when Chad takes her to a drive-in vampire movie which turns out to be Curtis' own production *The Night Stalker* (reviewed in this book). In the second, "Millicent and Therese," Black has a dual role as two antagonistic sisters, one prim and good, the other lascivious and evil. Although predictable, Black makes it entertaining and the nerves are kept taut by Robert Cobert's disturbing score. The third and the best is "Amelia," involving a fearsome little Zuni doll which has become a symbol of horror and the made-for-TV film. The evil doll is a favorite trope and done to perfection here. Although all the stories derive from Richard Matheson works, "Amelia" (based on his short story "Prey") is the only one he also adapted as a screenplay with Black's input. Amelia buys an African fetish doll, a scroll describing it as "he who kills... he is a deadly hunter," for a boyfriend, but when the chain around its neck detaches, it comes to life and begins its relentless murderous pursuit of her.

Twin Detectives (1976) 73 min.; Network: ABC; D: Robert Day; Charles Fries Productions; Release Date: May 1, 1976; Stars: Jim Hager, Jon Hager, Lynda Day George, Lillian Gish, Patrick O'Neal, Michael Constantine, Otis Young, Barbara Rhoades, David White, Fred Beir, Randi Oakes, James Victor, Frank London, Billy Barty.

Twin Detectives was the failed pilot for a TV series about identical twin private detectives played by Jim and Jon Hager who are part of the Thomas Detective Agency. The show screams the 70's from every frame, beginning with the identical 70's haircuts worn by the Hagers and the yellow and orange palette found throughout. The Thomas twins are hired by Marvin Telford (David White of *Bewitched* fame) to expose a ring of psychics who are conning an elderly lady Billy Jo Haskins (Lillian Gish) out of her money. Leonard Rainier (Patrick O'Neal) is the mastermind and Nancy Pendleton (Lynda Day George) is the conduit in the séances through which the spirit of Haskins' husband is channeled. His husky voice comes out of her mouth, sounding as freaky as Mercedes McCambridge talking through Linda Blair in *The Exorcist* (1973), although Day is less adept than Blair at lip synching. Pendleton then agrees to divulge what she knows to Tony Thomas, but is bumped off before she gets the chance. The words "HUD" are found scribbled on her purse in red lipstick. The Thomas twins decide to get to the bottom of things by tricking the tricksters, but not before there are some car chases with squealing tires. Yes, there is a dwarf in the movie – the wonderful character actor Billy Barty who appears as a bartender and would do a memorable comic turn in *Foul Play* (1978). The strong cast of supporting players keeps this enjoyable.

Two for the Money (1972) 73 min.; Network: ABC; D: Bernard L. Kowalski; Aaron Spelling Productions; Release Date: February 26, 1972; Stars: Robert Hooks, Stephen Brooks, Walter Brennan, Catherine Burns, Neville Brand, Shelley Fabares, Mercedes McCambridge, Anne Revere, Richard Dreyfuss, Skip Homeier, Michael Fox, Mady Maguire.

An Aaron Spelling pilot that didn't sell, *Two for the Money* is still a solid, stand-alone entry starring Stephen Brooks as Chip Bronx and Robert Hooks as Larry Dean, partners and buddies in the LAPD. The telefilm opens with a car chase, a staple of 70's detective shows that probably gained traction after *Bullitt* (1968) which was known for its breathtaking and breakneck car pursuit in hilly San Francisco. When Chip is wounded, the doctor pronounces that he can return to the force – but in a desk job. His stricken partner counters, "If a man is a policeman, that's the way he wants to live, that's the way Chip wants to live – not behind a desk." Larry then opens a detective agency for the two of them. Before they even have a chance to unpack their boxes in their new office space, Judith Gap (Catherine Burns), a 70's chick with a shag and bell bottoms, enters to hire them to find her brother Morris. He has been missing for 12 years after he murdered a family of five and the considerable bounty money would be their payment for finding him. The two detectives head out to Kincaid where the local law enforcement is hostile and uncooperative (what else?) towards the cocky city newcomers who think they can accomplish what they failed to do. Mrs. Gap (Anne Revere), who is seriously ill and wants to see her son one last time, tells them books were Morris' friends, so with the help of the cute, perky local librarian Bethany Hagan (Shelley Fabares), they learn of Morris' reading habits and Chip mixes business with pleasure. Amusing is when the two men go to a diner where their tab for breakfast is $3.00. Larry then grouses that Chip is overdoing it with his 85-cent tip! Also amusing is that Chip would be seen fit only for a desk job, yet is running all over the place unimpeded in his new assignment, the stunt double doing tumbles. This is a very tight, absorbing mystery with a supporting cast comprised of top notch talent such as Mercedes McCambridge, Richard Dreyfuss and Walter Brennan. Weirdly shades of McCambridge's creepy "Exorcist" voice can be heard; McCambridge would be the voice of the demon in *The Exorcist* the following year.

A Very Missing Person (1972) 90 min.; Network: ABC; D: Russ May-berry; Universal Television; Release Date: March 4, 1972; Stars: Eve Arden, James Gregory, Julie Newmar, Ray Danton, Dennis Rucker, Pat Morita, Ezra Stone, Woodrow Parfrey, Skye Aubrey, Bob Hastings, Robert Easton, Sherry Bain, Udana Power, Dwan Smith, Linda Gillin.

The original plan in 1972 was for a series called *The Great Detectives*, a program of alternating shows similar to *The NBC Mystery Movie*, but us-ing classic literary sleuths, such as Hildegarde Withers, the retired New York City schoolteacher turned amateur detective created by Stuart Palmer. *A Very Missing Person* was one of the three pilots crafted for the series and con-cerned Hildegarde Withers (the great Eve Arden) trying to locate 23-year-old Leonore Gregory who had run off to join a colony of hippies on a yacht called Karma; the "flower children" were planning to create a New Eden in the West Indies. Withers, described in the stories as a "tall, bony spinster" with trademark eccentric hats and a black furled umbrella, was originally created in 1931 and played by Edna Mae Oliver, and is well-embodied by Arden whose titian hair and blue eyes match the coloring of another female literary sleuth, Nancy Drew. The script was based on Palmer's last novel completed by fellow mystery author Fletcher Flora (great name), *Hildegarde Makes the Scene*. It was an obvious attempt to bring Withers into modern times, which only dated her. Christie never went "groovy" on her readers. Arden is wonderful, but looks as jarringly out of place among the hippies as Doris Day in the interminably mod *Caprice* (1967). *A Very Missing Person* is full of 70's lingo and types (think huge Afros and 1970's Sonny Bono loo-kalikes) and among them floats prim and fashionable Withers, but it does expose the cultish figures that the era gave rise to (i.e., Manson) and the hollowness and passive destructiveness of the "tune in, drop out" culture. Bodies begin dropping like flies and Withers enlists the help of handsome Aloysius "Al" Fister (Dennis Rucker) to delve into the cult. Gorgeous Julie Newmar (Catwoman in *Batman*) appears as Aleatha Westering, the spacy wife of the cult leader, and James Gregory ably embodies police officer Oscar Piper, Withers' friend and former love interest. *A Very Missing Person* is dated and unremarkable, but its sense of humor and the divine Arden infuse it with some liveliness.

The Victim a.k.a. Out of Contention (1972) 74 min.; Network: ABC; D: Herschel Daugherty; Universal Television; Release Date: November 14, 1972; Stars: Elizabeth Montgomery, Eileen Heckart, Sue Ane Langdon, George Maharis, Jess Walton, Richard Derr, Ross Elliott, John Furlong, George Jue, Michael Keller.

This was a chiller in the vein of *See No Evil* (1971) where the unsuspecting victim is in the house with a killer. Susan Chapel (Jess Walton) and her animals live in a remote Monterey beach house while Susan's sister Kate Wainwright (Elizabeth Montgomery) has sumptuous digs in a San Francisco high-rise. When Kate calls Susan to find out about her troubled marriage, she is told that Susan is going to start divorce proceedings. Unable to convince Susan to come to San Francisco, Kate decides to drive down to her sister's in spite of an impending thunderstorm. Meanwhile Susan was not alone and after hanging up with Kate, confronts an unseen presence to ask, "What are you doing here?" Cue fear. By the time Kate gets to the house, the storm is underway (what else?) and she shortly begins to sense something is wrong when the animals are there, but nary a sign of Susan. This is because Susan's body is in a trunk in the basement and the killer is in the house. *The Victim* is a good, absorbing thriller of its kind with a solid performance by Montgomery, wonderful atmosphere, great eerie music by Gil Melle, and most importantly, an isolated and scary setting, particularly the fabulous rustic beach house with its squeaky screen door. The initial glimpse of Susan in the trunk is quite terrifying, a technique Hitchcock used of showing the proverbial bomb beneath the table, and there are also a few red herrings for good measure. Eileen Heckart, a wonderful character actress, adds considerably as Mrs. Hawkes, Susan's maid and Sue Ane Langdon has a fun bit part as Susan's friend Edith Jordan. Dig Elizabeth Montgomery's posh San Francisco pad (where do they get these locations?) overlooking the bay and Golden Gate bridge. Above average chiller with fine acting.

Weekend of Terror (1970) 74 min.; Network: ABC; D: Jud Taylor; Paramount Television; Release Date: December 8, 1970; Stars: Robert Conrad, Carol Lynley, Lois Nettleton, Jane Wyatt, Lee Majors, Kevin Hagen, Ann Doran, Gregory Sierra, Byron Clark, Barbara Barnett.

When two escaped convicts, Eddie (Robert Conrad) and Larry (Lee Majors) kidnap a businessman's daughter for ransom and she accidentally dies under Larry's watch, they decide to get another hostage to take her place – a woman with a similar build who can pass as her double. Meanwhile three nuns, Sister Francis (Jane Wyatt), Sister Ellen (Lois Nettleton) and Sister Meredith (Carol Lynley), are driving across the California desert when their car breaks down. The comely Sister Ellen is in street clothes since, as she explained to Sister Meredith, she had "dropped out…tuned in…saw the world and man, it was really heavy!" Thus, in hipster clothes and with hipster hairdo, she's back to join the fold and is the one who gets out to flag down a passing vehicle. Lo and behold, Eddie spots her, his new victim, and picks her up, not initially seeing the two other nuns in the car, then decides to go through with his plan even in spite of them. With a cheesy story that he can give them a jack at his house, he takes the holy trio to his remote house in the middle of nowhere. Now he has gone from the frying pan straight to the pit of hell. This preposterous exercise in suspense is entertaining, because it serves up escapism, not realism. Who would really believe Carol Lynley with her spacy line readings was a nun or that a kidnapper would give his nun victim the money to go into a beauty parlor and buy a wig, telling her she's going to wear it at a party that night? At one point, Larry even knocks on the door of the room where the nuns are locked in and yells, "Hey, nuns! Want a beer?" Fun and basically wholesome made-for-TV fare with good on-location sites.

When Michael Calls a.k.a. Shattered Silence (1972) 73 min.; Network: ABC; D: Philip Leacock; 20th Century Fox Television, Palomar Pictures; Release Date: February 5, 1972; Stars: Ben Gazzara, Elizabeth Ashley, Michael Douglas, Karen Pearson, Albert S. Waxman, Marian Waldman, Christopher Pellett, Steve Weston, John Bethune, Larry Reynolds, Alan McRae, Robert Warner, Michele Chicoine.

When Michael Calls was one of the highly-anticipated Movie-of-the-Week offerings from ABC with the hook "Michael's been dead for 15 years. Now he's back to avenge his mother's death." Based on a novel by John Farris, it concerns a woman Helen (Elizabeth Ashley) whose ex-husband Doremus Connelly (Ben Gazzara) violates his visiting rights and shows up at her Vermont home to see his daughter Peggy. At the same time, Helen is suddenly beset by phone calls from a mysterious child who claims to be Michael, her nephew who died 15 years ago. Michael and his brother Craig (Michael Douglas) were taken in by Helen when their mother went insane and committed suicide in an asylum and Michael always held Helen responsible. Although Helen wants to dismiss the disturbing calls as a prank, the caller knows a nickname only Michael knew and things take an even more deadly turn when several people connected to Michael wind up murdered. There are attempts at red herrings, but the solution is fairly transparent. Still, *When Michael Calls* is a decent, if slightly predictable thriller. The remote setting (filming was actually in Ontario, Canada) and wintry Halloween season create a feeling of isolation like Bodega Bay in *The Birds* (1963). Note the peaked 70's cap worn by Ashley and her shag hairstyle.

Who is the Black Dahlia? (1975) 100 min.; Network: NBC; D: Joseph Pevney; Douglas S. Cramer Company; Release Date: March 1, 1975; Stars: Lucie Arnaz, Efrem Zimbalist, Jr., Ronny Cox, Macdonald Carey, Tom Bosley, Gloria DeHaven, John Fiedler, Rick Jason, June Lockhart, Mercedes McCambridge, Donna Mills, Henry Jones, Brooke Adams, Lana Wood, Ted Gehring.

Haunting, if anecdotal, recreation of the infamous unsolved murder of 22-year-old aspiring actress Elizabeth Short, dubbed "The Black Dahlia" because of her black hair and tendency to wear black clothes. The story alternates between scenes of Short's life after going to Hollywood and the investigation into her death by a determined detective Sergeant Harry Hansen (Efrem Zimbalist Jr.), the last frame of every scene involving Short dissolving into a black and white image. Against the objections of her mother Lucille Ball, Lucie Arnaz took the lead which proved a breakout role for her. Although her acting style sometimes evokes more of a live theater performance as it did on *Here's Lucy,* she effectively imbues Short with a naïve sweetness, longing and starry-eyed quality which evolves into a façade of slickness as Short's desperation to be someone increases. Arnaz also presents her as someone wary of being taken advantage of by the sailors who are on the make. Period detail is colorfully recreated in the manner of television movies with many familiar faces making appearances, such as June Lockhart, Tom Bosley, Brooke Adams and Mercedes McCambridge. Donna Mills does a particularly good turn as a flinty starlet who notes that Short seemed to be on the run from someone. The script, emphasizing the enigma of the tragic girl, has a tendency for sledgehammer anecdotal remarks, such as Short saying, "I feel alive" juxtaposed against the scene of the police finding the body and "Grandmama used to say nothing alive and pretty is ever permanent." The murder was gruesome in that Short was carefully bisected by someone with surgical skill, drained of blood with ear-to-ear lacerations and posed like a mannequin in an empty lot. High quality and solid retelling of a truly haunting and horrific unsolved case.

The Woman Hunter (1972) 74 min.; Network: CBS; D: Bernard L. Kowalski; Bing Crosby Productions; Release Date: September 19, 1972; Stars: Barbara Eden, Robert Vaughn, Stuart Whitman, Enrique Lucero, Larry Storch, Norma Storch, Aurora Munoz, Victor Hugo Jauregui, Sydney Chaplin.

The Woman Hunter is a silly and moderately campy bit of escapism and a must for Barbara Eden fans. As a party is in full swing under the Bermuda stars, a woman is murdered on the beach and the killer (who isn't shown) removes all her jewelry. Three years later, wealthy and beautiful Dina Hunter (Barbara Eden) is released from a hospital after having been cleared of manslaughter following a car crash and she joins her husband Jerry (Robert Vaughn) at a sumptuous cliff-side villa overlooking the beach in Acapulco. Along with the picturesque setting, Eden provides a feast for the eyes in her parade of fashion ensembles involving animal print bikinis with sarongs and coordinated scarves and outfits. Her navel is often exposed, unlike during her days on *I Dream of Jeannie* where she had to cover it with a jewel. An artist and mystery man and potential lothario Paul Carter (Stuart Whitman) meanwhile is observing her through binoculars and makes an excuse to meet her. There is some attraction between them, particularly since Jerry, who is dependent on her money, often neglects her. When she uncovers evidence that Carter has been stalking her, however, she panics. It results in a car chase along the winding cliffs. This is a fun bit of hokum with a story by Brian Clemens who wrote *The Avengers*. The true highlight is the hilarious "abandoned" Latin dance Eden does midway at a party in order to entice Carter with her jewels. It is as deliciously campy as Maria Montez's frenzied number in *Cobra Woman* (1944) and worth the price of admission and repeat viewings alone.

The Television Series

Mike Connors and Gail Fisher in *Mannix*. Photo courtesy of Desilu Productions and Paramount Television from the collection of JoAnn Paul.

William Conrad as Frank Cannon.
Photo courtesy of Quinn Martin Productions.

Cannon (CBS) (1971-1976) Executive Producer: Quinn Martin. Developed by Edward Hume. Production Company: Quinn Martin Productions. Starring William Conrad. 124 episodes. 5 seasons.

Cannon was another terrific entry in the detective genre, starring William Conrad as Frank Cannon, a former Los Angeles Police Department detective and widower who became a private detective. The gimmick with this particular series was that Conrad was a corpulent man and used it in his line of work, most notedly in his hilarious "belly bump" technique where he'd knock an opponent off guard with a thrust of his belly. Like Nero Wolfe, Cannon had very refined tastes in food and cars, and even used a mobile "car phone," which was fairly rare at the time, although unlike Wolfe, he was not an armchair detective.[1] Conrad gave a wonderful depth to the character that made him likeable and believable. Another thing that made *Cannon* unique is that he was shown as financially comfortable and although he wasn't as trim as some of his detective counterparts, he still did plenty of running in the line of duty and wasn't afraid to get physical. His stakeouts evoked the smooth intrigue of Jack Nicholson as Jake Gittes in *Chinatown* (one of Nicholson's finest roles) as opposed to the buffoonish methods employed by other TV detectives. Like several of his TV peers, he had served in the Korean War.

The pilot "Cannon" was terrific, as pilots usually are, and introduced Cannon after he had already embarked on his career as a private detective; this was the path he took after retirement from the LAPD following the death of his wife and son in a car accident. Fresh from an overseas assignment and enjoying the view from his Los Angeles penthouse, he is enlisted to help the wife of an old Korean war buddy who is accused of her husband's murder. Without missing a beat, Cannon heads to a backwater town in New Mexico to investigate. Once again, it's the sinister small town hostile to strangers with all residents seeming to harbor a collective secret. Cannon is shrewd and assured, in spite of the number of gratuitous shots emphasizing his girth, particularly one shot from below as he lies in bed that deliberately gives the illusion of a beached whale. He is not diminished by a joke, however, or anyone's fool. In response to someone trying to snicker or stare at his belly, he says, impatiently, "Yeah, I'm fat" and nips it in the bud, making his

---

1   William Conrad played Nero Wolfe in the 1981 series, quipping at the time, "I love his lifestyle. I don't have to run anymore."

detractors look petty, so he can get on with business. As Kevin Burton Smith of *The Thrilling Detective* put it, Cannon is the fat man as action hero. Conrad inhabits him so easily, we never doubt him.

Cannon was superior to some of the more celebrated series of the time, possessing a literate quality, which is not surprising since a number of scripts were derived from novels and a host of strong producers and writers were involved in it. As with a number of other popular TV shows, such as *Charlie's Angels, Columbo, Kojak, Hawaii Five-O,* and *Starsky and Hutch,* a series of tie-in novels were published in the 1970's, seven of which were written by Douglas Enefer under the pseudonym of Paul Denver and two by Richard Gallagher. The opening credits were dynamic and exciting when guest stars and "special" guest stars were sonorously announced as their faces appeared in circles just as the faces of guest stars appeared inside lifesavers on *Love Boat.* It gave a show extra drama and was a much-anticipated component. *Cannon* had the usual stellar roster of guest stars which were common to TV at that time as well, including Pamela Franklin, Martin Sheen, David Soul and Marcia Mae Jones.

In "Bad Cats and Sudden Death," Cannon once again has a client, District Attorney Mike Arnold (Michael Tolan), accused of murdering his spouse, although it smells of a frame-up. When Arnold asks what motive he could possibly have for murdering his own wife, Cannon tells him money, pointing out that Arnold was living way over his $17,500-a-year salary (yeah, it's the seventies!). Later when snooping in the D.A.'s apartment, Cannon is stopped by a woman with a gun who frisks him, saying, "A big one – and a little dangerous, too." It turns out she is an investigator for the D.A.'s office and he winds up making her a gourmet omelet as he pumps her for information. After she tells him she is 1/8 Cherokee, he tells her he believes the other 7/8ths of her was not there for the reason she claimed. There's a wonderful chemistry Conrad achieves with his co-stars which enlivens and elevates these scenes and makes one believe they were all genuinely enjoying themselves. He has a crackling rapport with the formidable Jessica Walter as an attorney he is hired to protect in "That Was No Lady." He was also good at putting across witty lines without making them sound kitschy, such as in "Dead Pigeon" when he says, plaintively, "Oh, Soapy, why do I have to be a sucker for your phony charm?"

Like *The Streets of San Francisco*, another Quinn Martin Production, the show is divided into four acts. In season one, a particularly sharp episode is "Death Chain" which guest stars William Windom as Harry Kendrix, a man who is implicated in the murder of his mistress Donna. Unlike some openings, the initial crime takes place in a way that is ingenious and plausible as Kendrix waits in a bedroom while Donna goes to answer the door. Donna is abducted into a car at gunpoint, which Kendrix witnesses from the bedroom window, and as he runs out the front door, distraught, while the car pulls away, another witness happens by to observe him at the scene. It doesn't look good for him. Cannon's interrogation of the client is full of great astute touches which also keeps the action believable. Such a wonderful through-line of superb and smooth acting is what kept *Cannon* in the lineup for six seasons.

Conrad was in fine form once again as Cannon in *The Return of Frank Cannon* (1980).

Jaclyn Smith, Farrah Fawcett and Kate Jackson, the original *Charlie's Angels.* Photo courtesy of Spelling-Goldberg Productions.

Charlie's Angels (ABC) (1976-1981) Executive Producers: Aaron Spelling and Leonard Goldberg. Created by Ivan Goff and Ben Roberts. Production Company: Spelling-Goldberg Productions. Starring Kate Jackson, Farrah Fawcett, Jaclyn Smith, Cheryl Ladd, Shelley Hack, Tanya Roberts, David Doyle, John Forsythe (voice only). 110 episodes. 5 seasons.

Charlie's Angels is like watching Breck Shampoo models fight crime. The premise involves three beautiful women who graduated from the Los Angeles police academy and were assigned to menial jobs until recruited to work as private investigators for millionaire Charles Townsend (voiced by John Forsythe who is never seen and uncredited) at the Townsend Agency. "Charlie" is sometimes depicted off-camera or his hands or feet are seen, but he invariably is surrounded by one or more beautiful women as he instructs his Angels about their newest assignment. The Angels themselves are not exactly heavyweights and their fluffy assignments often involve donning bikinis or going undercover where they unfailingly use their real names (which the criminals easily trace to the Townsend Agency). They also sometimes fall in love with the wrong person while investigating, but in spite of their feathered, coiffed hair and lip gloss and seeming lack of guile, they manage to defend themselves and get out of difficult scrapes and solve the mystery by the episode's end. Dismissed as "Jiggle TV" by critics initially, the show nonetheless became a runaway hit and star Farrah Fawcett Majors, in particular, became a pinup, fashion influence and popular part of the cultural lexicon.

The original "Angels" consisted of Kate Jackson as Sabrina Duncan, Farrah Fawcett as Jill Munroe, and Jaclyn Smith as Kelly Garrett with David Doyle[2] as their sidekick John Bosley. Originally a blonde, brunette and redhead were wanted for the cast, but Smith worked so well in the audition that they kept two brunettes and a blonde. Smith would not only be the Angel who endured through the show's run, but also came across as the most dignified, in spite of doing her share of cheesecake. The set-up of each episode was usually presentation of the crime, the Angels being given their assignment by Charlie via Western Electric Speakerphone, and then the Angels going undercover to unravel the case. In the last frame, Bosley and the Angels receive praise for a great job from the unseen Charlie as they lounge around back at the Townsend office. Sabrina Duncan was the most rascally of the trio and Jackson would sometimes fake Hollywood's idea of a New York accent, her undercover characters a blend of broad shtick and over-

---

2   Interesting that David Doyle would be given the last name of Bosley, since he was strikingly similar in appearance and personality to character actor Tom Bosley.

the-top caricature that would fool no one. Fawcett as Munroe was the most cutesy and girlish, often relying on her wide Colgate smile and baby blues to disarm her foes, although all the girls used sex appeal as part of their arsenal which gave the show a lightweight, escapist appeal. Episodes were plotted like the average procedural drama and the trademark eye candy was kept tasteful. Although the Angels had a layer of seriousness and capability beneath the trivial surface, their glamour fueled the addictive fantasy element of the show.

As always, storylines were recycled from other episodes or shows of the period. Like *Police Woman*, the girls went undercover in a variety of colorful professions, ranging from stuntwomen and roller derby queens to cheerleaders and prison inmates (cue Central Casting toughs and a prison matron a la Shirley Stoler). They were often required to put their lives in jeopardy and sallied forth into these hazardous assignments, at times completely unarmed. "Chorus Line Angels" gave Smith a chance to sing and dance, an audience-pleasing trope used in other detective shows like *Hart to Hart, Diagnosis: Murder* and *Murder, She Wrote*. Like many detective shows, particularly lightweight programs, *Charlie's Angels* had that "cops and robbers" horseplay element where the protagonists almost never were shot while running from foes, even when in clear sight, making the criminals impossibly poor shots. Jackson, in fact, was once directly on the other side of a car when her pursuer fired and missed, but this went along with other bits of silliness, such as when the Angels leave their car to run after a suspect on foot instead of driving (where they could easily overtake him) in "Waikiki Angels." In "To Kill an Angel," Smith became the only Angel to suffer from a gunshot wound when she was shot at close range by a young autistic boy, although like an MGM heroine, she managed to look near-flawless in the hospital. An occasional episode became slightly edgier when offering backstory on an Angel's life and many episodes, even with frivolous elements, were solidly absorbing.

The show underwent a notorious series of cast changes, beginning with the departure of Farrah Fawcett. Given that she was one of the drawing cards in the series, the producers worked out a deal for her to make a series of six guest appearances in future episodes. Fawcett was replaced by beautiful Cheryl Ladd who, like Smith, maintained a slightly more dignified and sophisticated aura. Ladd had been the singing voice of Melody on the animated series *Josie and the Pussycats* and would again showcase her abilities in "Angels in the Wings." She portrayed Jill's younger sister Kris and according to plan, Fawcett made guest appearances, revealed now as a daredevil race-car driver. The show was relatively unscathed by the cast change, but when Jackson's desire for film roles conflicted with her schedule on the series, she also departed and was replaced by cute and lanky Charlie (no pun intended) perfume girl Shelley Hack as Tiffany Welles. When ratings declined and Hack was released from her contract, she was replaced by model and actress Tanya Roberts as streetwise Julie Rogers. Roberts, a gorgeous redhead with electric blue eyes, brought an interesting edge and depth to the series in her debut "Angel in Hiding," but the show lost more of its audience and was canceled. *Charlie's Angels*, however, has earned a solid place in the cultural lexicon and an enduring fanbase. Its fans include Drew Barrymore who did a 2000 remake and a 2003 sequel.

Peter Falk as Lieutenant *Columbo* with Jose Ferrer in "Mind Over Mayhem"
(1974). Photo courtesy of Universal Television and Studios USA.

Columbo (NBC)(ABC) (1971-2003) Executive Producer: Philip
Saltzman. Created by Richard Levinson and William Link. Production
Companies: Universal Television and Studios USA. Starring Peter Falk and
"Dog" (basset hound). 69 episodes. 10 seasons.

Columbo was one of the greatest detective series in the history of television with movie-length episodes, the brainchild of Richard Levinson and

William Link. Peter Falk starred as Lieutenant Columbo of the LAPD's homicide unit, a disheveled, seemingly scattered detective of Italian descent, whose trademarks include a rumpled tan raincoat, a cigar and the catchphrase "Just one more thing." The format was the inverted detective story, in which the killer was known from the onset, and the show revolved around Columbo's ingenious methods of uncovering and exposing the perpetrator who has usually underestimated his shrewdness and intelligence. TV Guide ranked Lt. Columbo as no. 7 on the "100 Greatest TV Characters of All Time" and the show consistently ranks on lists of all-time greatest television shows. The character (played by Bert Freed) first appeared in a 1960 television anthology series in an episode adapted from a Levinson and Link short story and then Levinson and Link featured him in a stage play *Prescription: Murder* which opened in San Francisco in 1962 with Thomas Mitchell as Columbo. That same play was adapted into a two-hour television movie that aired on NBC with Peter Falk in the lead role which was so successful, it became a series that would play in rotation with two other shows, *McCloud* and *McMillan & Wife* as part of *The NBC Mystery Movie* wheel series. Falk won an Emmy in his first year on the show and would win a total of four more with seven additional nominations. *Columbo* received numerous awards and nominations from 1971 to 2005, including 13 Emmys, two Golden Globes and two Edgar Awards.

Because *Columbo* was part of a wheel series that rotated and did not play weekly, each episode was crafted with care and resulted in high quality, cinematic works that often painted a portrait of the many worlds of Los Angeles, including the Hollywood film industry. Sometimes famous Hollywood stars, doctors, mystery writers, singers, psychiatrists and other celebrities or esteemed professionals were the culprits. With great writing and a strong lead character perfectly embodied by Peter Falk whose squinting eyes seemed to glisten like that of a fox when observing his quarry, plus a multitude of terrific guest stars, the formula was foolproof. Like Jack Lord and *Hawaii Five-O*, Falk was deeply involved with the series, supplying his own wardrobe (including the iconic raincoat) and ad-libbing his character's eccentricities, which was also designed to keep fellow actors off-balance and therefore more impatient with Columbo. He also chose Columbo's car, a ramshackle Peugeot model 403 Grande Luxe Cabriolet and a great focal point for humor; it was as dilapidated as his wardrobe. In "Any Old Port in a Storm," the valet remarks, "Boy, you don't see many of these things around," to which Columbo responds, "I've got over 100,000 miles on it. You take care of your car, it'll take care of you." It was also quite hilarious when a tony, arrogant murderer was asked to climb into the car to ride down to the station. The car, like the raincoat and Columbo's fumblings, functioned as red herrings for the murderers and added to Columbo's underdog appeal.

Each episode was a cat-and-mouse game with the murderer trying to outwit Columbo and often involving him in a distinctive world related to the murderer's profession. He was sometimes pitted with formidable opponents whom he came to respect and even like with the feelings being mutual. In "Any Old Port in a Storm," he tangles with a wine connoisseur Adrian Carsini (Donald Pleasence) and his dedication to learning about wine in a short period charms the murderer who shares a glass of wine with him. In "Swan Song," his opponent is gospel singer Tommy Brown (Johnny Cash) who seems as amused as exasperated with Columbo; the episode treats us to wonderful singing from Cash, resulting in another great entry. Other times the murderer is so arrogant and nasty, his comeuppance is particularly sweet, most notably Robert Culp as Paul Hanlon in "The Most Crucial Game." There are also many references to "Mrs. Columbo" and Columbo's children, but the running joke is that Mrs. Columbo and certainly the children are never seen.

The many incredible episodes of *Columbo* are too numerous to mention, most of them produced when the series was part of *The NBC Mystery Movie*, although "Last Salute to the Commodore," which departs from the Columbo formula, uniformly ranks among the weakest episode in the show's history. Among my personal favorites are "Forgotten Lady," a *Sunset Boule-*

vard-type episode in which Janet Leigh prepares for a comeback; "Dagger of the Mind" set in England in which Honor Blackman and Richard Basehart are delicious as a venerated husband-and-wife theatrical team and pair of murderers; "Requiem for a Falling Star" with a fabulously melodramatic Anne Baxter; "A Stitch in Crime" guest starring Leonard Nimoy, the great Anne Francis and the always-memorable Nita Talbot; "Double Shock" with Martin Landau providing double trouble; "Murder by the Book" with the fabulous Jack Cassidy who would surface as a killer more than once in the series (and whose guest star appearances are all favorites with me); the pilot "Prescription: Murder" which remains brilliant; and "It's All in the Game" with a sensational Emmy Award-winning performance from Faye Dunaway.

Numerous books have been written about Columbo and the show retains a solid fan base akin to that of Sherlock Holmes, while the show continues to be broadcast on television. The last episode of the series was "Columbo Likes the Nightlife" in 2003 and Columbo went out on top, the episode being highly regarded and solid. Columbo – and Peter Falk's definitive portrayal – remain a highly-regarded and indelible part of mystery and television history.

Jim Hutton and David Wayne in the short-lived, but sublime *Ellery Queen*. Photo courtesy of Fairmount/Foxcroft Productions, Tom Ward Enterprises and Universal Television.

Ellery Queen (ABC) (1975-1976) Executive Producers: Richard Levinson and William Link. Writing Producer: Peter S. Fischer. Production Companies: Fairmount/Foxcroft Productions, Tom Ward Enterprises, and Universal Television. Starring Jim Hutton, David Wayne, Tom Reese, John Hillerman, Nina Roman, Ken Swofford. 22 episodes and 1 pilot. 1 season.

Along with *Columbo, Ellery Queen* was one of the finest detective series in television history without a single bad episode in its short but sublime run. Based on the novels and stories created by Brooklyn cousins Frederic Dannay and Manfred Bennington Lee who wrote under the pseudonym Ellery Queen, everything about this series was classy down to the "Stork Club" ashtray in the titles. The production values were stellar with rich saturated colors and meticulous period detail, a cut above many other programs with none of that "seedy" look that was commonplace in the 70's and still is to this day. The setting was the 1940's and mystery writer Ellery Queen lived in a

New York City townhouse with his father Inspector Richard Queen, whom he assisted regularly on cases. Jim Hutton was the perfect embodiment of Ellery with a wonderful, likeable, old movie star presence like Jimmy Stewart or Dean Jones and had a believable chemistry with the excellent David Wayne (memorable also as the Mad Hatter on the TV show *Batman*) who played his father. Each episode opened with the announcer telling the audience a specific character was about to be murdered and then an array of suspects was shown. ("Match wits with Ellery Queen and see if you can guess whodunit!") This method was in keeping with the format of early Queen novels and radio shows where the reader or listener was a participant in solving the mystery. Midway in the series, Ellery asks the audience if they think they've got it and lists a few cryptic clues for them to help them solve it. In the denouement, the cast of suspects is gathered in classic style and Ellery unravels the case, using flashbacks. Needless to say, like Agatha Christie mysteries, the complicated plots are not easy to decipher, even with all the clues presented.

Ellery Queen of the novels began as a dandified character like S.S. Van Dine's rather obnoxious gentlemen sleuth Philo Vance and evolved into his own person; it is likely he was inspired by Vance. Hutton's Ellery, however, is absent-minded and clumsy on the order of Columbo (who was also created by the Richard Levinson and William Link writing/producing team), often preoccupied with deadlines for his own novels, but sharp and perceptive beneath this bumbling exterior. He has a coltish charm and no shortage of girlfriends. The two strong leads are backed up by equally strong supporting characters, such as delicious character actor John Hillerman (reminiscent of Clifton Webb) as Simon Brimmer, a radio show detective who would like to be as clever as Ellery and tries to get the young mystery writer to contribute to his show and Tom Reese who plays Inspector Queen's thick-headed assistant Sergeant Velie. There is the usual abundance of fun dialogue and expressions, such as when Inspector Queen says, "Why don't we cut all the banana oil?"

With not a single stinker among the episodes, *Ellery Queen* featured a superb array of guest stars, including Guy Lombardo, Farley Granger, Ann Reinking, Joan Collins, Vincent Price, George Burns, Ida Lupino, Sal Mineo, Eve Arden and Dr. Joyce Brothers (who, like Angie Dickinson, seemed to have a great sense of humor and wasn't above poking fun at herself.) "The Adventure of the Two-Faced Woman" which guest stars Dr. Joyce Brothers, in fact, is one of my favorite episodes, using that great, old trope of the person-about-to-be-murdered recognizing his or her assailant and saying, "Oh, it's you!" before being dispatched. In "The Adventure of Miss Aggie's Farewell Performance," delightful Eve Arden and Betty White guest star in the tale of a radio soap opera star who is getting the axe and has a real-life enemy who wants her to bow out permanently. Both Arden and White performed in radio during their careers and are beautifully suited to the period ambience. "The Adventure of the Eccentric Engineer," which involves an inventor murdered in his electric train workshop, guest stars a cute and perky Ann Reinking as Ellery's girlfriend. Another great episode incorporates Alice in Wonderland in "The Adventure of the Mad Tea Party," a favorite theme for classic mystery writers, and uses that wonderful trope of the stormy night. Guest stars include TV favorites Larry Hagman and Julie Sommars and there is a wonderful bit on the train as Ellery tries to work out the details of his mystery novel which an attendant interprets literally.

The pilot "Too Many Suspects" introduces all the elements that made the show top-notch. It opens dynamically with fashion designer Monica Gray (stunning Nancy Kovack a.k.a. Nancy Mehta) staggering to her television to pull the plug while the news is being broadcast. It is the infamous "dying clue." Hillerman makes his debut as Simon Brimmer and amusing scenes of his mystery radio show "The Casebook of Simon Brimmer" with sound effects are featured. There is also a delightful, old-fashioned bit at Rockefeller Plaza where Ellery has taken his precocious cousin Penny (Frannie Michel, a child star similar to Lisa Lucas and Quinn Cummings) to ice skate. The precocious brat was a type that became popular in the 70's and it would surface again with Drew Barrymore in *E.T.* (1982). The great Ray Milland guest stars as the prime suspect in this excellent pilot which has richly detailed period sets.

Locked room puzzles, Tin Pan alley, and impossible murders are all woven into episodes of *Ellery Queen*, providing old-fashioned, classic fun for mystery lovers. The short run of this series was in no way a reflection of its quality and its brief one season allowed it to exit in the high style in which it began.

The stars of *The Hardy Boys/Nancy Drew Mysteries* who each became teen idols.
Photo courtesy of Glen A. Larson Productions.

The Hardy Boys/Nancy Drew Mysteries (ABC) (1977-1979) Production Company: Glen A. Larson Productions. Developed by Glen A. Larson. Starring Shaun Cassidy, Parker Stevenson, Pamela Sue Martin, Janet Louise Johnson. 46 episodes. 3 seasons.

The Hardy Boys/Nancy Drew Mysteries, which became merely *The Hardy Boys Mysteries* in the third season, was based on two popular children's books series, Nancy Drew and the Hardy Boys. The characters were created by American writer Edward Stratemeyer and saw many evolutions over the decades, best read in their original form when the language was at its richest. Nancy Drew first appeared in print in 1930 while the Hardy Boys made their debut in 1927. The television series was family friendly, but the heartthrob status and popularity of pouty Shaun Cassidy and cleft-chinned Parker Stevenson, who played the Hardy Boys, ensured a teen following and lots of pin-ups to drool over in magazines like *Tiger Beat* and *Teen Beat.* Pamela Sue Martin also became a teen idol, due to her work as Nancy Drew. Originally each series alternated independently until they became connected as *The Hardy Boys/Nancy Drew Mysteries* in season 2. The show was imaginative and fun, preserving the basic ideas of the books and with an opening that initially recalled *Ellery Queen* and *The NBC Mystery Movie*. The TV show also brought together the characters for the first time in a few episodes, something that never happened in the books up to that time, in the two-parters "The Hardy Boys and Nancy Drew Meet Dracula"; "The Mystery of the Hollywood Phantom"; "Voodoo Doll"; and the single episode "Arson and Old Lace." After Pamela Sue Martin left the series in 1978, due to the reduction of her role, she was replaced by Janet Louise Johnson who made three appearances as Drew before the "Nancy Drew" segment was eliminated and the series was retooled to feature only the Hardy Boys. It lasted only ten episodes in season three before being canceled.

Pamela Sue Martin was well-cast as Nancy Drew, the titian-haired, blue-eyed girl detective from Riverside (in the books, Illinois; in the series, New Jersey) and daughter of lawyer Carson Drew (played by William Schallert). Her adventures have an old-fashioned fun in keeping with the original source, such as "The Mystery of Pirate's Cove" in which Nancy and her friends see a ghost in a lighthouse. Martin possessed the forthrightness, confidence and intrepidness of her fictional counterpart, as well as her sense of leadership and popularity. Some recurring characters who also were featured in the books include Nancy's tomboyish pal George Fayne (played beautifully by Jean Rasey and later Susan Buckner), Bess Marvin (Ruth Cox) and Ned Nickerson (played by George O'Hanlon Jr. and later Rick Springfield). The characters maintain the wholesomeness and attractiveness they have in the Stratemeyer series, which was ghostwritten by various people under the pseudonym of Carolyn Keene. Martin comes off as that rare "most popular girl in school" who also happens to be a solid, unspoiled, unpretentious person with less popular, but no less valued friends.

Some delicious episodes include "A Haunting We Will Go" which has a plot familiar to cozy detective series in which someone is sabotaging a play that Nancy and friends are putting on to raise money for a youth center. The theater is said to be haunted, but when some notable thespians sign on, Nancy is suspicious and has cause to be. Besides featuring Carson Drew, George Payne and Ned Nickerson, it is chockfull of fun, scenery-chewing guest stars such as Victor Buono, Dina Merrill, and Bob Crane. "The Lady on Thursday at Ten," which has Nancy preventing a top British official's assassination, was Pamela Sue Martin's last appearance as Nancy Drew and fun in a hokey way. The episode featured stereotypical Irish cops right out of old Hollywood movies, a favorite trope about the protagonist (Nancy) witnessing something that is later covered up, and Nicholas Hammond who was Friedrich on *The Sound of Music*.

Shaun Cassidy and Parker Stevenson who played Joe and Frank Hardy, respectively, looked nothing like brothers, their only similarity longish, layered 70's hairstyles. The Hardy Boys are the preppie amateur detective sons of a famous private detective, Fenton Hardy, and live in Bayport, Massachusetts (in the books Bayport is in New York). Regulars in this series include their platonic female friend Callie Shaw (Lisa Eilbacher) who also assists their father part-time and Aunt Gertrude Hardy (Edith Atwater). Like Nancy Drew, the Hardy Boys featured wholesome, old-fashioned mysteries suitable for kids with a hip factor to draw in teens and a renowned father figure who supported his autonomous offspring's adventures. The ultra 70's episode "The Flickering Torch" showcased the music of handsome pop star Ricky Nelson; musical interludes reminiscent of *The Partridge Family*; and Nelson clad in the height of 70's hipness: a white pantsuit with bellbottoms. Although Cassidy and Stevenson undoubtedly had a teenybopper fanbase, the show was likely enjoyed by mystery fans of all ages. In "The Disappearing Floor," the boys investigate the disappearance of a missing scientist and stumble on an estate and house filled with bizarre illusions like a flying saucer, a room that gets larger, a door on the second floor that leads to a land filled with wolves, and trapdoors. This veritable funhouse is symbolic of the wholesome adventures offered by the series which are a throwback to simpler times like a Little Orphan Annie decoder in a cereal box.

Although the characters remained, for the most part, separate entities, in "Mystery of the Hollywood Phantom," Frank Hardy and Nancy Drew share a kiss. *The Hardy Boys/Nancy Drew Mysteries* was an entertaining adaptation of two famous children's mystery series. It respected the source materials while updating them with fresh-faced 70's teen hip.

Stefanie Powers and Robert Wagner in *Hart to Hart*. Photo courtesy of Rona II, Spelling-Goldberg Productions, and Columbia Pictures Television.

Hart to Hart (ABC) (1979-1984) Executive Producers: Aaron Spelling and Leonard Goldberg. Created by Sidney Sheldon. Production Companies: Rona II, Spelling-Goldberg Productions, and Columbia Pictures Television. Starring Robert Wagner, Stefanie Powers and Lionel Stander. 110 episodes, 8 TV movies and 1 pilot. 5 seasons.

Hart to Hart was a light, breezy mystery caper series starring Robert Wagner and Stefanie Powers as a glamorous and wealthy married couple,

Jonathan and Jennifer Hart, who sideline as amateur detectives. Both stars had an espionage series in the 1960's, Wagner starring as debonair, jet setter master thief Alexander Mundy in *It Takes a Thief* and Powers as the cute, kicky, gadget-using April Dancer a.k.a. *The Girl From U.N.C.L.E.* They also each starred in a mystery series related to con men in the 70's.[3] Recalling the urbane charm and warmth of William Powell and Myrna Loy in *The Thin Man* films, the Harts lead a jet-setting lifestyle where "their hobby is murder," as their loyal butler Max (Lionel Stander) says in voiceover in the opening credits. They are amorous, arch and attractive, a duo who sail through life and mayhem with aplomb and stylish cool much like Steed (Patrick Macnee) and Mrs. Peel (Diana Rigg) in Britain's *The Avengers*.

Jonathan is a self-made millionaire and CEO of the Los Angeles-based conglomerate Hart Industries, while Jennifer is a freelance journalist whom he first encountered in London ("Two Harts Are Better than One"). Their initial acrimony was laced with undeniable sexual chemistry. Max with his craggy face and voice and jaunty style is their cook, butler, friend and partner in solving crime, his relationship to Jonathan dating back to Jonathan's teens when Max rescued him from an orphanage ("What Murder?") and steered him away from a potential life of crime. A devoted family member, he calls them "Mr. and Mrs. H" and looks after their adorable Löwchen, Freeway, so-named because they found him on the freeway. He often finds time for romances of his own and brings a rascally air of Damon Runyon to the show, sometimes going undercover to assist in mysteries.

The pedigree of the show bleeds through. It had its seed in a Sidney Sheldon script called *Double Twist* about a pair of married spies. Producers Aaron Spelling and Leonard Goldberg wanted it updated for a potential television series and gave the task to screenwriter Tom Mankiewicz who had written three of the James Bond films. He made his directorial debut

---

3   Stefanie Powers was in *Feather and Father Gang* (1976-1977) while Robert Wagner co-starred with Eddie Albert in *Switch* (1975-1978).

with the pilot *Hart to Hart* and the feeling of Bond is in it. As Jennifer Hart speeds down a twisting road in that pilot film, feigning an uncharacteristic hostility towards a pursuing Jonathan (and endangering his life!), it recalls films like *On Her Majesty's Secret Service* and *Goldfinger*. Initially Cary Grant was visualized as Jonathan, but at the time he was in his 70's and retired from acting, so the younger Wagner was chosen. Perhaps Wagner's suave, globetrotting Alexander Mundy reminded producers of Grant's cat burglar John Robie in *To Catch a Thief*. Nixing the casting of his wife Natalie Wood as Jennifer, Wagner instead suggested Stefanie Powers who had appeared on *It Takes a Thief* in 1970. It proved a great choice. Their chemistry carried the series with a smooth blend of likeability, charm and class. Fashions were provided by designer Nolan Miller who would do clothes for *Dynasty*. Jennifer's trademark ensemble consisted of tailored suits, but she had plenty of evening wear, opulent floor-length furs and tasteful, expensive jewelry.

Hart to Hart is all about escapism, extravagance and romance. The Harts own a racehorse J.J. Hart ("The Hartbreak Kid"); a private jet (which is seen flying over Africa); and a multitude of expensive cars including a rare 1956 Bentley Convertible and a 1979 Mercedes Benz 300 TD Wagon which Max drove. Their fortified Bel Air estate, the exterior of which was actually the former home of actors Dick Powell and his wife June Allyson, is extremely easy to break into. In the course of the series, numerous and sundry villains gain access, holding Max, one or both of the Harts and sometimes Freeway hostage. But the Harts take most things in their stride, such as when they find the entire house stripped of furniture ("Max in Love"). "Well, it's all insured and we can replace it," Jonathan says with a smile. When Jennifer rues how much fun it was selecting those pieces, he says, "Think how much fun we'll have selecting the new ones."

Aside from a terrific cast, the series had some genuinely creative mysteries with good twists. My many favorite episodes include "Downhill to Death" guest starring Juliet Mills, which has as many sharp twists and turns as a slalom; "Murder, Murder on the Wall" which finds Jennifer running into an old friend in New York whose new husband mysteriously disappears; "Long Lost Love" in which Jennifer visits her father (the great Ray Milland) and meets another red-headed woman (Samantha Eggar) like herself who claims to be her half-sister; "Getting Aweigh with Murder" in which the Harts go undercover on a cruise; and the sensational pilot featuring delicious guest stars like Roddy McDowall, Jill St. John and Stella Stevens. Noel Harrison, Power's co-star from *The Girl From U.N.C.L.E.*, also guest starred on the show in "Murder in Paradise" set in Hawaii. Nearly a decade after the series ended, eight 90-minute telemovies were made, spanning 1993-1996, proving the dynamic duo still had that certain something that made the show a success. Lionel Stander appeared as Max in five of the films before his death from lung cancer in 1994. His last screen appearance was in one of the telefilms, *Secrets of the Hart*, a terrific entry that presents a mystery regarding Jonathan's past and a cameo by future president Donald Trump.

Aloha! Jack Lord as the formidable Steve McGarrett in *Hawaii Five-O*. Photo courtesy of Leonard Freeman Productions and CBS Productions.

Hawaii Five-O (CBS) (1968-1980) Executive Producer: Leonard Freeman. Production Companies: Leonard Freeman Productions and CBS Productions. Starring Jack Lord, James MacArthur, Kam Fong, Gilbert Lani Kauhi, Al Harrington, Herman Wedemeyer, William Smith, Sharon Farrell, Moe Keale, Doug Mossman, Danny Kamekona. 279 episodes and a pilot. 12 seasons.

"Book 'em, Danno!" This fierce line spoken by star Jack Lord as detective captain Steve McGarrett, head of a fictional elite branch of the Hawaii State Police known as "Five-O", became a trademark of one of the greatest and longest-running detective shows ever created. Lord as McGarrett was sensational, a stick of dynamite. The 12-year success of *Hawaii Five-O*, and the fact that it continues to be broadcast in syndication worldwide, is a testament to his commitment, perfectionism, and charismatic embodiment of the lead character. McGarrett is tough, sensitive, no one's fool, stalwart, handsome and sleekly fit, attired in tasteful suits and ties at all times (uncommon in Hawaii), and brings the respect and dignity to the image of policemen that is often lacking in the media. Like Gene Kelly, Lord is described by co-stars as a tough taskmaster, but that meticulousness and the standards he demanded from himself and others paid off handsomely. Lord and the original *Hawaii Five-O* crackled and the setting couldn't be bested. The show was shot on location in Honolulu, Hawaii and throughout other Hawaiian Islands with occasional filming in Los Angeles, Singapore and Hong Kong. Five-O was named in honor of Hawaii's being the 50th state and the memorable, Emmy award-winning theme music was created by Morton Stevens.

The pilot "Cocoon" was cinematically crisp and dynamic with intriguing camera angles and ample doses of the local culture, including hula dancers, Polynesian cultural shows and sightseeing buses with tourists in "Aloha" shirts. It establishes all the best elements of the show, including Five-O's occasional involvement in international espionage and U.S. intelligence. Like Joan Crawford in *The Damned Don't Cry,* Lord is shown in constant movement, the pace set for excitement and action and establishing that McGarrett is in command. In his entrance, he strides through the building in an impeccable blue suit, wearing a pink lei, his hair sleek with one tousled forelock. He is a former U.S. naval officer, a detail which is worked into many plots, and appointed by the Governor, Paul Jameson. He is depicted as working in a suite of offices in the Iolani Palace in Honolulu and heading a special state police task force that was based on an actual unit that had existed in the

1940s. His small unit consisted of Danny Williams (played by Tim O'Kelly in the pilot who was then replaced by Disney star James MacArthur), veteran Chi Ho Kelly (Kam Fong, an 18-year veteran of the Honolulu Police Department) and Kono Kalakaua (played by an affable local DJ, Gilbert Lani Kauhi a.k.a. Zulu) for seasons one through four. Officer Duke Lukela (Dennis Chun, Kam Fong's son) would later join the team and Ben Kokua (Al Harrington) replaced Kono in season five.

Like all great fictional detectives, McGarrett battled some arch enemies and nasty villains, including his nemesis, communist rogue agent Wo Fat (Khigh Deigh) who was like a top Bond villain and the Professor Moriarity to Steve McGarrett. Wo Fat, who was named after a local restaurant, is introduced fittingly in "Cocoon" as a master spy for the Red Chinese and later evolved into an independent super villain. He proves a formidable and worthy opponent and adds much fun to the series. Other great villains included Ricardo Montalban as the seemingly indestructible and evil Tokura in one of my top favorite episodes "Samurai" and Gavin MacLeod as narcotics dealer Big Chicken (played almost like Bond's Blofeld). In the last episode, McGarrett at last sends Wo Fat to jail, perfect closure to the series.

Hawaii Five-O offered rich local color and unlike many detective or cop shows of the period, had a cinematic quality akin to *Columbo*, as was observed in the pilot. People of all races and classes were shown as perpetrators or good guys and native Hawaiians with no previous acting experience were used liberally in the cast. A lot of issues unique to Hawaii, such as the resentment of locals over Hawaii's development, the depiction of poverty in contrast to that development, and even the surfing culture, were worked into scripts, allowing for a fascinating cultural perspective. There were the requisite car chases, which could sometimes be amusing, such as when a kidnapped McGarrett can be seen conversing amiably with his abductors in the car in a long shot. Also amusing were certain stakeouts when the glaringly red Mercury cougar of Five-O is in plain sight while a caper is going down or when the Five-O team was visible with their binoculars at the top of a hill watching their suspect. These occasional idiosyncrasies and bloopers were part of the escapist fun.

My numerous favorite episodes, aside from the pilot and those mentioned above, include "Clash of Shadows" involving a Nazi hunter, "Retire in Sunny Hawaii…Forever" featuring legend Helen Hayes (James MacArthur's adoptive mother), "Turkey Shoot at Makapuu," "Good Night, Baby – Time to Die" which features some of the intriguing close ups of character's eyes the series was known for, "Time and Memories" featuring McGarrett's lost love Cathy (Diana Muldaur), the highly cinematic "Yesterday Died and Tomorrow Won't Be Born," "The Singapore File" and "The Big Kahuna" with a young Sally Kellerman.

Best of all were the numerous terrific speeches of Lord as Steve McGarrett: "You think it's any easier to kill a grown man? You think the next one will be easier than this one? God help you if you do. It had better hurt every time. It better tear your guts out every time you pull that gun, whether you use it or not. You learn to live with it, but don't get used to it."

Raymond Burr as the wheelchair-bound detective *Ironside*.
Photo courtesy of Harbour Productions Unlimited in association
with Universal Television.

Ironside (NBC) (1967-1975) Created by: Collier Young. Production
Companies: Harbour Productions Unlimited in association with Universal
Television. Starring Raymond Burr, Don Galloway, Barbara Anderson, Don
Mitchell, Elizabeth Baur. 199 episodes and a pilot. 8 seasons.

In spite of an extensive background in film, theater and radio, Raymond
Burr became best known for his portrayal of Erle Stanley Gardner's criminal attorney Perry Mason on the television show of the same name. The

year after *Perry Mason* ended, he was cast as Robert T. Ironside, a former San Francisco Police Department Chief of Detectives who was wheelchair bound after being paralyzed by a sniper's bullet in the line of duty and became a special consultant to the police. The 1970's was the era of the detective/cop show and there was always a novel spin being put to the genre. The wheelchair-bound detective was yet another gimmick, but solid writing and the strong presence of Burr made it work. With his sonorous voice and large somber eyes, Burr managed to suggest depth and toughness. Rather than being depicted with pity, Ironside was shown as smart, capable and resourceful enough to compensate for any physical limitations; he, in fact, was as formidable and "active" as any man with use of both legs. It is somewhat ironic that Burr would play a man confined to a wheelchair when he had played a villain menacing a man in a wheelchair in Alfred Hitchcock's *Rear Window* (1954), one of his best-known film roles.

Ironside was not spectacular, as detective series went, but it was well-done and garnered six Emmys for Burr. Ironside (referred to as "the Chief") was assisted by Detective Sergeant Ed Brown (Don Galloway) and plain-clothes officer/society girl Eve Whitfield (Barbara Anderson) who was later replaced by another attractive policewoman, Fran Belding (Elizabeth Baur). There was also a bodyguard and former delinquent Mark Sanger (Don Mitchell) who became a lawyer and married during the run of the series. The crew would ride around in a paddy wagon that served as a surveillance vehicle, although it did not make the team invulnerable to attack. Surveillance and wiretapping were a significant theme in *Ironside*, as in undercover officers being wired so that the crew could listen in on what was going down. The episode "Amy Prentiss a/k/a The Chief" utilized a wired operator and became a spinoff for the short-lived detective series *Amy Prentiss* starring Jessica Walter as an investigator who becomes the first female Chief of Detectives for the San Francisco Police Department. "Amy Prentiss," like many other episodes, is peppered with colorful 70's dialogue like "Let's get it on" and "Show me the bread and I'll take you to the man" and "The heat might have taps on your phones." Predating *Prime Suspect*, it dealt with the same issues of feminism and women entering male-dominated fields, issues that were prevalent in the 70's, and did so without political correctness, resulting in a very strong character and episode.

The episode "The Priest Killer" also was a "crossover" episode where, after a priest is murdered, Ironside teams with Father Samuel Patrick "Sarge" Cavanaugh (George Kennedy), a priest at the St. Aloysius Parish and a former homicide detective. Kennedy would star as Father Cavanaugh in a short-lived series, *Sarge*, yet another unique spin on the detective series. *Sarge* was introduced by a pilot and appeared in the crossover *Ironside* episode before the actual series premiered. It's a pity, because the homicide-solving priest as embodied by Kennedy seemed a promising idea, predating *The Father Dowling Series* with Tom Bosley and Tracy Nelson which debuted in 1989. The priest-killing episode also recalls "For the Love of God," an episode on *The Streets of San Francisco* which dealt with Lieutenant Mike Stone's loss of a priest-friend to a serial priest killer. Burr is particularly strong in this episode, perturbed by Father Cavanaugh's involvement in the case. After accusing the priest of being unable to really retire from homicide, he snaps, "What do you want? My blessing?"

A little insight into Ironside's romantic life came with the episode "In the Forests of the Night" guest starring Dana Wynter as an art thief and lost love of Ironside's. Although many series allowed episodes to humanize their protagonists by bringing in lost loves, family members or romances, the pairing of Burr and Wynter, to my mind, felt uncomfortable and without believable chemistry. One somehow couldn't imagine Wynter falling for a man like Burr, besides which Wynter had guest starred on the show before as a completely different character. But one saw the softer side of the somewhat irascible Ironside and it was an opportunity to lend some shading to the character. The show allowed all the characters to have backstory and development; the episodes themselves ran the gamut from character studies to action-filled plots. In the two-parter "Downhill All the Way," Ironside begins behaving erratically, drinking heavily and living like a bum after retiring from the force. The team is alarmed, but is it a ruse? Burr's wonderful *Perry Mason* co-star Barbara Hale guest stars in the intriguing episode "Murder Impromptu" which is set in the world of nightclub improvisation theater and has Roddy McDowall playing a former child star.

In the '70's, the era of the detective and cop show, writers were working overtime to come up with new twists on the genre. *Ironside* gave us a Chief of Detectives who was confined to a wheelchair and not about to slow down. Already beloved for his long and successful run on *Perry Mason,* Raymond Burr had the drawing power and goods to create another, long-running success, and the eight seasons of *Ironside* are a testament to this. He would reunite with the old gang in the TV movie *The Return of Ironside* (1993) which found him married to Dana Wynter (as yet another character!).

Telly Savalas as Theo Kojak: "Cootchie-coo, baby."
Photo courtesy of Universal Television.

Kojak (CBS) (1974-1975) Executive Producers: Abby Mann, James Duff McAdams and Matthew Rapf. Production Company: Universal Television. Starring Telly Savalas, Dan Frazer, Kevin Dobson, George Savalas, Mark Russell, Vince Conti, Andre Braugher. 118 episodes. 5 seasons.

"Who loves ya, baby?" Telly Savalas as Detective Lieutenant Theofilies ("Theo") Kojak was the epitome of "Brat Pack" cool and swagger, working in New York City Police Department's Eleventh Precinct and using toughness, humor, tenacity and less-than-savory methods to bring his perps to justice while sporting a dandified style including shades, 1970's bling and lavish suits. The show also was unique at that time for depicting cops as not above the law and abusive, because of the realm they lived in, but also decent and compassionate. They were fully-fleshed, fallible human beings. As observed in *Cop Shows: A Critical History of Police Dramas on Television*, Kojak had "cop knowledge," keen instincts from "twenty years of sniffin' the garbage," as he himself put it. As a former long-time resident of New York City, I can vouch that Kojak rang true as both cop and New Yorker. He was simultaneously real and larger-than-life. It wasn't hard to see how Savalas became an unconventional sex symbol after appearing on this show. Originally depicted as a smoker, he partially switched to lollypops and Tootsie Roll Pops when smoking became unpopular because of its health risks. The lollypops and his catch phrases, including "Cootchie-coo" and especially "Who loves ya, baby", became his trademarks, although some of his less well-known phrases were masterstroke as well, such as "Dead is not guts. Dead is dumb" or "That's the way the crookies crumble, baby!" Savalas' Greek heritage was a significant component of the show.

Like many detective shows of the seventies, *Kojak* started with a pilot film *The Marcus-Nelson Murders* (1973) which was based on a true-life event. Kojak, then spelled "Kojack," was allegedly a composite of several people, including a real detective Thomas Cavanagh who got a poor black teenager exonerated after he was falsely accused of murder, the plot of the pilot. In the true case, the real killer was a Puerto Rican drug addict. Kojak was also allegedly based on other people involved in the case, but the personality of Telly Savalas remains first and foremost in the character. *Kojak* was effective at capturing the banter and ribald humor in the squad room, an atmosphere that was echoed in many other shows of the period and in cop shows that followed. Frequently at the butt of Kojak's jokes was his subordinate Detective Stavros (played by Savalas' real-life brother George Savalas who looked identical to Telly except for his distinctive Harpo Marx curls and portlier body.) Stavros' weight was used rather cruelly for comic relief. The cast was rounded out by plainclothes detective Bobby Crocker (Kevin Dobson), Detective Saperstein (Mark Russell), Detective Rizzo (Vince Conti) and Kojak's supervisor Frank McNeil (Dan Frazer) who became Chief of Detectives.

The opening credits to *Kojak* featured the split screens favored in the sixties and seventies depicting action scenes, including a kitschy and amusing shot of Savalas bending down to seemingly look under the frame and point his gun at the audience. As always, certain tropes and storylines were used that were common to other shows of the period. One familiar bit was the perp from the past resurfacing with a decades-long grudge intact to extract revenge on the protagonist ("Cop in a Cage") which featured a squirrely Peter Ibbotson as the madman. Another involved a strangler terrorizing a hospital ("The Halls of Terror"), an always-fun scenario. Crime novelist Joe Gores won an Edgar for writing "No Immunity for Murder" in which a seemingly mild-mannered businessman is killed by a blonde hooker and her accomplice. In this episode, shots of the garment district capture the area's slightly seedy flavor. New York City was as much a character in the show as everything else which lent *Kojak* an extra edge of authenticity. Unlike contemporary police shows which often have a home video quality, production values were high and the show teemed with life and grit.

A fairly solid episode which incorporated Greek culture was "Night of the Piraeus" in which a beautiful woman maces several men at the docks where a deal is going down and a Greek sailor is murdered for his belt. Later the double crosser is double crossed by her associates and killed. A third murder connects all three corpses to rare stamps hidden in the belt. Kojak finds plenty of instances to deliver flippant dark humor. Examining the body at the docks, he remarks, "The guy is perfect, except he's dead. Well, he's almost perfect." Later a prostitute named Betsy (Elizabeth MacRae) gets one in on him by saying, "Have you ever noticed, lieutenant? Besides having a very bald head, you have a very large nose." Given the number of wiseacre detectives and cops in seventies television, it becomes clear why a contemporary reality show like *Judge Judy* is so popular. Audiences evidently find

some sort of vicarious release from smart asses who take charge and are em-
powered by attitude. As with Judith Sheindlin, a former family court judge
and the star of *Judge Judy*, Telly Savalas as Kojak repels as often as he delights
with his edge of gratuitous meanness and ego, but that swagger is key to the
entertainment factor.

"Bad Dude" reflects the seventies at its most funky, incorporating *Shaft*-
like blaxploitation types from Harlem who call everyone "baby" (like Kojak) and wear flamboyant, "fly" clothes that look like zoot suits, but which
were urban black fashion at the time. It reminds one how everything old is
new again. In this one, music is also predictably *Shaft*-like as well and Kojak
utters the laugh-out-loud line, "I've got a badge that's bigger than both of us."

Theo Kojak ranked number 18 on TV Guide's 50 Greatest TV Characters of All Time list. Cootchie-coo, baby!

Darren McGavin as Carl Kolchak in Kolchak: *The Night Stalker,*
an unconventional reporter/monster hunter. Photo courtesy of
Francy Productions, Inc. and Universal Television.

Kolchak: The Night Stalker (ABC) (1974-1975) Producers: Cy Chermak,
Paul Playdon and Darren McGavin. Created by: Jeff Rice. Production Companies: Francy Productions, Inc. and Universal Television. Starring Darren
McGavin, Simon Oakland, Jack Grinnage, Ruth McDevitt. 20 episodes and
2 television movies. 1 season.

The highly-acclaimed television movie *The Night Stalker* may have
failed to stand out for me against the numerous other supernaturally-ori-
ented made-for-TV films of the decade, but such was not the case for the
series it spawned, *Kolchak: The Night Stalker. Kolchak: The Night Stalker* was

a delicious and thoroughly entertaining spin on the detective series and featured an unconventional reporter/monster hunter, Carl Kolchak (Darren McGavin), a world-weary middle-aged average Joe who wrote for the Chicago wing of the Independent News Service (INS). His trademark was an old straw hat and seersucker suit. He pursued his stories with a camera and portable cassette recorder and typed them on an old-fashioned typewriter, usually narrating the episodes. Like most classic detectives, he was not popular with the police force because of his unconventionality and often disbelieved by those around him, but he inevitably managed to prove his detractors wrong. The look of the production resembled the top-notch, but short-lived *Ellery Queen*, and like *Ellery Queen*, *Kolchak: The Night Stalker* only ran one season, but it did so with great ingenuity, a sense of humor and old-fashioned and sometimes genuinely chilling horror. The monsters were just that – straight-up monsters sometimes disguised as ordinary folk who were often awaiting their victims in the shadows at nightfall, although some struck in broad daylight as well. They ran the gamut from vampires, werewolves, headless riders and mummies to Native American and Creole spirits and a witch played by everyone's favorite witch, beautiful Lara Parker who was best known as Angelique on the Dan Curtis daytime horror soap *Dark Shadows*. Curtis produced the telemovie *The Night Stalker* (reviewed in this book), in fact.

Although it was set in the present (at that time, the 1970's), *Kolchak* had a retro feeling like *Ellery Queen*, almost reminiscent of the original *Superman* series with "stock" or theatrical bit players, such as the little old lady with feathered hat and her white terrier Randolph in "Firefall." The character of Carl Kolchak originated from an unpublished novel by creator Jeff Rice called *The Kolchak Papers*. It was published in 1973 by Pocket Books as *The Night Stalker* as a movie tie-in after the success of the TV film. Its sequel *The Night Strangler* was also turned into a Pocket Books novel in 1974. The first telefilm *The Night Stalker*, adapted by Richard Matheson and starring McGavin, debuted to the highest ratings of any TV movie at that time. Simon Oakland, who appeared in both telefilms as Tony Vincenzo, Kolchak's combative editor, reprised his role for the series and other regulars in the cast included Jack Grinnage as Ron Updyke, Kolchak's tony rival at INS; the adorable Ruth McDevitt as Emily Cowles, an elderly advice and riddle columnist and aspiring novelist; Monique Marmelstein as Carol Ann Susi, an intern at INS; and John Fiedler as morgue attendant Gordy "The Ghoul" Spangler. Each episode opened with Kolchak typing and whistling and then giving a startled look at the audience as the lights begin to dim and the clock's hands jump.

The series improved on the pilot films with tighter and stronger writing and an appealing blend of wit and suspense. It also featured the usual strong array of guest stars including Hollywood veterans and delightful character actors. Some terrific episodes included "The Vampire," which was a sequel to *The Night Stalker* and involved a road crew accidentally unearthing the grave of Catherine Rollins (a terrific Suzanne Charney), the victim of the original film's vampire and now a vampire herself. Hidden beneath "six layers of cosmetic skin cake," as Kolchak puts it, the sexy she-beast lures her prey and then savagely attacks like a feral animal which results in an exciting confrontation between Kolchak and Catherine. Also hilarious is seeing this monster with alleged superhuman strength stumbling over weeds as she pursues Kolchak. "The Werewolf," although it doesn't feature the greatest werewolf ever committed to film (the werewolf on *Dark Shadows* gets those honors), guest stars one of my favorite character actors Nita Talbot as Paula Griffin, one of the guests on a cruise ship terrorized by a werewolf. Talbot interjects her usual likeable blend of wit, color and quirkiness into the proceedings. As she shares a table with Kolchak on the ship and alarms begin to go off, she asks, "Did you ever see *Lifeboat* with Walter Slezak and Tallulah Bankhead?" and "I happened to overhear a couple Italian stewards talking. They thought I couldn't speak Italian. Yo capsico tutti." "Firefall" featured a doppelganger and was one of the episodes spliced together with another episode and new footage to become a TV movie *Crackle of Death* (1974). In this episode, Madlyn Rhue does a delicious stint as a gypsy fortune teller,

Maria, whom Kolchak consults regarding the peculiar demon he must overcome. She mentions an acquaintance who was a doctor. "His friends always
want free advice," she says. "Gypsies have the same problem." In fan favorite
"Horror in the Heights," the plights of the elderly are highlighted as a car-
nivorous monster targets a Jewish community of seniors.

Kolchak was canceled after only 20 episodes, although three unproduced
scripts survive and it was credited as having inspired *The X-Files*. It remains a
highly inventive, entertaining and family-friendly spin on both the detective
and supernatural series like a *Weird Tales* comic brought to life.

Mike Connors with co-star Gail Fisher in *Mannix*. Photo courtesy of Desilu Productions and Paramount Television from the collection of JoAnn Paul.

Mannix (CBS) (1967-1975) Created by: Richard Levinson and William Link. Production Companies: Desilu Productions and Paramount Television. Starring Mike Connors, Gail Fisher, Joseph Campanella. 194 episodes. 8 seasons.

Mannix was a class act and, in many ways, a cut above the rest, primarily due to high production values, great cinematography and a solid star in the form of Mike Connors as Los Angeles private investigator Joe Mannix. The split screen opening credits were dynamite with terrific theme music by Lalo Schifrin in triple time. The editing throughout the series was superb. When it began in 1967, it had the feeling of the Cold War and espionage about it and a striking use of camera angles, movement and color (color never looked so vivid or good). Crisp cinematography showcased the beauty of Southern

California with its palm trees, shimmering swimming pools, tawny deserts and snow-capped mountains. Air travel was captured at its most glamorous, along with babes in kicky fashions. In the first season, Mannix worked for a posh detective agency called Intertect where computers (the archaic blinking kind) were used to research and solve crimes and they featured significantly in the opening credits. There was also the use of surveillance cameras throughout the agency by Mannix's boss Lew Wickersham (Joseph Campanella), although Mannix remained the renegade against the neat, corporate environment. By the second season, the computers were removed and Mannix worked for himself in a Spanish-style office with a grate facing the street, his set-up somehow reminiscent of Nero Wolfe. In the outer office, he had a feisty black secretary Peggy Fair (Gail Fisher), a single mom and widow of a police officer. As with *The Rockford Files,* bad guys had easy access to the detective's office (in Rockford's case, his trailer) and were always busting in to rough up Mannix and hold Peggy hostage.

The debut episode "The Name is Mannix" has Joe Mannix investigating a missing woman with plenty of double crosses and twists in the storyline. The plot is intriguing, if not entirely shocking, but the shots are spectacular and at times Hitchcockian. Even the pale blue of an actor's eyes in close-up is breathtaking. The Palm Springs Aerial Tramway has been a location site for a number of television movies and series, but rarely has it been filmed with such immediacy where you can almost taste the snow. Barbara Anderson, best known for *Ironside,* guest stars as the missing woman and her lime green dress is used to great effect. The first season was arguably one of the strongest, but *Mannix* is best-remembered for the seasons following, probably because those seasons were most frequently broadcast. Whether or not there may have been occasional repetition of storylines over the show's run, as some critics claim, *Mannix* found a solid groove with its strong star, stylistic imagery and at times intricate plots.

Writer Kevin Burton Smith accurately summed up the appeal of *Mannix* in *The Thrilling Detective,* saying, "[T]here was a certain edgy style to it . . .

Joe might have been the hippest square on television at the time." A rugged Armenian-American like Connors, Mannix had been in the Korean War where he was a prisoner of war until he escaped; he had also been a college football star. There was a refreshing lack of political correctness in that he did lots of smoking and drinking and brawling, as did many other characters on the show. He had a car phone and drove various cool convertibles. Much is made of the level of physical punishment Mannix sustained, particularly blows to the abdomen, and Connors did enough of his own stunts to suffer injuries, but said violence never struck me as being any more extreme or realistic than that of many 70's detective shows. There were enough larger-than-life elements, sometimes humorous, to assure viewers this was entertainment and not real life. In "The Shadow of a Dream," for instance, Mannix battles several assailants -- in a straight-jacket. In "Huntdown," his foot is in a cast and he is chased by a tractor.

Although mainly functioning as a supporting player, beautiful Peggy had the opportunity to shine in a few episodes and was an integral and memorable part of the show. Like Della Street in *Perry Mason*, Peggy Fair goes above and beyond the call of duty, including being kidnapped and injured on the job. In "The World Between," she is shot by a stray bullet in the office (workplace violence?) and while recuperating in the hospital, she falls in love and gets caught up in a mystery. Fisher would become the first black actress to win an Emmy for her role on *Mannix*, as she was the first black actress to do a national TV commercial with lines in the early '60's. One of the partners of Peggy's late husband, Lieutenant George Kramer (Larry Linville) would occasionally help Mannix on cases.

Mannix was assisted by several other members of the Los Angeles Police Department during the show's run, including Lieutenant Art Malcolm (Ward Wood) and Lieutenant Adam Tobias (Robert Reed of *The Brady Bunch* fame). A number of his old comrades from the Army would surface to create trouble, as well as other stray characters from his past, and Mannix's relationship with his estranged father was explored in "Return to Summer Grove." The latter relationship would ultimately be favorably resolved. (Summer Grove was shown to have a large Armenian immigrant population.) Like many protagonists of detective/mystery shows, Mannix was shown to be a marvel at a variety of sports and pursuits, including as a pilot, golfer, horseback rider, and basketball player. Connors would reprise his role as Mannix on other TV shows. In 1971, he appeared on *Here's Lucy* and in 1997, he was on *Diagnosis Murder* in an episode that would be a sequel to the *Mannix* episode "Little Girl Lost."

Dennis Weaver, a cowboy cop in the Big Apple in *McCloud*.
Photo courtesy of Universal Television.

McCloud (**NBC**) (**1970-1977**) Executive Producers: Glen A. Larson and Leslie Stevens. Created by: Herman Miller. Production Company: Universal Television. Starring Dennis Weaver, J.D. Cannon, Terry Carter, Ken Lynch, Diana Muldaur. 45 episodes and 1 TV movie. 7 seasons.

Along with *Columbo*, *Ellery Queen* and a few select others, *McCloud* ranked with the finest detective series of all times, each episode crafted like a mini-film. Rotated with *Columbo* and *McMillan & Wife* as part of the *NBC Mystery Movie* wheel series after debuting as part of the *Four in One* wheel series, it concerned Deputy Marshal Sam McCloud (Dennis Weaver) of Taos, New Mexico assigned to New York City as a special investigator and riding its mean streets on a horse like a transplanted cowboy in the big city. Weaver had already been a cowboy in *Gunsmoke* and wore the Stetson hat, bolo tie and sheepskin coat well, bringing an easy drawl, self-effacing charm and humor to the job. Like Columbo, his attire and persona served as a red herring to criminals and in his case, to the New Yorkers he encountered who dismissed him as a hayseed, which made their comeuppance all the sweeter. Like many classic detectives, such as Hercule Poirot and Miss Marple, he found antagonism and conflict with the police because of his unconventional appearance, methods and success. His superior, the irascible, flint-eyed, Peter Clifford (J.D. Cannon), Chief of Detectives, reminiscent of Editor-in-Chief Perry White of the original *Superman* series, constantly took him to task ("Try not to get any more ideas!"), but it never phased McCloud who got the job done and knew how to disarm his detractors.

After the social turmoil and violence in the sixties, New York City was on a decline in the 1970s, fueled by economic collapse and rampant crime, as captured in the film *The Panic in Needle Park* (1971). The city was, in fact, teetering on the edge of bankruptcy and the building of the World Trade Centers, in various stages of its construction, meant to aid its return, could be glimpsed in early title cards of *McCloud* and throughout its run. Although filmed partially on location with occasional forays to exotic locations like Hawaii, Mexico, and Australia, *McCloud* was also filmed on the Universal backlot and the cute set and neatly-dressed extras populating a scene made some locations look less like New York City and more like Disneyland or Mayberry from *The Andy Griffith Show*. The cardboard backdrop feeling never detracted from the strength or integrity of the show but added some movie fun like Hitchcock's use of rear projection. Episodes featured terrific guest stars like Bernadette Peters and Della Reese in "The Day New York

Turned Blue," which dealt with the city's fiscal crisis and had Peters as a hooker who paints her clients blue, or the delicious "The Barefoot Stewardess Caper" which featured gorgeous Britt Ekland as part of a trio of female cat burglars. Lorna Luft and Tina Sinatra made rare guest appearances in "Park Avenue Pirates" and "The Stage is All the World," respectively.

In many 70's detective shows, in fact, a stable of talented and reliable character actors were ubiquitous as guest stars, a key strength like the regulars in Hammer horror films who functioned as a veritable repertory company. These included James Olson, Patrick O'Neal, Roddy McDowall and Jack Cassidy who made great, oily villains; Val Avery, brilliant at playing sleazy, marginal types and toughs; and women like Nita Talbot. In "The Disposal Man," Talbot as prostitute Rosaline Hudgins tells McCloud, "You vice squad guys are too much. These weird disguises. What are you supposed to be – Midnight Cowboy?" One lovely ubiquitous face on television, Diana Muldaur became a regular part of the *McCloud* cast as sophisticated *New York Chronicle* writer Chris Loughlin, McCloud's on-again off-again love interest. In one of my favorite episodes, "'Twas the Fight Before Christmas," the last of the four highly-regarded "Alamo" episodes, Chris is held hostage in a children's ward at a hospital where grumpy Clifford is playing Santa. In "Return to the Alamo," Chris becomes a feminist champion of Sergeant Phyllis Norton (Teri Garr whose qualities were similar to Goldie Hawn). Tellingly, Norton, who was often relegated to fetching donut and coffee for her male colleagues, demands Chris fetch coffee and donuts, once she assumes a position of command. Muldaur would also appear in the reunion TV movie *The Return of Sam McCloud* (1989).

The series was not deficient in groovy 70's fashions either. In "Encounter with an Aries" which guest starred Sebastian Cabot as an astrologer, Susan Strasberg wears a long red dress and fascinating, rimless, red sunglasses a la Gloria Steinem and has a psychedelic pad replete with beads and hanging machete baskets. There were also broadly drawn characters played by guest stars, such as the tough girl who invariably chews gum, acts insolent and shuffles like Carol Burnett's Mrs. Wiggins. One such type was played by Stefanie Powers in "Top of the World, Ma" who gets that anticipated, amusing dig at McCloud's cowboy attire with, "What are you dressed for?" When the bad guy who is paying to photograph her in a bikini says, "I've never met a New York model before," she says, "Well, neither have I." This episode contained fun, quirky touches like a saloon called "The Lavender Doily" and some typical McCloudisms. As Clifford tries to confine him to "stolen cars," McCloud says of the elusive murder suspect, "If we'd a had this Jack Faraday character down in Taos, New Mexico . . . we'd a had him tied so tight, he couldn't fight the flies off." The cowboy element and nods to Hollywood were evidenced in a number of episodes which put McCloud back in big sky locations like Colorado and Oklahoma. "The Colorado Cattle Caper," in fact, featured an apropos guest star for the setting, John Denver.

McCloud had creative scripts and a great cast headed by a terrific and likable hero, Dennis Weaver as Sam McCloud. While presenting an offbeat detective and fish out of water, Weaver never let the easygoing McCloud be dismissed as a hayseed, but rather made him charming and smart and a gentleman. Gallon hats off to this fine series and cowboy.

Rock Hudson and Susan Saint James as television's groovy *McMillan &*
Wife. Photo courtesy of Talent Associates-Norton Simon.

McMillan & Wife (known simply as McMillan from 1976–77) (NBC)
(1971-1977) Executive Producer: Leonard B. Stern. Production Company:
Talent Associates-Norton Simon. Starring Rock Hudson, Susan Saint James,
Nancy Walker, John Schuck, Martha Raye, Bill Quinn, Mildred Natwick,
Linda Watkins, Richard Gilliland, Gloria Stroock. 40 episodes including a
pilot. 6 seasons.

McMillan & Wife was part of Universal Television's wheel series NBC
Mystery Movie, in rotation with the superb entries of *Columbo* and *Mc-*

Cloud, and featured Rock Hudson and Susan Saint James as 40-something San Francisco police commissioner, Stuart "Mac" McMillan and his twenty-something, freewheeling wife Sally. The NBC Mystery Movie was a wonderful addition to the lineup and rotated these three, 90-minute detective series within the same time period throughout the season to great success. The NBC Mystery Movie opening was memorable and exciting with superb theme music by Henry Mancini, and *McCloud* and especially *Columbo* went down in history as two of the finest detective series ever created. Although *McMillan & Wife* was the lesser of the three, it still remained an entertaining addition to the rotation, due to the strong and attractive leads and a solid supporting cast.

The McMillans move into a new home in the first episode "Murder by the Barrel" where Sally discovers a body in one of the moving barrels which later disappears. The interiors of the pilot were actually filmed in Hudson's own home, but the exterior shots of the home changed throughout the series. Hudson was Saint James' senior by twenty-one years and with his handlebar moustache, long sideburns and occasional bellbottoms, he came across as an aging hipster, although undoubtedly he and Saint James were the epitome of 70's cool at the time. Sally was a pretty, carefree and slightly kooky character who often wore typically 70's hippie dresses and a long shag hairstyle. She was a blunderer and somewhat helpless, often getting into trouble and relying on "Mac" to come to the rescue, although she was also feisty and funny. "Murder by the Barrel" introduces the McMillans' alcohol-loving and wise-cracking maid Mildred, played by character actress and comedienne Nancy Walker (who also played Rhoda Morgenstern's mother on *The Mary Tyler Moore Show*). She recalls Thelma Ritter's alcoholic housekeeper in the Doris Day film *Pillow Talk,* which co-starred Hudson, with her New York sarcasm and common-sense bluntness. The series was rounded off by goofy sidekick Sergeant Charles Enright (John Schuck).

Maintaining a light tone, *McMillan & Wife* had a running trope where Sally would think of something and reach over to Mac's side of the bed to snap on his light. He would make a comment and turn off the light and several minutes later, Sally would again think of something and reach over to his side to turn on the light. The days of showing married couples in twin beds on television were long over and like Jonathan and Jennifer Hart in *Hart to Hart*, Sally and Mac were often depicted canoodling in bed without it ever being crude or graphic. They would go over points of the case there. Unlike the Harts, however, who seemed genuinely smitten with one another and were equals in terms of sophistication, age and experience, radiating maturity and security, Sally was written essentially as a scatter-brained flower child and her pairing with the much-older Mac with his graying temples and calm, paternal tone made her seem even more childlike and dependent. Her trademark was raspy cries of "Oh, Mac" and perhaps she was meant to evoke Gracie Allen with cutesy and flighty remarks such as, "I bought you that [tie] because you liked the other one so much." Sometimes solutions to the mystery were found in her offbeat remarks. Displays of jealousy, also meant to be cute, crept up between the McMillans, furthering the impression of inequality and insecurity in their relationship.

McMillan & Wife incorporated some of the things unique to San Francisco into the storylines, such as the earthquake that takes place in "Aftershock" which guest stars Julie Newmar or "Night of the Wizard" where Mac chases a suspect through a series of moving cable cars on Russian Hill. The couple attend trendy parties and have socially prominent friends who sometimes get them involved in mysteries, but a lot of common tropes of the period were also used in storylines, such as "The Deadly Cure" where Mac, wounded and recuperating in the hospital, witnesses another patient being smothered or "Reunion in Terror" where a killer stalks Mac's football class reunion. Another deliciously far-fetched trope was that of the doppelganger used in "Terror Times Two" and again in "Cross & Double Cross" where Mac has a double, affording Hudson the opportunity to play two distinct personalities. Even a straight show like *Hawaii Five-O* featured a doppelganger for star Jack Lord, as would *Murder, She Wrote* and *Hart to Hart* and others.

Saint James' pregnancy was incorporated into the storyline, but after a few references, the baby was never referred to or seen again. By the sixth and final season, Saint James left after a contract dispute, as did Walker. The explanation given was that Sally and her son were killed in a plane crash and Mildred left to open her own diner on the East Coast, allegedly a reference to Walker's gig as Rosie the waitress in the Bounty Paper Towel commercials. Martha Raye, who played Mildred's sister Agatha in "Greed," came to fill in the gap as Mac's new housekeeper and Mac moved into a luxury apartment and had a revolving series of girlfriends. Sergeant Enright was also promoted and Richard Gilliland was sent in as Sergeant Steve DiMaggio, his replacement. With all the comfortable familiars removed, the series faltered and ended, but during its run, it enjoyed and continues to enjoy great popularity, due to its two likeable and attractive stars.

Angie Dickinson as Sergeant Pepper Anderson goes "undercover" in *Police Woman*. Yeah, baby, yeah! Photo courtesy of David Gerber Productions and Columbia Pictures Television.

Police Woman (NBC) (1974-1978) Executive Producer: David Gerber. Production Companies: David Gerber Productions and Columbia Pictures Television. Created by Robert E. Collins. Starring Angie Dickinson, Earl Holliman, Ed Bernard, Charles Dierkop. 91 episodes. 4 seasons.

Police Woman was considered groundbreaking in its time for depicting a female police officer in the Los Angeles Police Department and allegedly being the first drama with a female lead (there were plenty of females heading comedies on television.) Like Teresa Graves in *Get Christie Love*, Angie Dickinson as Sergeant Pepper Anderson was a police woman straight out of Central Casting. She was a platinum blonde who wore sundresses, big hoop earrings and halter tops. Her numerous wardrobe changes included form-fitting ensembles such as a suede, powder blue pant outfit with rhinestones and a velvet, emerald ensemble with a pale green cashmere sweater that made her look more like a high-end shopper on Rodeo Drive than a sergeant in the L.A.P.D. In these clearly expensive outfits, she occasionally tackled bad guys, a very incongruous image like seeing a farmer tilling a field in a tuxedo. She and her partners Detective Joe Styles (Ed Bernard) and Detective Pete Royster (Charles Dierkop) worked in the criminal conspiracy department.

Episodes frequently exploited Dickinson's sex appeal by having her go undercover as a hooker or a go dancer and don skimpy outfits or also cozy up seductively to bad guys right before she let them have it or they let her have it when her cover was blown (as it frequently was). ("You live by the rules?" she purrs to one perp. "I don't. Not when I see something I like.") She also donned many other hats undercover, including as an investigative news reporter, a waitress, a porn queen, a fashion model, a prisoner, a revolutionary, a high school teacher and a caterer. In spite of Pepper's too-precious attire, Dickinson exuded an underlying boldness. She was a fine actress with easygoing charm who could facially express ambiguities in feeling or thought. By all accounts and interviews, in real life, Dickinson was a great gal and that also came through. She was no less believable than her partner, Pete who looked like an extra from the cast of *Godspell* with his florid caps and impish slouch.

It's also easy to see how exciting the debut of a show featuring a police woman would be, especially as portrayed and embodied by Dickinson – with more than a touch of natural glamour. Well over forty when *Police Woman* premiered, she was a woman, not a girl, with a sense of knowingness and maturity. Women were inspired to apply for jobs in the police department and cited *Police Woman* as the reason they stayed on their jobs which shows its impact. *Police Woman* was also allegedly President Gerald Ford's favorite show.

Although *Police Woman* tackled hot topics for the time like baby brokerage, rape, white slavery, Marxism, spousal abuse, terrorism and cop killers, it was entertainment, not graphic realism, and one never lost sight of that. It was populated by broadly drawn 70's types – badass black pimps who called cops "pigs"; trippin' teenagers who wanted "bread" (the 70's lingo for money); even a trio right out of *Bonnie and Clyde*; and lots of choice 70's dialogue like "Freeze, turkey!" In "The Death of a Dream," Pepper goes against the orders of her supervisor Sergeant Bill Crowley (Earl Holliman), who often treats her like a big brother, and sneaks into a motel where three domestic terrorists on the order of the Weather Underground (including an electric Sharon Farrell) are holding hostages. It's a very exciting, action-packed episode until one notices that as Pepper is slithering on her belly along the corridor outside the motel room doors, she's dragging her pouchy bag and wearing heels. At this point, credibility shrivels. In "Fish," where Pepper goes undercover as an inmate, she is in a prison full of platinum blondes – yep, right out of Central Casting. In "Blast," her assumed name is Flaxie DuPres – said with a straight face. Dickinson showed good humor and a lack of pretention towards everything, saying during a 2014 WE TV and Paley Center for Media panel, "If we went too hard and made her too tough, people weren't going to like that. I wasn't Marilyn Monroe, but I was middle of the road and it worked." She had played another gun-toting combination of grit and glamour in *Big Bad Mama* (1974) which had a retread in 1987. The film came out the same year *Police Woman* premiered and both vehicles presented the star in heels and flashy ensembles, absurdly juxtaposed against rough and tumble violence.

Police Woman featured people of all races. It wasn't made into a big deal, as it shouldn't be. There were references made to Pepper's autistic younger sister in the first season which were eventually dropped, but it was an attempt to bring the marginalized into the forefront. Sometimes *Police Woman*'s attempt to break barriers backfired, such as in the episode "Flower of Evil" where Pepper investigates a group of lesbians who are robbing and killing elderly residents at a retirement home they head. Lesbian rights groups, feeling the image was negative and stereotypical, protested and occupied the

NBC offices until NBC agreed in 1975 not to rebroadcast the episode. Unfortunately, oversensitivity by once-marginalized groups caused them to often object to their own representation on the large or small screen if it wasn't positive, a phenomenon that still occurs. With so many civil rights movements bringing people out of the shadows, the concern was negative images would set them back, thereby misguidedly perpetuating a "white hat/black hat" mythology. The episode was included in the DVD release.

Frank DeCaro of *The New York Times* summed it up, that even though she wasn't that tough, Pepper spiced up 70's TV. She also paved the way for female-led crime shows and encouraged countless women to become the next Police Woman.

Jack Klugman fights corruption as a principled coroner in *Quincy*. Photo courtesy of Glen A. Larson Productions and Universal Television.

Quincy, M.E. (NBC) (1976-1983) Creators: Glen A. Larson and Lou Shaw. Production Companies: Glen A. Larson Productions and Universal Television. Starring Jack Klugman, Garry Walberg, John S. Ragin, Val Bisoglio, Robert Ito, Joseph Roman, Eddie Garrett, Marc Scott Taylor, Lynette Mettey, Anita Gillette. 148 episodes. 7 seasons.

Quincy had its inspiration from a book *Where Death Delights* by former FBI agent Marshall Houts and was also loosely based on Thomas Noguchi, a former Los Angeles Chief Medical Examiner and Coroner known as "Coroner to the Stars" because of all the high-profile autopsies he performed (including Marilyn Monroe's). It was originally one of the 90-minute rotations in the NBC *Sunday Mystery Movie*, along with *Columbo, McCloud* and *McMillan*. Having achieved success, it became its own weekly one-hour series. As Dr. Quincy (called "Quince" by colleagues, family and friends), Jack Klugman often erupts and butts heads with his boss, Dr. Robert Asten (John S. Ragin) and the police. He lives on a sailboat in Marina Del Rey, California and is a widower and retired captain in the U.S. Navy. He has a steady girlfriend, Lee Porter (Lynette Mettey) who occasionally assists on cases, but in "Quincy's Wedding," an episode at the end of the final season, he marries Dr. Emily Hanover (Anita Gillette who played the wife he lost to cancer in a flashback in another episode "Promises to Keep"). *Quincy* was one of the first series to use its platform to address political or social agendas and as a result of being in the series, Klugman himself testified before U.S. Congress about several issues that he had learned about through the show. It was also one of the earliest shows to depict in-depth forensic investigations or "crime scene investigations," which became the focus of a number of shows that followed. Its seven seasons are a testament to a winning alignment of elements.

Quincy was often shown enjoying his life on the water, although ironically, he appeared to have a type A personality with his frequent explosions (doctor, heal thyself!), his frustration compounded by the lack of cooperation he encountered from the powers that be around him. Like Hollywood's idea of waitstaff who invariably are depicted with sweat stains under their arms (something I've never personally observed in real life), Anita Gillette's Dr. Emily Hanover was earthy to a fault. Her personality meshed well with Quincy's equally earthy brashness. In "Go Fight City Hall to the Death," a woman is founded raped and strangled on the beach and Quincy is positive the wrong young man is being targeted for the murder. In this episode, as in others, Quincy frequently ribs his lab assistant Sam Fujiyama (Robert Ito) in ways that would now cause a coronary, although Sam returns the horseplay with equally silly digs. When Sam tells him, "I keep telling you I'm Japanese, not Chinese," Quincy responds with tongue firmly in cheek, "What's the difference?" Television was blessedly not under the stranglehold of political correctness in the seventies, so this remark was taken as the tease it was intended to be and goes in line with Quincy's shoot-from-the-hip, but principled personality. A tireless crusader, he was often obnoxious in his behavior, sometimes inconsiderate with his female companions and prone to barking at anyone who disagreed with him ("If I tell you you've got a homicide, buddy, you've got a homicide!"). This also falls in line with those types who are great at big causes and saving the world, but not as good in day-to-day relations or manners. Quincy, in spite of or even because of his flaws, remains likable and relatable, however, and a believable, comfortable world is created on the show that viewers can instantly sink into. The rich premise also lends itself to intrigue and reflects the era's dismantling and questioning of sacred cows and institutions (like hospitals).

In "Images," in which a celebrated female newswoman is killed in a fire and a preposterous doppelganger shows up to prove it was a mistake, the emphasis is on mystery and unintentional humor. Jessica Walter has the pleasure of playing the two identical personalities, one good, one evil (what else?) in the type of episode which offers much in the way of escapism. Grouchy Quincy shows up on the scene, irate with the press who are prematurely asking his opinion; one of his favorite expressions seems to be a scowl, although he has an opportunity to irascibly flex his superiority by correcting the false assumptions of those around him regarding cause of death and even positive identity of the victim. Walter, as always, knows how to expertly play off her co-stars and makes a great villainess, finding herself up against a tenacious foe. What many of the detective series of the seventies had in common was the average Joe or Josephine raging against the machine and triumphing against the odds. Quincy falls in line with this type of underdog who is underestimated by all, but sticks to his guns and proves his instincts are correct. Along the way he is willing to risk all for the sake of integrity and pursuit of truth.

"Who Speaks for the Children" represents a socially conscious episode where Quincy delves into the disturbing area of child pornography, a topic that was rarely addressed on television at that time. *Quincy* was not afraid to explore controversial subject matters and bring awareness to the complexity surrounding specific situations, but one never lost sight of the fact that its primary mission was to entertain. Quincy invariably triumphs over evil as the hero, noticing things that the audience may have been aware of practically from the start, but the satisfaction is in seeing this unconventional professional buck the system and be powerful where in reality, he would most likely be powerless. *Quincy* received over a dozen Emmy nominations during its run, including the nomination for Outstanding Lead Actor in a Drama Series.

James Garner as Jim Rockford carried his series *The Rockford Files*
with easy charm. Photo courtesy of Roy Huggins-Public Arts
Productions, Cherokee Productions, and Universal Television.

The Rockford Files (NBC) (**1974-1980**) Executive Producers: Stephen
J. Cannell, Meta Rosenberg. Production Companies: Roy Huggins-Public
Arts Productions, Cherokee Productions, and Universal Television. Starring
James Garner, Noah Beery Jr., Joe Santos, Stuart Margolin, Gretchen Cor-
bett. 122 episodes and 8 TV movies. 6 seasons.

The enduring popularity of *The Rockford Files* rests largely on the affable, easygoing charms of James Garner as unconventional Los Angeles-based private eye James Rockford who lives in a dilapidated trailer on the Malibu beach and handles missing person investigations, cold cases, insurance scams and assorted convoluted situations for "$200 a day plus expenses." His clients often manage to reduce or skirt that fee, lending to the "marginal" feeling about Rockford. Having served time in San Quentin in the 1960's, due to a wrongful conviction, he often finds his past dogging his present and stoking up antagonism with the police. He maintains a dubious friendship with a duplicitous former prison cohort, Evelyn "Angel" Martin (Stuart Margolin) which repeatedly gets him into trouble. His relationship with his father, a retired truck driver, Joseph "Rocky" Rockford (Noah Beery Jr. who bears an uncanny resemblance to Garner), is a significant and endearing part of the show and he also has warm relationships with Sergeant Dennis Becker (Joe Santos) of the LAPD and his lawyer and sometimes-girlfriend Elizabeth "Beth" Davenport (the cute Gretchen Corbett). But one of the show's many assets is Rockford's cheeky sense of humor, such as when several villains hold him at gunpoint inside a car and Rockford responds, "I'm sorry I forgot the peanut butter sandwiches" or "Cataloguing my virtues won't work. I hold them to a minimum, so they're easy to keep track of" or "I've got this little problem. Every time I get indicted for murder, I seem to lose my manners." Each episode opens famously with Rockford's answering machine where you hear him tell his caller to leave a message at the sound of the beep and some quirky message is left.

The Rockford Files was ranked Number 39 on TV Guide's 50 Greatest TV Shows of All Times, has remained continuously in syndication and was also rated one of the greatest TV shows of all times in TV (The Book): Two Experts Pick the Greatest American Shows of All Times (2016) by Alan Sepinwall and Matt Zoller Seitz. Besides offering entertaining P.I. capers with the requisite car chases and plot twists, it had "comfort food" appeal. Rockford wore "off the rack," 70's Brooks Brother-style clothing that was reasonably attractive in an era known for screamingly bad fashion and like Garner, he served in

Korea. Garner was also known to do his own stunts, resulting in numerous injuries. Not only did he do fights, but he also did some of his own fancy driving maneuvers and racing in Rockford's gold Pontiac Firebird. When Rockford went on stakeouts in this fairly conspicuous car, infallibly it was with the window down, so bad guys could easily stick their guns through the windows or bodily remove him from the car. At this point, they would be treated to the impudent, off-the-cuff sarcasm Garner delivered so perfectly.

The writing remained consistently good in the show or maybe it was Garner's ability to create a consistent, easygoing, relatable and likeable character. Aside from the regular supporting characters, there were those who made repeat appearances on the show, such as roughhewn Gabby Hayes (Louis Gossett, Jr.) from Rockford's prison days who calls Rockford "Rockfish" and Rita Capkovic (Rita Moreno), a former call girl and police informant who shares a mutual attraction with Rockford. These recurring characters helped lend a depth and authenticity to Rockford's life. The handsome P.I. also had a soft spot for the ladies, which led to countless romances and the opportunity for a multitude of terrific female guest stars, such as Susan Strasberg, Lindsay Wagner, Sharon Gless, Jill Clayburgh, Lara Parker, and Linda Evans. Lauren Bacall also guest-starred on the show in a two-part episode called "Lions, Tigers, Monkeys and Dogs."

The many superb episodes include "Say Goodbye to Jennifer" in which Rockford is hired by an old war buddy to find a beautiful fashion model; "Black Mirror," an exciting two-parter which introduced Dr. Megan Dougherty (Kathryn Harrold), a blind psychiatrist who hires Jim when she is being terrorized by a stalker (she would resurface again in the series); "The Hawaiian Headache" in which Jim and his dad believe Jim won a trip to Hawaii which turns out to be a scam; "The Farnsworth Stratagem" which guest starred beautiful Linda Evans; and "Trouble in Chapter Seventeen" which involved a female author, urging women to return to their traditional roles, who believes a feminist group is trying to murder her. Garner's older brother Jack Garner also did a variety of bit parts on the show and eventually had a regular role as Captain McEnroe in the final season, altogether appearing in over sixty episodes.

The Rockford Files had an enormous amount of heart and charm, chiefly due to its lead James Garner, that made it a welcome addition to the detective series canon. James Rockford was said to have influenced Tom Selleck as Thomas Magnum in *Magnum, P.I.* Both brought an easygoing charm and humanity to their roles, as well as conveying the perils of an unstable and undependable career choice that often put them in jeopardy. Like *Hart to Hart*, *The Rockford Files* was followed by eight reunion movies in the 1990's, which reunited many of the original cast members.

The four teenagers and the titular Great Dane of *Scooby Doo, Where Are You?*
Image courtesy of Hanna-Barbera Productions.

Scooby Doo, Where Are You? (CBS) (1969-1970) ABC (1978) Executive Producers: William Hanna and Joseph Barbera. Production Company: Hanna-Barbera Productions. Voices of Don Messick, Casey Kasem, Frank Welker, Nicole Jaffe, Stefanianna Christopherson, Heather North, Pat Stevens. 41 episodes. 3 seasons.

Scooby-Doo, Where Are You is fondly remembered by any child growing up in the 70's and had several incarnations since its debut in 1969. It involved the adventures of a loveable, cowardly Great Dane called Scooby Doo (voiced by Don Messick) who had a memorable chuckle and four teenagers: Norville "Shaggy" Rogers (voiced by disc jockey Casey Kasem) who was distinguished by shaggy brown hair and an unshaven chin; pretty Daphne Blake (voiced by Stefanianna Christopherson in season one and later Heather North) who had a groovy purple dress with piping, a headband and pink leotards; bookish Velma Dinkley (voiced by Nicole Jaffe) who always wore a turtleneck, skirt, knee socks and glasses; and hunky blond Fred Jones (voice actor extraordinaire Frank Welker) whose attire was mildly preppie. The gang tooled around in a funky psychedelic van called the Mystery Machine and solved supernatural-themed mysteries which they invariably stumbled into in a variety of unexpected ways. Scooby Doo and Shaggy loved eating Scooby snacks (i.e., pizza, sandwiches or hamburgers) and "Scoob," as he was sometimes referred to by Shaggy, found treats wherever they traveled. Each episode opened with the memorable groovy theme song composed by David Mook and Ben Raleigh and performed by Larry Marks and George A. Robertson, Jr. The show was originally part of the Saturday morning cartoon fare and also one of the first cartoons of its kind to feature a laugh track. Although it survived through the generations, *Scooby Doo* was quintessentially a creation of the '70's.

Scooby Doo followed the blueprint of many other cartoons, such as *The Flintstones* in terms of the way the animated figures moved; the resemblance to *The Flintstones* is not surprising, since both cartoons originated from Hanna-Barbera, the animation studio that dominated television from its creation in 1957 by former MGM animation directors William Hanna and Joseph Barbera through the mid-1980's. Joe Ruby and Ken Spears were the story supervisors and the storylines always involved monsters of various types who were investigated by the teenagers and Scooby Doo and eventually unmasked. Investigations featured much skulking around in creepy environments like haunted houses where the kids were invariably chased by the supernatural villains in an *Abbott and Costello* or *Three Stooges* slapstick style. "Like no one seems to be here, Scoob," Shaggy might say. His other favorite expression was "Zoinks!" The culprits were usually scam artists of some sort, not particularly threatening, and Scooby Doo often had a good hand in capturing them, if inadvertently. Although like all detective/amateur sleuth series, there was a formula, it never made the episodes less entertaining or mysterious. The set-ups presented impossible situations, such as the ghost of a Yeti known as the "Snow Ghost" encountered on a skiing vacation or a two-million-year-old caveman frozen in ice that Shaggy and Scooby Doo accidentally reel in while fishing who later thaws and goes on a rampage, which all prove to have logical explanations. The fun is arriving at the solution to the mystery.

Episodes had wonderful alliterative and clever titles, such as "Haunted House Hang-up" (total 70's), "A Creepy Tangle in the Bermuda Triangle," and "Jeepers, It's the Jaguaro." "Jeepers" was the favorite expression of Velma. They also took the gang to a great variety of fun and exotic locations, such as Turkey ("The Tar Monster"), Scotland ("A Highland Fling with a Monstrous Thing"), Brazil ("Jeepers, It's the Jaguaro") and Venice ("A Menace in Venice"). Background visuals and fantastic music enhanced the air of mystery and intrigue considerably, sometimes including twisted trees, shadows and full moons. In the opening episode "What a Night for a Knight," the gang find a black suit of armor in an abandoned pickup truck and return it to the museum. After learning that the archaeologist who was transporting it has disappeared, they return to the museum to snoop around and discover that the black suit of armor has come to life. Like many classic mysteries, the last scene involves the summing up of the solution to the mystery with much praise for the kids who were clever enough to solve and thwart a crime. "A Night of Fright is No Delight" involves Scooby being included in the will of an eccentric millionaire where the will stipulates that the heirs must spend the night in the mansion to collect their fortune. The mansion, as it turns out, is haunted and the gang arrives there in the middle of a thunderstorm. The episode is filled with characters with witty and silly names like Sweet Cousin Maldahyde, Cousin Slicker, Cosgood Creeps and Mr. Crawls. A message is left on the mirror to threaten the gang, saying, "The first is gone, the rest will go, unless you leave the island and ROW! ROW! ROW! Phantom Shadow." Strangely, although Shaggy and Fred are shown in pajamas, the rest of the gang wear their usual attire in the middle of the night.

The *Scooby-Doo* characters would eventually appear in various specials outside of their Saturday morning slot and in 1979, Scooby's nephew,

Scrappy-Doo was added to the series in an effort to boost ratings, just as Ricky Segall was added to *The Partridge Family* as their four-year-old neighbor in the show's fourth and final season. The 1979 episodes were then billed as *Scooby-Doo and Scrappy-Doo* and fired up new interest. The series would have several other incarnations, such as *The New Scooby and Scrappy-Doo Show*, and even a 52-chapter televised novel presentation, *Scooby-Doo! Mystery Incorporated*. A blend of comedy, mystery and music, *Scooby Doo* has been a surefire winner and continues to attract new generations.

Karl Malden and Michael Douglas with the Golden Gate Bridge in the background.
Photo courtesy of Quinn Martin Productions and Warner Bros. Television.

The Streets of San Francisco (ABC) (1972-1977) Executive Producer: Quinn Martin. Developed by Edward Hume. Production Companies: Quinn Martin Productions and Warner Bros. Television. Starring Karl Malden, Michael Douglas, Richard Hatch. 121 episodes and a pilot. 5 seasons.

The Streets of San Francisco was a typical 70's cop drama featuring a streetwise, 20-year veteran and widower Lieutenant Mike Stone (Karl Malden) and his college-educated partner, rookie Inspector Steve Keller (Mike Douglas) who solve homicides as plainclothes detectives on the streets of San Francisco. The success of the series was due in part to the genuine connection and chemistry between the two stars who had a father/son relationship in real life, and whose easy bantering and multi-generational dynamics and mutual affection resonated with audiences. That wonderful juxtaposition of worldly wisdom with brash youth would find success again with the BBC's Inspector Morse series where John Thaw as misanthropic, snobbish Detective Chief Inspector Endeavour Morse had perfect counterpoint in young, earthy, working class Sergeant Lewis (Kevin Whately). The pilot of *Streets* was based on the detective novel *Poor, Poor Ophelia* by Carolyn Weston and the series was developed by Edward Hume who also wrote the teleplay for the pilot. Like many cop shows of the 70's, the series featured plenty of car chases with squealing tires and burning rubber. Although filmed entirely on location in San Francisco, one of the most picturesque cities on earth, in keeping with the 70's desire for grit and "realism," *Streets* also maintained an air of seediness and did not glamorize the city. Malden and Douglas did their homework and spent time with the San Francisco Police Department to imbue the show with authenticity, but it was the depth of Malden's characterization coupled with the handsome swagger and brashness of Douglas that made the show a hit.

Another reason behind the success of the series was high quality, tight scripts which maintained the integrity of the series and the characters consistently. Episodes were divided into four acts and incorporated many storylines that were timely and interesting. As always, television detective shows of the decade mirrored each other's plotlines which were in keeping with events and concerns of the day. Vietnam was touched upon and homegrown terrorists a la Patty Hearst were covered, such as in the two-parter "Thrill Killers" which featured Patty Duke Astin as a homegrown terrorist killing off members of a jury. *Streets* had its fair share of far-out hippies and counterculture clashes as well. Malden functioned more as an establishment guy with paternal concern for his young partner, while Douglas was at the hip epicenter of the 70's with an eye out for the ladies.

Another story setting that would be used in numerous detective shows, including *Magnum PI* and *Murder, She Wrote* involved the slimy talk show host that everyone loves to hate. A particularly fine incarnation of it is found in "Dead Air" in which a woman is murdered who may be pregnant by arrogant radio host Terry Vine (Larry Hagman, always a great villain) whose show is "Vine, Women and Song." Arlene Golonka is wonderfully flinty as his girlfriend Barbara Tyler, while beautiful Ina Balin, proving men makes passes at ladies with glasses, is his sexy secretary Penny, with whom he is also involved. This superb episode has plenty of suspects including the on-air lothario. Along with Hagman, other guest stars often elevated episodes by virtue of their extraordinary performances, such as John Davidson as a female impersonator in fan and cast favorite "Mask of Death." His unhinged portrait recalls the demented ventriloquist in "Dead of Night" (1945).

With his bulbous nose and twinkling eyes, Malden had a face like the cartoon Mr. Magoo and brought intensity, relatability and humor to Lieutenant Stone. His distinguished career spanned Broadway, radio, film and television, and he was considered one of the great character actors of his time. Episodes established the backgrounds of both men. In "For the Love of God," Stone goes undercover as a Roman Catholic priest when a serial killer is targeting members of the clergy. When Keller jokes about it, Stone retorts, "What did you expect? Bing Crosby in *Going My Way*?" We learn about his rough-and-tumble background where the choice was to become a cop, a criminal or a priest. He then admits his unwillingness to "carry a piece" while posing as the priest, because he believes it's sacrilegious and when he genuflects and crosses himself before the altar, he reveals his deep-rooted religious convictions.

Stone's daughter Jeannie Stone (Darleen Carr) would be featured in a dozen episodes in the series and Michael Douglas' mother Diana Douglas guest starred in "Chapel of the Damned." As the series progressed, Keller would be promoted to full inspector and in the fifth and final season, Douglas left the show. The absence was attributed to Steve Keller taking a teaching position at a local college and Lieutenant Stone was partnered with a new detective, Inspector Dan Robbins (Richard Hatch). As is often the case with cast changes in a successful series, the change did not go over well with audiences and *The Streets of San Francisco* declined in popularity and ended in 1977. The five seasons of *The Streets of San Francisco*, however, bear testament to fine craftsmanship, strong acting and good storytelling. Most especially they showcase the beautiful connection and camaraderie between Karl Malden and Michael Douglas as Lieutenant Mike Stone and Inspector Steve Keller that kept this show an enduring favorite.

Vega$ star Robert Urich with his iconic 1957 red T-bird.
Photo courtesy of Aaron Spelling Productions.

Vega$ (ABC) (1978-1981) Executive Producers: Aaron Spelling and Douglas S. Cramer. Created by: Michael Mann. Production Company: Aaron Spelling Productions. Starring Robert Urich, Phyllis Davis, Bart Braverman, Tony Curtis, Naomi Stevens, Judy Landers, Greg Morris. 69 episodes and a pilot. 3 seasons.

Vega$ takes a new spin on the private detective series by setting it in glittery Las Vegas, the city -- like New York City -- that never sleeps. The opening shows the Las Vegas strip at the peak of its gaudy 70's excess. The camera quickly pans casinos and card dealers; lines of leggy showgirls wearing huge headdresses; brightly lit neon signs of such clubs as the Sultan's Table, Saharas and the Dunes; and headliners like Tom Jones, Lola Falana, Joey Heatherton and Liberace. The breezy theme music sets the stage for the Aaron Spelling formula of beautiful people and escapist, action-filled plotlines. Heartthrob Robert Urich stars as private detective Dan Tanna, a Vietnam vet who lives in a converted theatrical warehouse for the Desert Inn near Circus Circus Hotel Casino. One of his clients is Phillip Roth (Tony Curtis), also known as Slick, who owns a number of hotel casinos and is seen as a Big Man Around Town type, greeted obsequiously by showgirls and fast-talking into his phone ("Sammy wants to switch his dates with Liza. Tell him it's okay.") (What a time capsule of 70's Vegas!) Tanna is assisted by Beatrice Travis (Phyllis Davis), a former showgirl, and her friend Angie (Judy Landers), also a fellow showgirl. Unlike Travis who is capable and smart, Angie is dithery and a fixture of overblown sexuality, recalling ditzy blonde bombshells like Carol Wayne. The buxom Landers makes her entrance into the series wearing a thin pink shirt that ties under the breastbone and white-hot pants. Her delivery is very breathy and giggly, playing to type, a shtick that could be tiring if not handled with the comedic brilliance of a Judy Holliday, but the character works and fits within the setting. Part of the show's escapist appeal is the fact that it's populated by extraordinarily good-looking people and the beefcake is as prevalent as the cheesecake (Tanna is often shirtless). The city itself is a character and all the humans are offshoots of it. Besides members of the Las Vegas Metropolitan Police Department and the two comely ladies, Tanna also has assistance from a college-age kid who has a record, "Binzer" (Bart Braverman). Characters like "Binzer" date back to Sherlock Holmes and his Baker Street Irregulars who were street kids employed as intelligence agents.

Aside from featuring crazy, offbeat characters that are quite believable in places like Las Vegas, as they are in Key West, *Vega$* also represents a fascinating time capsule of this Oz-like city in the seventies. There are many glimpses of live acts, including circus acts, the aforementioned headliners and dazzlingly beplumed showgirls, as well as of behind the scenes, in the parking lot and on the floor of the casinos. The series sometimes strayed from Vegas. The meat of the two-parter "The Golden Gate Cop Killers" takes place in San Francisco where someone has been killing cops. Since one murdered cop was his friend, Tanna gets involved in uncovering the culprit and runs across two glamorous gals with guns strapped to their thighs (Tanya Roberts and Michelle Phillips) who are not what they seem to be. *Bad Gurl in Vega$* goes in line with a popular trope of a character who is not the gender they seem to be and guest stars Christopher Morley. With all the glam in Vegas, it is already pretty difficult to tell who the drag queens and biological women are, but Morley is more convincing than most. The series got a lot of mileage out of its setting and featured quintessentially 70's Vegas guest stars in its roster like the Captain & Tennille, Wayne Newton, Lola Falana, Sid Caesar, Dean Martin and Barbi Benton. Stalwarts of the period like lovely Lynda Day George and Michael Cole (of *The Mod Squad* fame) also made appearances on the show.

Urich's handsomeness made him ripe to be exploited as a heartthrob with all the shirtless and romancing scenes, but aside from this, he proved to be a good actor with glimpses of greater depths that the show rarely allowed. Although it was an entertaining, colorful series, *Vega$* also never reached the levels of a *Columbo*, and perhaps it wasn't trying to. There were plenty of good-looking private detectives on television with cool cars who always had babes on their arms and who had a background in the military, i.e., "flashbacks to Nam." Perhaps Urich was younger and cuter than most, but the series didn't remain indelible like some, in spite of achieving success and earning several Golden Globe nominations. With such a plethora of television detectives and amateur sleuths, it was a challenge for any new series in the 70's to stand out from the pack. It reminded me of a circus performer I saw interviewed who said it wasn't enough just to dangle from one's hair in a high wire act; you also had to spin and contort and juggle, if necessary, to keep the audience amused. *Vega$* also did suffer as Noel Murray of A.V. Club put it, "from more than a little *Love Boat*-ification." A few years later *Miami Vice* would come along and appear to reinvent the wheel with its New Wave vibe and music, Art Deco style, gritty storylines and distinctive beach colors (pink, blue, fuchsia, peach). Don Johnson was handsome, cool, a trend setter in slouchy Armani and also a damn good actor (which came through even in a show where substance was nearly overshadowed by style). In spite of the flash and bling and a sexy star with a 1957 red (yes, red) Ford T-bird, *Vega$* failed to remain indelible in the general public's imagination the way *Miami Vice* would, but it still remains a unique, solid show and an engaging time capsule.

Robert Urich did a crossover as Dan Tanna in the *Charlie's Angels* episode "Angels in Vegas" a week before the premiere of the *Vega$* series.

The awe-inspiring Lynda Carter in *Wonder Woman.*
Photo courtesy of Warner Brothers Television.

Wonder Woman a.k.a. The New Adventures of Wonder Woman (ABC and CBS) (1975-1979) Executive Producers: Douglas S. Cramer and Wilford Lloyd Baumes. Production Company: Warner Brothers Television. Starring Lynda Carter, Lyle Waggoner, Debra Winger, Carolyn Jones, Richard Eastham, Norman Burton, Beatrice Colen. 59 episodes and a pilot. 3 seasons.

If anyone was going to perfectly embody the Amazonian Wonder

Woman of the DC comic strip, that person was Lynda Carter, a former Miss World USA. With her statuesque beauty including dazzling blue eyes and an equally dazzling smile, she truly is a wonder, as the title song by Charles Fox and Norman Gimbel puts it. She brings the right touch of integrity, purity and light to the role, conducting herself with dignity and kindness and a message of female empowerment. Based on the comic strip by William Moulton Marston, the Lynda Carter TV show followed a 1974 TV movie starring Cathy Lee Crosby as Wonder Woman and a 1975 telemovie billed *The New, Original Wonder Woman* starring Carter. In *The Secret History of Wonder Woman,* author Jill Lepone contends that to radical feminists, *The New Original Wonder Woman* looked like a sellout of everything the feminist movement stood for in the 1970's. However, in retrospect and especially as played by Carter, Wonder Woman, while appealing also to adults, is a great role model for little girls like a Super Power Girl Scout where kindness and integrity matter. Wonder Woman is not only compassionate to other women, but is also kind to animals with a unique ability to communicate with them. She is omnipotent yet never morally ambiguous. Her mix of power and goodness is on point and Carter keeps her savvy and believable.

The pilot with Carter was set during World War II and faithful to the original comic book to a large degree, establishing the basic storyline and background. It involved American pilot Steve Trevor (Lyle Waggoner) bailing out over the Bermuda Triangle and tumbling into the secret location of Paradise Island. On Paradise Island, home to an Amazonian race of women with superior strength and intelligence, he is nursed back to health by Amazonian Princess Diana (Carter). The comely women in togas frolicking on Paradise Island could be mistaken for Playboy Bunnies at Hugh Hefner's Mansion, but no matter; they are strictly anti-men. Diana's mother Queen Hippolyta (Cloris Leachman in the pilot) suggests they have an Olympic game to decide who escorts Trevor back to America and Diana competes in blonde disguise and wins. She is then sent to America as Wonder Woman in an American-themed, red, white and blue uniform designed by her mother.

She has a gold belt for strength, bullet-defying bracelets, and a golden lasso which forces the ensnared to tell the truth. (Comic creator Marston was the inventor of the lie detector test and also, according to *The Secret History*, into bondage which crops up frequently in the series). In America, Wonder Woman winds up stopping a bank robbery and defeating Nazis.

At the conclusion of the pilot, Brigadier General Blankenship (John Randolph) is talking about the new secretary hired for Trevor who is not only exceptional clerically, but plain in appearance —Yeoman First Class Diana Prince – Wonder Woman in disguise. Like Clark Kent in Superman, glasses are the simple device used to hide the super hero's true identity and also allegedly make him or her less attractive or "weak." Amazingly, no one seems to spot the resemblance between Prince and Wonder Woman.

The TV show originally kept the World War II setting with Wonder Woman battling the Nazis and then switched to contemporary times where Diana Prince became an agent for the Inter-Agency Defense Command (IADC), a covert government agency. Debra Winger appeared as Diana's younger sister Drusilla in several of the World War II episodes, affording her an opportunity to also wear the "satin tights" and red, white and blue costume and Carolyn Jones was Queen Hippolyta. There was coincidentally a striking family resemblance between Carter, Jones and Winger. Waggoner was a good choice for Trevor. Besides being a hunk, he had comedic abilities similar to Leslie Nielson, an almost "Dudley Do-Right" campiness befitting a comic book figure. Carter suggested the spin Diana Prince does to become Wonder Woman and comic book elements were maintained throughout each episode, such as animated starbursts and exposition through comic book panels or images fading into panels.

The plotlines mixed fantasy, mystery, horror, sci fi and other genres deftly. The special effects were quite good for the time on par with *The Six Million Dollar Man*. Wonder Woman is able to leap to or from the top of buildings gracefully, knock out dozens of assailants, and move cars and other heavy objects as sound effects similar to *The Six Million Dollar Man* play. As in a number of the TV series from the 70's, she is also frequently shown running, often at superhuman speeds. The many fantastic episodes include my favorite "Death in Disguise" in which brilliant female impersonator Charles Pierce guest stars as a villain equal to the infamous Rosa Klebb (Lotte Lenya) in *From Russia With Love* whose shoe tips had poison-laced blades. Teen heart throb Leif Garrett, an icon of the 70's, and his sister Dawn Lyn guested on "My Teenage Idol is Missing" in which Garrett performs some of his top hits like "I Was Made for Dancing" at an actual concert and Wonder Woman rides the Wonder Motorbike in a Wonder catsuit. Carter, a singer, also performs songs from her own album *Portrait* in "Amazon Hot Wax."

Not just a pretty (read spectacular) face, Carter projected intelligence, kindness and capability as the caped crusader. For children and adults, *The New Adventures of Wonder Woman* was and remains good, clean fun.

Memories of Those Who Were There

The lovely Diana Muldaur, a ubiquitous face on 70's television.
Photo courtesy of Eva Alfhild Jonsson.

Sharon Farrell as a young starlet. Photo courtesy of the Movie Store.

Sharon Farrell ~ Actor

Sharon Farrell, the "Hollywood Princess from Sioux City, Iowa", as she titled her autobiography, was a familiar face in numerous television shows and motion pictures for forty years, making her debut as a teenager in the 1959 film Kiss Her Goodbye. *Of Norwegian ancestry, she had been born Sharon Forsmoe and took the professional name Sharon Farrell, combining her father's name Darrell with an "F" for Forsmoe. Throughout the 70's, the lovely blonde was active in a variety of television shows and made-for-television movies, including* Banyon, The New Perry Mason, The Eyes of Charles Sand, The Wide World of Mystery, Love American Style, Petrocelli, The Six Million Dollar Man, Police Woman, Kolchak: The Night Stalker, McCloud, *and* Mrs. Columbo. *She appeared as Florence Webster in the long-running daytime soap opera* The Young and the Restless *from 1991 until 1996. Her private life has often been as turbulent as her onscreen life. After the birth of her one child, Chance Boyer, she suffered an embolism that caused brain damage, including memory loss. In spite of this, Farrell resumed her acting career in full force, keeping her illness a secret on the recommendation of friend actor Steve McQueen. She has been married six times, twice to the same person, and her famous lovers included revolutionary Che Guevara, Bruce Lee and Steve McQueen. She currently lives in Los Angeles.*

Q. I know you began in live television. What was that like?

A.   I was on the *U.S. Steel Hour* and they had fifteen minutes of us really live. This was back in New York. I lived on 7th and then I lived between Avenues B and C on 6th Street. I did *Naked City* back then and I did a lot of these religious programs. There were a lot of religious shows that were on in the morning and I did four or five of those. I did commercials. I did Alberto VO5. They wanted me to be the Alberto VO5 girl and I did Spic 'N Span and Zest. I was just trying to work, trying to pay the rent. It's always been great.

I lived in New York for a while until Bob Hope brought me out here [to Los Angeles.] There was an Alfred Hitchcock I did with Franchot Tone ("Final Performance") and Franchot Tone was like an old-style vaudevillian in it. I did a few Hitchcocks. Do you know who Franchot Tone is?

Q. Oh, yes, I do.

A.   I got to work with some really amazing people. Eve Arden. I worked with her. In New York, I lived with Andrew Prine for a while. I think I was married to him for ten days. We got married out here and then we broke up. I felt safe with him while he was there. He was always a kind of cover. He was more my friend. When I met him in Cuba, he covered for me when I was having an affair with Che Guevara. When I got back, he was my only friend that I had in New York and I was going to meet Che in Bolivia. My girlfriend that I was living with then wouldn't let any calls come through from Che. She was from Puerto Rico. She said, "He's married. You're one of many. He's going to dump you. You're going to get killed." I said, "Well, I know how to use a machine gun. I can do this. I want to go fight. I want to be a revolutionary." I wanted to go. I had to have an abortion, too, because I was pregnant. It was against the law to have an abortion at that time. Andy found this place for me to have my abortion and sat outside. He knew it was Che's baby. He said, "You can't go to Bolivia. You can't do this with your career. You just did this movie. [*40 Pounds of Trouble.*] You're hot now." He was my real friend. I was like his sister. He didn't want to be married, though, and did break my heart when we got a divorce.

Q.   Were there any people who were seminal in helping you develop as an actress?

A.   Joanne Linville. Joan Hackett. I had an embolism and my heart stopped for four and a half minutes and I really couldn't read, walk or talk. It took me a while to get back. Steve McQueen called Steven Spielberg and Steven

Spielberg was directing Gene Barry in this trilogy. It was *The Name of the Game*. Robert Stack would do one episode one week, Gene Barry the next and then [Tony] Franciosa would do one. I was playing a robot, so I didn't have to be very good. I didn't know what upstage, downstage was then. I really didn't. Steven Spielberg let me look through the camera and he was teaching me about the camera while I was on that show. He was incredible. He was just so sweet and nice.

Q. I was reading your autobiography. What a dramatic life you've had!

A. My life is a total soap opera. I think everybody's life is! I had retired. I went to the Fiji Islands and built a house there. While I was in Fiji, someone climbed over the wall of the compound where there was barbed wire on top. I woke up with a guy on top of me, trying to smother me with a pillow and the bed was soft and I got some air. He hurt me really badly, [though]. He raped me and beat me up and punched me with a nail and everything else. It's a soap opera. It's like, "Is this going on?" The guy ran out and confessed. The police were after him for some other things that he had done, too, but they put him away for 15 years.

Q. That's good that they got him. There's often an intensity in your performances like in *The Eyes of Charles Sand*.

A. When I was doing *The Eyes of Charles Sand*, I had a really long drive, because I was living in Suma. I was living on Broad Beech Road and it would take me an hour to get to the Pacific Coast Highway and it would take me another 45 minutes to get back to the beach. My son Chance was really young then. Chance was born in 1970, so when I did *The Eyes of Charles Sand*, he was under five. Gosh, he must have been two or three – he was really little. Whenever I was screaming for Raymond, I was screaming for my son Chance, not being able to be with him. While I was shooting, it was night for night and I was running through the woods and falling down and I just let out everything. I'm a method actress. Any time I had any kind of problem, I'd always have some kind of a job and I always played abused women -- and that was my life. It seemed like the roles that I played are the roles of my life. I had somebody trying to kill me [in real life]. My sister was trying to kill me in *The Eyes of Charles Sand*. You know, Barbara Rush – who I adored. She took one look at me and I think I had a Pucci dress on and she said, "Oooh, you look rich. You look like you come from money." We went to singing lessons with David Craig and to Richard Simmons for working out. I followed her around until she wanted to take this pastry class. I thought, "This I cannot do." She said, "Oh, we've got to go downtown and buy some lard!" I thought, "This is where our friendship ends. There's a fat lady inside of me. If I'm going to be cooking pastries with you, I'm going to be eating them and the fat lady is going to come out." (laughs)

When I was doing shows that you're interested in like *The Eyes of Charles Sand*, I didn't know what marijuana or what anything was. X____ [1] really got me into drugs and stuff. I met him while I was working on a film that was shot in Mississippi. I flew in and I was so exhausted and you had to go to these parties and the Governor was there and all these people were there and they were asking me how I started and how do you get to be an actress. These are stories you tell over and over until you want to throw up. X____ was there and said, "I've got a joint. I'll meet you outside." I thought, "Oh, a joint. That's marijuana. I never tried that." It wasn't a joint he had; it was this white powder and he put it under his pinkie fingernail that was longer than the other nails and I didn't know, but it was laced with heroin. He got me on heroin. I became his doormat for the next thirty years. I always played victims, so I guess I was a mark right off to a certain type of man.

I was always playing drug addicts, which was easy for me, because I was one. Because X____ kept me out of my mind most of the time and it went very nicely for the roles I was playing. I didn't even have to work, I could just go in and film. I got sober when I got off the plane from Fiji which was 2007, so I've been clean – no smoking, no drinking, no drugs, no heroin, no cocaine, no nothing. It's been ten years now that I've been clean.

---

1   Editor's Note: The name of the individual is being withheld to protect his privacy.

Q. Congratulations. While we're talking about your work in the 70's, I wanted to also ask you about the film *It's Alive* from 1974 where you played Lenore Davies, a woman who gives birth to a monster. It's become a cult hit. What was that like?

A. Larry Cohen, the director, was really wonderful to us all and got the most out of us – free locations, etc. We all would contribute as much as we could. I was married to an accountant and we used his office in Beverly Hills for scenes with Guy Stockwell, for example. We used Larry's house for where the Davies lived. The baby crib was that of my son's. When the father came out of the sewers with the baby wrapped in a blanket, that was my dog Tippy under there. At my first meeting with Larry, he was worried that I might be too glamorous and I immediately used the bathroom and washed off all my makeup and convinced him on the spot that I could play dowdy Lenore. Everyone in the film was an actual friend of Larry's and his wife Jenelle at the time. When I first saw the plastic baby, I just about died. I still can't believe how Larry made it look so scary and great/realist. I thought the audience would get up and leave at that point; they didn't. I still have people come up to me, telling me how they saw the movie and it scared them to death when they were little and that they were afraid to walk home from school for years after seeing it. Richard Pryor's daughter Rain was a little girl at the time and she decided she wanted to give out Oscars and sent me one for Best Actress. It looked just like an Oscar. It is against the law to have such a copy, but Richard Pryor got someone to make them up for her. Mine says: "To Sharon Farrell from the Black Rain Arts and Science Awards for Her Moving Performance in *It's Alive*." The Oscar came to my agent and he was afraid to open it. *He* thought it was a bomb, so he called the police and me. I went to his office. The police had a dog-sniffing bomb detector with them and they opened it to find my Oscar from that sweet little girl, Rain. The music by [the] great artist Bernard Herrmann is a good part of [the movie's] success.

Sharon Farrell at the Oscars. Photo courtesy of Sharon Farrell.

Q. Tell me about your experiences on detective series during the seventies. You were in practically every series I'm profiling.

A. *Police Woman* was before my binge on drugs. I love Angie Dickinson. She was great, she was wonderful. I loved that show. It was great working with her. At one time the producers called me in because it was somewhere in some gossip column that I was dating Burt Bacharach. I'd never met him. They said, "I thought you were a friend of Angie Dickinson's." They threw some rag, some movie magazine down and it said I was dating Burt Bacharach. But Angie? She could care less. She was just wonderful. Everybody loved Angie Dickinson.

Angie Dickinson turned down a role that I was able to play. It was a Janis Joplin kind of role that I played on *The Name of the Game* with Robert Stack. It was a real big hit, "Hard Case of the Blues." That was one of my best performances, I think. Sal Mineo was in that and Keenan Wynn. Robert Stack was the one that got away. I had such chemistry with him. He was incredible. But I was straight and narrow until I met X___. Then I went haywire.

Q.   What about *Hawaii Five-O*?

A.   I learned a lot from Jack Lord on *Hawaii Five-O*. I learned to pick up my clothes, because here in Hollywood, if you have wardrobe people, you cannot dress yourself, you cannot pull up a zipper, you cannot do anything. The unions would get after you. If you did take something, you can't pick it up and put it on a hanger, but in *Hawaii Five-O*, because it was not on the mainland, we worked six days a week instead of the five days a week. Jack Lord called me in the office and said, "What do you mean by leaving your clothes on the floor? Don't you know how to pick up your clothes and put them on a hanger?" and I just stood there. I'd never been reprimanded. For years, I'd climb out of my clothes and I thought, 'Well, I won't hang them up, because I'll really get them in trouble if I do that.' It's really horrible what actors were forced to do, because we were not able to dress ourselves, we're not able to put on our makeup, we're not able to comb our hair, we're not able to touch anything except our words. Say our words, hit our marks, say our line. But Jack Lord – God bless that man. He really, really cared about me. He would be checking on me and making sure I didn't have any bugs in the apartment. There were these cockroaches that would fly around. They were five inches long with wings. He had bug inspectors come over.

I think I was making $5,000 a week [then]. Jack Lord had promised me $10,000. He did the negotiating. He told me not to get an agent. I listened to him and I didn't have an agent for it. I took him at his word.

I had gone to the airport to pick up my son and X____ and the first thing X____ did was say, "Here, take this" and he put this thing in my mouth that was LSD. I came back and Jack Lord called me into the offices and he was ranting and raving and all upset, because I was supposed to have a meeting with him and I had called and said I had to pick up my son and X____ at the airport. I had some reasons why I was unhappy with Jack. He liked me a lot. He was trying to protect me, but I kind of took it the wrong way, especially with picking up my son at the airport. The fact that X____ was with Chance gave Jack the power to say, "Your duty was to be here [for the meeting.]" He was right in a way, but I missed my son so much and I figured he'd understand. He kicked X____ off the set a couple times. He wouldn't let him anywhere around. Jack just despised X____. I never realized Jack had a built-in psychopath detector. He was so intuitive. It was an experience. Of course, Bill Smith was always ready to sock him. He was on his best behavior, because he had such a bad boy reputation in Hollywood. He'd go through sets on his motorcycle. He's now over at the Motion Picture Hospital and he sits in a wheelchair. This man spoke seven languages and now he has dementia. I went to his last birthday party over at the Motion Picture Hospital.

Q. Did Jack Lord have a lot of input into your acting? I know he was a perfectionist.

A.   Oh, he was wonderful. I played two roles in "Why Won't Linda Die?" and Jack Lord was up for best director for that. I was playing sisters, a blonde and a brunette. I was one person, but I thought I was two people. Or maybe I had a sister and killed her and pretended that I was her. I had my hair in a bun. Jack would say, "I want you to walk like a bull dyke." He used to call me a broad and say, "You're a good looking, broad." He called me into the office once, because I wasn't wearing a bra. He said, "I don't like that. You've got to be a lady." I told him, "Look, I came from Sioux City, Iowa." He'd say, "Be like my wife Marie" and I'd say, "I never had a man like you. I'm sorry. I don't know how to be a lady."

When I played the cop, Det. Lori Wilson in the last season, the first show was great. "Who Says Cops Don't Cry" was a really good show, but after that, the writing wasn't the same. It just developed into nothing. CBS kind of dropped Jack, because Jack wanted me and Bill to take over the show and he wanted to go off and play a captain of a boat. He had a script written for that, but anyway, CBS cancelled *Hawaii Five-O*.

Q. You did *McCloud* also and *Kolchak: The Night Stalker*.

A.   Dennis Weaver was one that got away, too. He was very spiritual and wanted me to come to his meditation room. He was such a gentleman and so nice, but he did want me to come to visit his meditation room and I was too scared to do that. Sparks were flying and I couldn't handle that at the time.

I tried to do a New Jersey accent in *Kolchak: The Night Stalker*. That was fun. You'd laugh your head off at that one. (Ed. Note: I'm from New Jersey).

I've got to get started in the business again. Everything is digital now. It's all changed so much. I did one of these digital YouTube shows – Indie TV. I did the show, but golly, the kids don't know what they're doing and they're all inexperienced. They don't know anything.

For instance, a TV repair guy just left here. The sun comes in this one window and I've got this flag that I use. It says "Sharon Farrell, *My Favorite Martian, Gunsmoke, The Reivers, Wild Wild West, Night of the Comet*." It's got all these things and it's got a bunch of pictures and I hang it up, so it doesn't get all wrinkly and to keep the sun out. When people come in, they see this "Sharon Farrell, Actress" thing. The TV repair guy said, "I just came from Steve McQueen's son's place down in Malibu" and I didn't say anything. He said, "I know who Steve McQueen is, but I've never seen any of his movies." I'm thinking, "Oh, God, Steve would just turn in his grave." When I did *The Reivers* with him, Steve McQueen was the biggest star in the world and got paid more money than anybody in the world at that time. But they do know who Chuck Norris is. They do know who Bruce Lee is. It's amazing.

Q. I know what you mean.

A.   But I know I can break into the business again. I've got to get an agent. Gosh, my agent Morgan Paull died. He said, "Sharon, I've got to get everything in order, because I'm going to die in two weeks." I couldn't believe it. He was a fine actor in his own right. There's got to be an agent that handles old timers, except there are so many of us old-timer actresses. I've gotten my health back. I've gone through a bunch of stuff here. I go from one scrape to another, from one frying pan into the next. (laughs) I have one more operation to get at Cedars-Sinai. [My current doctor] comes from an old doctor/friend of mine, Richard Grossman, that I knew back in the day; he was like his son. I'm going to go to him because Richard Grossman is up above watching. He's a Guardian Angel of mine. I've got all these people who are dead that I call upon to help me and they do. Then I fall into another hole and I have to get on Facebook and I tell everybody my woes and somebody on Facebook says, "Hey, Sharon, try this" and I try it. [At this time] I can't get into my house and I'm living in my garage, but my garage is so cute and it's so fun. Goldie Hawn's daughter has a 10-acre parcel next to my 17-acre parcel. I bought this place way back in 1975 from a guy named Alden Rollins and there were two houses on the property. I thought I could live in one and rent out the other one. One of them is the original Ranger Station from Topanga and it's a split log cabin. He covered it up with cedar siding and he built a garage next to it. In this garage, he built a little apartment upstairs and that's where I'm living. It's so great with windows all around. It's like living in a treehouse.

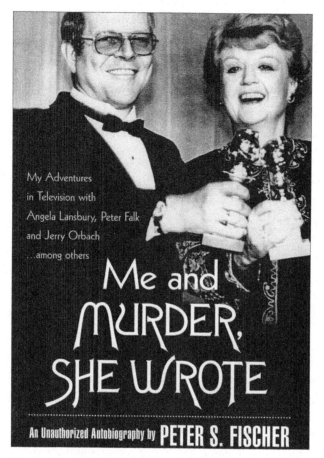

Peter S. Fischer with Angela Lansbury on the cover of his
unauthorized biography *Me and Murder, She Wrote (2013)*.

Peter S. Fischer ~ Producer/Writer

*Peter S. Fischer is an accomplished and prolific producer and writer who has
worked on some of the most celebrated mystery series in television history. He
served in the Army and attended John Hopkins University, originally planning on
becoming an actor, but a stint in summer stock changed his mind. His script for*

The Last Child *became a 1970 television film starring Michael Cole, garnered a Golden Globe nomination from the Hollywood Foreign Press and started him on a fulltime career in television. His many credits include* McMillan & Wife, Kojak, Ellery Queen, Baretta, *the mini-series* Once an Eagle, The Eddie Capra Mysteries, Walt Disney's Wonderful World of Color, Dead Man's Island, Stranger at My Door, Delvecchio, A Cry for Help, Columbo *(for which he was a story editor, writer and producer) and* Murder, She Wrote, *which he co-created with Richard Levinson and William Link. On* Murder, She Wrote, *he was Executive Producer for the first seven years, wrote numerous scripts and received an Edgar for best television episode for "Deadly Lady." He also garnered three Emmy nominations for outstanding drama series and won two Golden Globes. A resident of Pacific Grove, California, he now pens the delightful Hollywood Murder Mysteries which feature a Warner Brothers press agent, Joe Bernardi and wrote the equally delightful* Me and Murder, She Wrote *about his adventures in television.*

Q. **I know you were editor-publisher of your own small trade magazine when you sold a script for the 1970 TV movie *The Last Child* which would star Michael Cole. It changed your life. Tell me about that transition.**

A.   I was 35 years old and living in Smithtown, a small town on Long Island. I had a wife, three kids and operated a small publication called "Sports Car News." The publication allowed a few weeks a month to really get serious about my writing. It took a month to write my first movie and I sent it to my brother Geoff, a casting director at Universal Studios, for feedback. I thought he could pass it on to someone. A few days later I got a three-page letter with lots of notes. He also sent a few shooting scripts so I'd know how to properly format a script. Although he couldn't pass it around, he felt I had a knack for it. I was determined to try again with something fresh. I got my idea from a news article about a law passed in China, limiting couples to one child. Suppose it was the U.S. Congress that passed the law, not Beijing. I was very excited about the concept. I made a likable young couple who lost a child and the government only allows one child. She becomes pregnant again and they find out. The couple has to go on the run. There was a lot of back and forth, but it resulted in Geoff getting it to an independent producer Bill Allyn who took it to Barry Diller, who was behind ABC's new Movies of the Week, and then it went to Aaron Spelling. Aaron wanted to film it. Aaron Spelling sent it to one of my heroes, Rod Serling, for a possible rewrite and Serling returned it to him with a note that said "This script doesn't need rewriting." I almost cried. It became *The Last Child* with Michael Cole, Janet Margolin and in his last performance, Van Heflin. The ratings were phenomenal and it got an Emmy nomination for Best Made-for-TV Movie. My brother Geoff gave me some advice. If I really wanted a career in television, I couldn't remain in Smithtown. So I sold the magazine, my wife quit her job, we sold our house and moved to California. My friends thought I'd lost my mind.[2]

Q.   What are the different hats you wear as writer and producer? What is involved in producing a show?

A.   Writing and producing television is much different than doing the same in films. For example, in films, the writer is a necessary inconvenience once the script has been delivered. In television, the writer is king. First of all, the chief writer or writer-creator of the series is often also the executive producer which is the equivalent of a CEO.

All decisions stop at his desk. In addition, he tries his best not to be caught doing minutia like wardrobe approvals, props, location scouts. This the exec producer leaves to underlings. In my case, my chief interests were writing scripts, working with the casting director and ultimately editing the first or second cut down to 44 minutes and 30 seconds. This is extremely critical in a mystery show because an editor, left to his own devices, might

---

2   In *Me and Murder, She Wrote,* Fischer describes the dry period that followed his initial success: "[A very experienced old pro] said that they way business was conducted in Hollywood, it was a miracle that anything ever got made. The number one time-filler for writers and producers was doing lunch. You don't eat lunch. You don't meet for lunch. You DO lunch. . . . [t]he time-honored tradition of 'doing lunch' does not result in actual business being transacted but sets the stage for another lunch months or years down the road where no business can again be not transacted."

unwittingly cut out a clue or something else basic to understanding the plot line. The executive producer also is required to schmooze with studio execs and the network. I did little of this. I didn't have the time or the inclination, except in one or two cases where I really liked the guy/gal. The subordinate to the executive producer is the line producer who does all the heavy lifting (see above). He also has a table reading of the script with all departments in attendance, firming up wardrobe selections, locations, props needed where and when. Necessary, but time consuming and all of this must be done within a six-day window of preparation. The filming begins while simultaneously prep starts for the next episode, leaving the producer having to keep an eye on two episodes at once.

Being a line producer is not a fun job. As to writing, if you are an executive producer who writes, then you are constantly writing or you should be. You are also rewriting sub-par material which you have bought from freelance writers. If you are smart and efficient, you have at least one story editor on your staff to meet with freelancers and who also write scripts of their own. Often you will sit in on a final story conference to okay an assignment (or kill it). You may contribute to the storyline or help resolve a plot snag. Television writing is a never-ending process and the pressure to create decent scripts every six or seven days is crushing. Some shows succeed, some don't, but only a handful of shows succeed week after week.

Q. Did you always have an interest in mysteries -- either reading or writing them or both? Which authors did you admire?

A.   Yes. I was fascinated by Agatha Christie when I was about 12 and read them all which is where I think I learned the mechanics of the whodunit. As an aside, writing whodunits is a skill almost no freelancer brought to the table when I was producing *Ellery Queen* and I ended up having to write many of the scripts. Others were written by story editor Bob van Scoyk and we found one solid freelancer named Bob Swanson who later became a story editor on *Murder She Wrote*. As I aged, I started reading Hammett, Chandler,

James Cain, Ed McBain and Erle Stanley Gardner and finally graduated to writers like Scott Turow and John Grisham and David Baldacci, to name just three. Even now my favorite reading involves cops, lawyers and private eyes.

Q. What is the key to writing a good television mystery? How did television shape you as an artist?

A. In simplest terms, it is your obligation to keep your storyline simple enough so that the viewer can and will stay with you. This simple storyline may in reality mask a narrative which, when finally revealed (The butler did it!), will prove to be fair and surprising. Very astute mystery fans should identify the killer early on because a good television mystery is not designed for the smartest guy watching but the ordinary Joe and Jenny Six Pack. I can't stress this enough. If your plot is too complicated, no matter how clever, your viewer will turn off the episode and the series as well. As for shaping me as a writer, I don't think it did. I studied playwriting in college and when in my twenties, I would watch TV and say, I can do that, and when I finally got my chance, I proved that I could.

I had my chance with *Marcus Welby*. Six months after moving to California, I was running out of money. Then my agent set up a meeting with Nina Laemmle, the story editor for *Marcus Welby*, a Universal show and the highest-rated show on television. I thought my brother Geoff who was at Universal had something to do with the meeting, but he never said. Nina had liked *The Last Child* and asked if I'd be interested in working on an idea she had. Would I? I went home to the typewriter and sent over a fleshed-out story the next day. She gave me the go ahead and wanted to see a first draft within 8-10 days. Two days later I finished and sent her the script. A week later, with her blessing, I was in Van Nuys where the Welby company was shooting my episode. I was carrying my script which said "Written by Peter S. Fischer" on the cover page.

Q. Tell me about your work on *Columbo* and *Ellery Queen*. To me, they were two of the finest television mystery series ever created. What was most satisfying to you about each show?

A. This is too broad a subject to answer here. You can take excerpts from my book *Me and Murder, She Wrote*. On *Columbo:*

> Good characters, good settings, good dialogue, all of it went for naught if Peter [Falk] didn't like the cluework, not only at the end, but throughout the script. Apparently I had passed muster [with my first script] and he didn't mind telling people about it.
>
> A few weeks before the show aired, I had gotten a call from Peter complimenting me on the script and asking if I could drop by his office for a chat. I was flabbergasted. I was finally going to meet "Columbo" and I couldn't wait. And as it turned out, I actually did meet Columbo because in so many ways, Peter was much like his character. It wasn't only his speech cadence, it was the twinkle, the sense of humor, the lack of sartorial elegance, the quick mind and the down-to-earth intelligence that would show itself only if you dug for it. Unlike some of his contemporary TV stars, he was one of the good guys, though there were those in Universal's executive suite who would violently disagree. It was my experience, then and in the years to come, that Peter was a hard-working dedicated co-worker with his fellow actors, directors, writers, and sometimes even his producers. He did not, however, have much patience with the "suits" (executives) that populated the executive offices. In fact, I think he got a real satisfaction out of making them squirm because to Peter, the true test of the show was its quality and not budgets or shooting schedules.
>
> . . . I was told in no uncertain terms by someone who would know that Peter Falk had been up in the executive offices, pounding on desks, and threatening to quit *Columbo* for good if

the studio didn't sign me up to work on his show. I'm sure this
is an exaggeration, but with Peter's flair for theatricality, I can't
guarantee it. . . . In my long career writing for various stars and
their roles, Peter and the lieutenant were at the top of my fun
list. No question about it. Not being an actor, I did not "act" my
dialogue when writing except for Peter. I would be sitting at my
desk at home on a Saturday afternoon, banging away on a script
and now and then one of my kids would peer in and yell to my
wife, "Mom, he's at it again!"

On *Ellery Queen:*

Cut to 1975 and suddenly NBC is very interested in a weekly
Ellery Queen series and they want Dick [Levinson] and Bill
[Link] to produce it. . . . Which brings me to the offer I could
not refuse. The boys asked me if I would join them as a producer on the series. They would executive produce, and . . . I
would be the "writing producer", working with the story editor to develop scripts as well as writing a few myself. Was I flattered? Hell, yes. Was I scared to death? Yes, indeed. . . . We had
a lot of fun that year turning out what we thought were pretty
good shows, ever mindful that the viewing public didn't agree.
At least not in large numbers. We garnered a lot of good reviews
but realists will tell you these are good for wrapping fish. . . .
All 22 of the episodes we aired were entitled "The Adventure
of. . ." and every episode featured an all-star cast of one-time,
big-name movie stars or television personalities. Our opening
show starred Joan Collins, Farley Granger, Barbara Rush, Ray
Walston and even bandleader Guy Lombardo.

. . . Despite anemic ratings, we were hoping for a second season.
Sadly, it eluded us. . . . . In the years it went off the air, *Ellery
Queen* has become something of a cult favorite. . . .. It helps take
away the sting of that second season we never got. Cult favor-

ite? Absolutely, but cult favorites don't pay the rent. Let's just say that our best efforts resulted in a noble ratings and financial failure. But why? I have my theories.

A major problem was our mystery solutions. Though I loved Dick dearly, I always thought he was fashioning the show, perhaps subconsciously, for the critics and other murder mystery aficionados and not for the viewing public. In some episodes, the solution was so obscure and contrived that it almost defied explanation. That is not the way to hang onto a mass television audience...

As far as which was more satisfying, that's tough. I wrote a spec script for *Columbo* which was my favorite TV show at the time and while it was never made, it opened doors for me and led to my first assignment on the show, "Publish or Perish." I can truly say that I loved writing every one of my *Columbos* because I knew Peter Falk and the character so well. With *Ellery*, Jim Hutton as Ellery never really gelled in my mind and it was also my first stab at writing a "closed" mystery (i.e. whodunit). I always enjoy writing and *Ellery* was no different, but I found myself writing to please Dick Levinson who was the exec producer and my boss and when ratings were bad, I found myself second guessing what I was doing. Satisfying? Merited or not, I always felt satisfied with my work on *Columbo*, less so on *Ellery* wherein I felt my foundation was wobbly.

Q. **"Publish or Perish" was a fantastic episode with a great villain and I wondered what inspired that story.**

A. Yes, I loved that one. As I recall, the plotline was all my idea, but to be fair, it's possible that either Dean Hargrove or Roland Kibbee put a one-line "what if" into my head. But the plot was all mine and the casting of Jack Cassidy was brilliant. Later on, these two did hand me a great "what-if" in the episode where Columbo goes up against the police commissioner. I love all my Columbos, but my two favorites are this one with Richard Kiley ("A

Friend in Deed") and a later one, "Rest in Peace, Mrs. Columbo." "Negative Reaction" with Dick Van Dyke is a millimeter behind them. Dick Van Dyke, I thought, was very good. He did a nice job and in those days, he wasn't known for doing straight stuff. He was basically doing his comedy show and that was it. That's all people knew about him.

Q. What kind of problems or difficulties do you encounter working on a show? What do you do to resolve them?

A. There are two sets of problems. One is the network and the other is the studio. And they have different agendas. Let me see if I can put this in a proper perspective. The networks hire young hotshots out of film school or relatives, one or the other, nephews or nieces. These people are put in a position of power over the creators, the producers and the emissaries of the studios. If Universal does a show – let's say *Murder, She Wrote*, then we will have somebody from the network attached to it. It's this person's job to make himself or herself look as important as possible, so they are constantly harassing you with minutiae which means absolutely nothing, so you have to deal with them in a way that doesn't really humiliate them, which is very hard to do, because they're generally fairly stupid. (laughs) I didn't have a bad time with *Murder, She Wrote*, because the lady who was in charge of keeping tabs on me was a sweetheart. She was an old-timer, she knew what she was doing, she knew what she was talking about and she knew that I knew what I was doing, so it was marriage made in heaven, but I've had other experiences that were much worse.

So the guy calls me up in bed. "Oh, for God's sake, I just saw the dailies!" I said, "Whoa, what's the matter?" He says, "Why is that guy wearing a red sweater? That should be a blue sweater!" I say, "What?" He said, "The red – it just doesn't jive. You've got to get him in a blue sweater." I said, "You want me to throw out and shoot this entire scene with him in a blue sweater for no Goddamn reason?" That's typical. Or there's "I found misspellings in your script." No kidding. You found misspellings. You know how the monks used to whip themselves? I said, "I'm going to flagellate myself for the next 15 minutes." That's what the problem is with the network. They all want to be important, they all want to save their job, they all want to be the head of programming, so they'll make your life miserable now.

When it comes to the studios, they are penny pinchers. No matter what you do, they want to make sure that you don't spend too much money. They make a fortune, a *fortune*, on episodic hits, but they won't tell you that. They say, "I don't know how we're going to survive. You're $50,000 over budget." I said, "Oh, my God, really, am I? What does that mean? Does that mean you're going to have less than a million dollars in profit this week?" (Laughs) So that's a game they play and I don't play it. I think in the book I did talk about that.

Q. Yes, you did.

A. *Ellery Queen,* where they said they were going to shut me down. I said, "Fine. Shut me down. I'm going up to the Tower. I'm going to tell them we're going to shut down for the week. See how they like what that costs them!" (Laughs) If you have a bully, all you have to do is bully back and you almost always win.

Q. What would you say was the key to *Murder, She Wrote*'s enormous success? Who shaped the Jessica Fletcher character? How would you describe the show and the sort of direction it took?

A. Angela Lansbury. It never would have been the major hit it became without her.

Given that, the next best thing we had going for us was our time slot right after *60 Minutes*. Harvey Shepherd, director of programming, planned to put us there from the beginning knowing that the audience for *60 Minutes* would stick around for a warm, non-threatening hour of fun and mystery. Third, little or no onscreen violence.

We were an old-fashioned show like Poirot or Marple in the midst of up-to-date, hip offerings like *Miami Vice, Hill Street Blues* or *NYPD.* Jessica was down-home America, apple pie and vanilla ice cream, honest and true-blue and as comfortable as an old shoe. It still is. As far as shaping Jessica's character, I started her out in the pilot, but as she moved along, Angela was in charge of Jessica and did a wonderful job of it. And that was great for all us writers, because if your character is indelible, it makes the writing so much easier. Toward the end when I was no longer involved in running the show (after year 7), I worried that Jessica was becoming too sophisticated, but the audience didn't seem to mind.

Q. What different kind of slant did you take when you crafted a script for *McMillan & Wife* and *Kojak*? Where do you get your ideas?

A. I wrote only one episode of *Kojak*[3] and the background came out of my own experience as an investigator for an insurance company, a job I held for three years after getting mustered out of the army and getting married. As for *McMillan*, the episode "Downshift to Danger" was inspired by my involvement with auto rallying on Long Island where I was living prior to moving to Los Angeles. One of my five favorite scripts I wrote for TV was "Love, Honor and Swindle", my other *McMillan* effort, a charming story on love, marriage and double-crossing. This one, like most of my ideas, sprang forth from my head and I am never sure of the source of the inspiration. I do know that my first made-for-TV movie *The Last Child* was inspired by the Chinese government's ban on multiple children in a household.

Sometimes an idea comes from watching an episode on TV, sure of where it is going, and when it doesn't, at some time in the future, I will find myself doing a similar storyline the "right" way.

---

3   In his book *Me and Murder, She Wrote,* Fischer describes the license given to stars, such as Telly Savalas, who called the shots: "During his *Kojak* years, Telly liked to jet off to Vegas for the weekend. He would show up on the set on Monday a little worse for wear. Often he would pull the director aside and ask for his opinion of the script, the writer's intent, the subtext, etc. This was the code for the fact that Telly had not read the script and had no idea what it was about or what scenes they would be shooting. Did anyone care? Not really. He was Telly and if the episode made it to the air on time, no harm done."

Q. Tell me about the Hollywood Murder Mysteries, your delightful series. You said in an interview that you had to exercise different muscles as a novelist as opposed to a screenwriter. Is your protagonist a blend of various people you've known?

A. I love my Hollywood Mysteries and Walter Mitty would be the first to tell you that my hero, Joe Bernardi, is me. Not that I would ever get involved in his adventures, because I am a homebody at heart. I mean that in spirit and attitudes and lifestyle, likes and dislikes, I am very much Joe who speaks for me in the first person in each of the books. I came up with the idea because it blended my two passions, mysteries and old movies, and so far, the work has kept me happy and young at heart. Joe starts out in the series as a studio publicist because I didn't want to repeat the cop, lawyer, private eye clichés and I think I have succeeded. By 1973 my current book, which involves the filming of *The Exorcist*, Joe has become a screenwriter and an author and watching him grow and develop has been a joy.

As for muscles, screenwriting involves mainly dialogue and sketchy descriptions of action which the director will interpret, costuming which the wardrobe people will handle, etc. Writing prose forces the author to paint word pictures accurately and in an entertaining or provocative way to force the reader to participate in the process, rather than sit like a toad on a lily pad and observe. Writing descriptions of locales or a character's unspoken reactions is hard to do and to me, for one, it has been a long learning process. In a script, all you need say is "It is raining." The reader of a short story or a novel will demand more than that. Is it a light rain, is it a downpour, are the streets awash or is it what the Irish call a "soft day"? If you paint the picture well, your reader will visualize your book like a movie as yet unfilmed. Do it wrong and the reader will be looking for a different author.

Q. What do you think made television mysteries in the seventies special?

A. That's a hard question. TV comes and goes and the hits that survive are sometimes not the best shows in the world, but they can be entertaining. I remember when we used to watch Buddy Ebsen doing *Barnaby Jones*. The trade papers were all full of "Last season for *Barnaby Jones*. He's been on two years. We don't need to see anymore. This is not a very good show and they're gonna cancel it." And so that happened the third year, the fourth year, the fifth year, the sixth year. By the time we got to the seventh year, they were singing the same, old song and *Barnaby Jones* had survived for yet another year. The other thing about watching television is the more you like the show, the more likely it is going to get canceled. Watching shows and programming television is not an easy job, because so much depends on what night you're on, what your competition is, what your demographic is. Harvey Shepherd had decided that the demographic from *Sixty Minutes* to *Murder, She Wrote* was perfect. I didn't know what the hell he was talking about. I thought we were going to be on Saturday night. That 8 o'clock slot was a blockbuster. You have the world by the – er, throat. (laughs) That used to be Ed Sullivan's slot and he was huge. Then, of course, when *Murder, She Wrote* moved to Thursday night at 8 o'clock, it died and I mean it died so fast, it was incredible, because it was up against entrenched comedies that everybody loved. They weren't about to switch off from that, so it basically killed the show and I think they knew they were doing it and why, I don't know. They may have been scared of the demographic of *Murder, She Wrote*, because it was older and they wanted the younger 35s to 55s or whatever the hell they were looking for. So when you're programming shows, so much depends on when they're on, who's up against them and how good it is the first three or four episodes out of the box, because, as Dick Lindheim, who would become the head of NBC programming said, you get them in the first two episodes or you don't get them at all.

Veteran stuntman Bob Herron with Ernest Borgnine. Photo courtesy of Bob Herron.

Robert Herron ~ Stunt Man

Born on September 23, 1924, Robert Herron is a Hollywood stunt legend. He grew up in Hawaii and relocated to California where his stepfather, Ace Hudkins was a famous supplier of horses to films. After serving in the Navy in the South Pacific, Herron began wrangling horses for his stepfather on movie sets and moved onto stunt work and acting gigs. While in Hawaii, he already was doing high dives, surfing and marital arts, which acquitted him well for the daredevil world he entered. In a career that has spanned over fifty years, he performed stunts of all kinds in over 300 films and television shows, ranging from westerns to detective shows to comedies, science fiction and horror. In the 70's alone, his many credits included the Bond film Diamonds are Forever, Prime Cut, Kojak, Cleopatra Jones, Cannon, Blazing Saddles, Dillinger, Columbo, The Day the Earth Moved, Earthquake, Petrocelli, Kung Fu, Rocky, The Streets of San Francisco, Silver Streak, The Rockford Files, McCloud, The Six Million Dollar Man, They Call Me Mister Tibbs! *and* Charlie's Angels. *He was a regular stunt double on* The Wild, Wild West *and doubled on many other shows and films, including* Father Dowling Mysteries, Batman Returns, Melrose Place, The District, Matlock, Star Trek *and* Magnum, P.I. *Other appearances included* Naked Gun, Buffy the Vampire Slayer, The X Files, *and* LA Confidential. *Highly regarded in his field, he was on the board of directors of the Stuntmen's Association, the S.A.G. board of directors, the Chairman of the National S.A.G. Stunt and Safety Committee, and is a past president of the Stuntmen's Association. He currently resides in Los Angeles, California.*

Q. Were you an intrepid kid? How did you go from being a horse wrangler to doing other stunts on movie sets?

A. My stepfather rented horses to the movies, Hudkins Stables. I wrangled horses for the barn. I took the horses to the set and then took them back to the barn after they were finished. As a wrangler on the set, I watched the stuntmen perform and I knew I could do that! I played football in high school and was all city in track (Narbonne High School) in Lomita, California. Shot put, long jump (200-yard dash, now 200 meter).

Q. What did you do to stay in condition? Did you lift weights, do gymnastics? What was your secret to staying fit to perform so many stunts?

A. No weights in the gym, but a lot of physical labor, including lifting hay bales and manual exercise in general. Heavy punching bag in the gym. Lots of running in parks.

Q. Did the studios send you to special classes to learn stunts?

A. No, you learned from other stuntmen. That's really the only way.

Q. What were some of your special skills as a stuntman?

A. I was raised in Hawaii, surfboarding, diving, swimming. I boxed in the Navy in World War 2 after learning from my stepfather who was a famous boxer in the 20's. I raced sports cars back in the 1950's. I trained in judo also with Gene LaBell who is the guru of the art.

Q. Can you tell me anything about working on the sets of *Rockford Files, Columbo, McCloud, The Streets of San Francisco?* Were any sets more pleasant than others? What kind of stunts did you do on detective shows?

A. I'm 92 as of this month, so my memory is not that great. All of the lead actors were great to work with. Very professional and not temperamental. You shot so many set ups all day, there wasn't much time for being social. There were mostly horse stuff and fights, a lot of car chases and a lot of fights.

Q. How did you protect yourself?

A. You put on pads – stunt pads – knees, elbows. Usually in explosions, you have to make sure you're not too close.

Q. I wanted to hear about your experiences on *Naked Gun* and *Mad, Mad World.* What made working on those particular movies so much fun?

A. Both pictures were a lot of fun. Very talented people. Comedies are great to work. Actors are pretty relaxed. O.J. (Simpson) on *Naked Gun* was not very likeable and was not very professional.

Q. What kind of injuries did you sustain as a stunt man? Did you break many bones?

A. On *Sheriff Lobo*, I broke three ribs (falling) off of a horse and I broke a foot and an ankle and that's been it as far as breaks go. I suffered seven concussions that I know of.

Q. Were there any TV directors that you enjoyed working with in particular? Or actors?

A. Dave Cass, Mike Preece, Len Katzman, Irving Moore. I worked with so many TV directors so long ago, I don't remember them. Movie directors: Raoul Walsh, John Huston, Bob Wise, Stanley Kramer, Clint Eastwood, Cecil B. DeMille, Blake Edwards.

Q. What kind of stunts most often can go wrong?

A. Fist fights – actors hitting each other, horse stunts – two horses not cooperating, car filming – cars with engine or brake failure, etc.

Q. What did you love most about stunt work? What were some of your favorite stunts?

A. Working with all the famous actors and directors and doubling them sometimes (actors). In films, it's all camera angles. In fights, a punch can miss by a foot but look like a hit. The punch can miss by an inch but the wrong angle, it will look like a big miss. On *Convoy*, doubling Ernest Borgnine, I jumped a car through the air 165 feet – through a billboard, then through the roof of a barn and 100 feet beyond that. That was a goodie. Another one was doubling another actor riding a horse bareback leading three head of horses on a halter. Going full tilt, I had to transfer from one to the other. I was going to tire out the guy I was chasing who was on one horse.

Q. Did you find things changing in television over the decades?

A. There are changes in stunt equipment and stunt procedures and then of course the new technology is certainly different from what we used to do. We used to drive rear wheel cars. Now most of the cars you drive are front wheel drive which makes for a different technique.

Lance Kerwin as a successful young teen actor.
Photo courtesy of the Movie Store.

Lance Kerwin ~ Child/Teen Actor

Lance Kerwin was one of the most talented child and teen actors of his generation. Raised in Lake Elsinore, California, his father was an acting coach and his mother was a performer and later a talent agent. He is the youngest of five brothers and his brother Shane sometimes functioned as his stand-in. Throughout his youth, he appeared in commercials and numerous television shows, including Wonder Woman, The Bionic Woman, Little House on the Prairie, Emergency, Gunsmoke, Police Story, The Wide World of Mystery, Simon & Simon, Family *and* Cannon. *He was a cast member of the television series* The Family Holvak *with Glenn Ford and Julie Harris and the star of* James at 16. *His many made-for-television films included* The Death of Richie; Young Joe, the Forgotten Kennedy; *The Mysterious Stranger; Reflections of Murder; Children of Divorce; and the highly-acclaimed adaptation of the Stephen King novel* Salem's Lot. *During his teens and 20's, he suffered from drug and alcohol problems and spent time in rehabs, but then succeeded in becoming clean and sober and worked as a counselor and ordained minister with U-Turn for Christ. Having departed the business in the 90's, he currently is happily married and lives with his wife and five children in Kauai, Hawaii.*

Q. How did you get started in the business and do you feel it took away from your childhood?

A. No, it did not take away from my childhood. It *was* my childhood and I loved it. I don't think I missed out on anything. I gained a lot. It helped my education in terms of the tutoring. My mom was raising five kids that were all musicians and entertainers and surfers. My parents were basically hippies and we all wanted to be actors and we did summer stock and theater and community theater and local plays and things around the house. I wanted to be an actor as much as everyone in my family did and it just kind of happened for me in a bigger way than it did for the rest of the family. Then my parents had to put their path on hold because they would have to go on auditions with me and be with me on the sets and that kind of became their career also.

My stepdad was a jack of all trades in the motion picture industry, but at one point, he was an extra and knew some guys who were working on *High Plains Drifter,* a Clint Eastwood movie. So we had our summer vacation down in Mono Lake where they were filming *High Plains Drifter.* At the wrap party the town did in honor of *High Plains Drifter,* I met and talked with Mr. Eastwood. Well, a month later at home, I told my mom, "I want to write Clint Eastwood a letter." She encouraged me to do so. I wrote him and told him that I wanted to be an actor and I was doing everything to get ready. I was taking tap and ballet and acting workshops. At this stage, I was maybe ten. My mom had told me, "Look, there are two types of people and the way they approach becoming actors. There are the ones who spend all their time trying to get their foot in the door who are looking for that opportunity wherever they can and then there are the other type who are doing everything they can to be prepared for when they get that opportunity" and she encouraged me to be that [last] type. "If you want to be an actor, start taking acting, singing, dancing. When you do get your break, you'll be ready." I relayed that to Mr. Eastwood in the letter, that I wasn't in a rush, but if he needed someone, to give me a call. A week went by. "Gee, Mom, how come no letter back?" She said, "You've done your part." Well, lo and behold, we get a phone call from Ted Post who was the director of a lot of Clint's movies and this particular one was *Magnum Force.* He said that Clint had given him a letter from me and that he wanted to meet me.

We were living way out of L.A. at that time, a pretty rural lifestyle, and we loaded up and went to L.A. to meet Ted Post. I auditioned for him. I played the flute, I tap danced, I sang and read for him. I spent some time with his wife. I do not know. But he was a short guy and I was a short guy and was really thin for my age and he really liked me and said, "We're going to give you a part in this picture. You gotta go get an agent." I went and got an agent.

Let me back up just for a second. The year before that when we were living in Hollywood and then I told my parents that I wanted to be an actor, I went on interviews, but I wasn't in the union and the case is such that you can't do a show if you're not in the union. You can get in the union if you've done a show, but you can't do a show unless you're in the union. Every audition I was too tall, too small, too short, just not right. It's pretty discouraging. You have to spend a lot of time going on union interviews to finally get someone willing to sign a waiver and get you into the union to do your first show. And they made a choice for the family, my mom and stepdad, to move out of L.A. and move to the country. Here we were in the country with really no opportunities, but we did what we could. So flash forward. We get the call from Mr. Post, the director, so we go up and meet him and he says, yes, he's going to use me. Get an agent. Based on that, this agent took me who actually was a family friend. At the last minute, the show didn't work out. They recast for an infant. I was pretty disappointed, but saw my brother-in-law that summer and when I came back, I still had the agent who said, "Let's start again." I went on auditions and finally got an audition in, I guess it was '73, for a remake of *Diabolique*, the film with Simone Signoret. Anyway, this was Sam Waterson, Tuesday Weld and Joan Hackett.

Q. Reflections of Murder.

A.   Yes. It was a 20th Century Fox film and it was a cattle call with at least 200 kids and I did my homework and they took me for the second callback and the third callback and while they were on the fourth, they were frank with me. "Look, we like you, but we just don't know if it's going to work out. You don't live in LA." The director wanted me, so they told me why don't you come to the last callback anyway. They gave me the script to take home and I did what I'd learned from my stepdad and in acting school and did my homework and knew the character and his through line from all that stuff we were studying on building the character and creating the role. When I came back, I was prepared and for whatever reason, they took a chance and hired me and gave me the waiver. I was twelve and that year I did thirteen shows. After that one, I was in *Adam 12, Gunsmoke, Emergency, Wonder Woman, Bionic Woman*. I did about six *Afterschool Specials*. I did a couple Movies of the Week, one of which was *The Greatest Gift* with Glenn Ford that NBC decided to turn into a series. Glenn Ford had called us and said, "You know, Lance, I enjoyed working with you. They're offering this series. I just want to tell you a series is a big commitment. You'll miss a lot of roles. You better make sure you want to do this and you better ask for everything you want. Because I told them I wouldn't do it without you."

We wanted to do it. I really like that part of the industry, creating roles. We really didn't care too much about the money, because we'd never had money before, so we asked for a whole bunch, they gave it to us and we began the series. That was *The Family Holvak*. Then after that was *The Loneliest Runner*, Michael Langdon's story about the kid who wet the bed. By then, they'd written *James at 15* for me and we did *James at 15*. My senior thesis was about how the positive aspects of a minor working in the motion picture industry far outweighs the negative aspects which had been highly publicized. Everybody talks about drugs and losing the chance to play Little League and exposure to lewd, immoral kind of stuff, but my experience was way different. I loved the craft of it. I liked cinematography and the set dressers and the building of it and the lighting. Every aspect of the motion picture industry was my childhood. I hung out up on the catwalks on top of the soundstage and would watch the building. Before I got my work permit to act, I think I got four Fs and one D one year, so I wasn't a great student, really couldn't read. In order to work in the industry, you had to have a work permit, so with the flip of a switch, I was getting all As. Whatever it was that motivated me to pay attention, I was interested. You had to read scripts. My parents would read with me all the plays and scripts – you know, stuff that I was interested in.

So you're talking about how I got in the motion picture industry. I was determined and desperate to do it and so was my family and that's just what we did until it happened. My parents taught me a really good work ethic, so I was prepared. I wasn't one of those kids who had the day off from school or was looking for an autograph or was, you know, enamored with celebrities. I really took it seriously. And I think, as humbly as I can try to say this, that's what Hollywood liked about me, that I was pretty professional. At least that's what was shared with me over the years when I talked with directors and producers I worked with. A lot of kids at that time were adults portraying teenagers like *Welcome Back Kotter* and *Happy Days*. I was one of the few teenagers who was really doing a teenager show. *James at 15* was all minors and I was in every scene in every show, so it was pretty much working around the clock. I couldn't say at all I missed my childhood. I loved my childhood. It was awesome.

But I never really learned how to do anything else for a living. (laughs) That's what I did, I could pretend to be anything. Every time you do a show, you'd get some instruction on that. If the character you're playing is a musician, they'd teach me how to play the instrument. Some of the characters I played afforded me the opportunity to have some pretty neat experiences – you know, hockey playing with Scott [Baio] in *The Boy Who Drank Too Much*, riding horses. I guess about every kind of lifestyle a kid could have, whether country or city, I got to have it. In the show, *P.J. and the President's Son*, it was kind of a modern-day *Prince and the Pauper* and I played the president's son and another boy who just looked like the president's son and we swapped places. We were at the White House filming and that was during the Ford administration. What better life could a kid have than that?

We did one of those "Whatever Happened to Child Actors" things for – I don't want to say which one. You know, *Entertainment Tonight, Access Hollywood* – they all like to do them and the story they want to tell is that Hollywood is what went wrong with kids. That's just not the case. My family was part of the drug culture before acting ever was and Hollywood just gave us enough money to do it to the point of ruin. I loved acting and think that's a separate thing. With drugs, I couldn't get off that rollercoaster. I had never learned any coping mechanisms other than escaping and so then when I retired from acting and got involved with Calvary Chapel, helping other people, it was the only other thing, other than acting, that ever occupied and fulfilled me. Helping other people overcome drugs then became my main passion.

Q. Tell me about some of your experiences on *Salem's Lot* with David Soul. What was it like on that shoot?

A. *Salem's Lot* for me was pretty neat. It was a departure from most of the television, because I did mainly television, not feature films. I did a few feature films and didn't really have lead roles in feature films. In television, the main goal was usually to get it done. If it was close enough, if the mike wasn't in the room, if the actors were happy enough, they'd say, "Check the gate. Moving on." You know, is there a hair in the gate – meaning, beyond the camera lens. Quiet on the set. Rolling. Sound. Cut and print. Because that's what television is about, it's about the timing and the budget. And *Salem's Lot* wasn't that at all. Tobe Hooper, the director, was more interested in getting the effect he wanted than how long it took or how much it cost. It was one of the most expensive, high-budgeted movies of the week that was done at that time. Some of the effects that they used were really different. There was a scene where one of the kids comes to my character's window—my character, Rob Petrie [Mark Petrie], I don't know, whatever my character's name was, but the little vampire kid comes to the window and he's scratching at the window and saying, "Let me in, let me in." I go to the window and almost succumb and almost open the window. Then I get this strength and back away, "Go away, go away" and go back to bed. Well, we shot that scene backwards. We put film in the camera running in reverse. It was the weirdest thing I've ever seen. We started at the end of the scene and walked backwards and we went all the way until we figured out how we were going to do it. That's one of the reasons that scene has such a weird feel to it and the way the smoke is going in an odd direction.

They let rats go on the set, they had glycerin oozing through holes in the back of the walls so the walls would look like they were moving and alive, and it was the first time really it wasn't about "quick, let's do it and finish it." But "let's go ahead and do whatever it takes to make this thing as good and as scary and affect the audience in the biggest way we can." What a departure for me where I could really dig in. I can remember doing commercials where you had to hold your hand on a can in such a way that it shows the label of the product. You would have to shoot the scene off balance, so you would get the shot and keep going and where with *Salem's Lot*, it was like, "No, no, no. We don't want that. We'll move the camera. We'll knock the building down, whatever it takes. The finished product is the most important thing." I loved that. James Mason had quite a sense of humor. I was surprised at that. I think everybody on the set was. James Mason would tell a joke, so there was a bit of that. David Soul was trying to dig into it. He was supposed to walk into the house. He was like, what was his motivation. After a few times, I can remember someone saying, "Come on. It's Friday. It's our last scene. We're losing the light. Walk into the house. That's your motivation."

The set was pretty neat. The exteriors that were shot in Ferndale, California, they put that house together in one night. They got the parts from United Warner Brothers backlot. They tried to use a bunch of parts of different scary films from throughout the years. I don't know if you knew that or not.

Q. No.

A. The interior set as well. They used one wall from *Mommie Dearest*, they used some parts from *Psycho*, they used some parts from something else. These pieces of sets that they put together were all different sets from old classic horror films. So our call, the first day we went to the exterior of the Marsten house was like 5:30, 5 a.m. makeup call. We showed up early and the craftsmen and the set builders were just finishing it. As you know, the house looks old, it looks weird, it's rock wall, it's off balance. They had painted and thrown it together in one night. There was a little tavern and there was a guy driving home drunk. I remember seeing this guy pulling his car over and getting out of his car and kind of stumbling and scratching his head like, "I lived in this town thirty years and I never saw that."

About the time I finished *James*, I was taking a break to recover from the sheer amount of time I put in and I had broken my foot, so I had some time off at a time when careerwise it probably wasn't the best thing. My agent didn't think so, anyway. It wasn't a time to take a break, it was a time to ride the roll. But I took time off and then I got hurt and went to Europe and worked for a while and took a couple of shows that my agent didn't think I should have. There's a lot of pressure between parents who have a big say in how a child's actor's life and career goes, the manager/producers and then the kid himself.

I liked doing parts. I wanted to do parts that were challenging. My parents and agents were more about doing shows that advanced my career and paid more each and every time, and I really wasn't into climbing that ladder, so we had a conflict with regard to that. There were parts that we turned down that I wouldn't have turned down, because I liked the role, but it didn't pay what they thought it should pay, and there were parts I took that they really thought I shouldn't take, but I was having fun. I wasn't really interested in becoming a celebrity. That was just a part that kind of went with it.

Richard Chamberlain had said one time that there's really only three reasons you do it. It doesn't pay that well, it's not going to be that much fun, but it's a part you really want to play. The other one is it's not a part you really want to play and it doesn't pay that well, but it's going to be some fun. It's a swashbuckler or it's shooting in Europe or it's shooting in Hawaii. Of course, the third reason is that it's not a part you want to play nor is it going to be any fun, but the premium is so much, you can't afford to turn it down.

Right when I took the break from *James at 15*, I was getting offered a lot of horror parts, because it was right when all the horror shows were coming out and what I thought was exploitative stuff and stuff I didn't want to do. So I said "no thank you" to *Porky's*, said "no thank you" to a bunch of horror shows that were going on at the time, but *Salem's Lot* wasn't so much horror as it was suspense. At least that's the way I saw it.

Q. You did several mysteries, didn't you?

A. *Reflections of Murder* started it. There was another one, *The Chancellor*. I always loved mysteries and whodunits. Some of my most fun moments were actually just doing guest spots. In the 80's, I did this one called *A Killer in the Family* with Robert Mitchum, James Spader and Stuart Margolin who was Angel in *Rockford Files*. It's a story about these kids who broke their father out of prison. They thought their father was unjustly accused and they broke their father out and he turned out to be a homicidal maniac and went on this rampage of killing people, tagging the kids along.

In the 70's, gosh, between *The Loneliest Runner* and *Young Joe: The Forgotten Kennedy* where I was fortunate to meet some Kennedys and got autographs from them, working in the White House, it was a wonderful childhood and a great career. Had I not found joy in helping people get off drugs and have victory there, I'd probably still be in the motion picture industry, because it's one of the things I really know how to do. I'm raising five kids and living in Hawaii and loving it. I just have a great life here, but I do miss the motion picture industry. I miss the set. There was a show that was shooting over here and I knew a couple of the producers and I asked can I just help out and be a PA and hang around. They said, "Yeah, sure." It was the most fun I'd had in so long. I can't imagine that it's any different from some guy who was a football star in high school who goes to see a football team or some guy who was in band and his kid takes band.

I am so proud this week especially, because my fourteen-year-old just finished her production of *School of Rock*. She did Hawaii Children's Theater. And I'm watching her and her excitement for it and getting ready for the play and memorizing her lines and learning everything and for me, it's pretty nostalgic. I feel like a father who was a football star whose kid is in Pop Warner – you know what I mean?

Q. Do you think you'll go back to it at any point?

A. Well, I would definitely be open to it. I'm not pursuing it, only because I'm busy raising kids and like the other day when I was supposed to talk to you, the surf came up and was like ten feet. So like at five in the morning, we were all out surfing. Here in Hawaii, the surf comes up. Everything stops. Like every commitment stops. And when you're out in the ocean and the waves are that big, you don't really think about anything. You're not missing a career, you're not missing money, you don't care about anything but not drowning. So between raising my kids and surfing here, I haven't been chasing it. And then my fourteen-year-old has the bug, so we may move over there [to L.A.] to give her a shot at it. I'm trying to keep her focus on school.

I'm trying to do it a little bit different than my parents did it. My parents certainly encouraged me, but we neglected some other areas in my life that would have given it some balance. So, yeah, that's a possibility. In the meantime, I'll stay involved at this level doing church plays and doing acting lessons for kids over here.

Diana Muldaur. Photo by Albert L. Ortega
from Getty Images and the collection of
Eva Alfhild Jonsson.

Diana Muldaur ~ Actor

Lovely Diana Muldaur (Dozier) has been one of the most ubiquitous faces on tele-vision, although her multi-faceted and accomplished career also spanned theater and film. Born in Brooklyn, New York, but raised in Martha's Vineyard, Massa-chusetts, she began acting as a teenager and continued through college and beyond. Among her numerous credits, she appeared in the soap opera The Secret Storm *as Ann Wicker; five episodes of* Dr. Kildare *with Richard Chamberlain; Gun-*

smoke; Bonanza; The Courtship of Eddie's Father; Dan August; The F.B.I.; The Incredible Hulk; Murder, She Wrote; I Spy; *and* Matlock. *Her seventies output included* Marcus Welby, M.D.; The Hardy Boys/Nancy Drew Mysteries; Mod Squad; Walt Disney's Wonderful World of Color; Cannon; Hawaii Five-O; Police Woman; *and* Fantasy Island, *among others. She appeared in the original* Star Trek *series which led to a friendship with creator Gene Roddenberry who cast her in other projects. Later she starred as Dr. Katherine Pulaski on the second season of* Star Trek: The New Generation. *Her motion pictures included her critically acclaimed role in* The Swimmer *with Burt Lancaster;* The Other *with Uta Hagen; and* McQ *with John Wayne. Among her recurring roles, she starred as Chris Coughlin during the seven-season run of the mystery series* McCloud *and as Joy Adamson in the television drama* Born Free, *for which she received an Emmy nomination. She also was twice Emmy-nominated for her role as power-hungry attorney Rosalind Shays on the hugely popular and acclaimed series* L.A. Law. *The ruthless Shays famously met her demise by falling down an elevator shaft. Muldaur was the first woman to serve as president of the Academy of Television Arts and Sciences and a board member of the Screen Actors Guild. Once a breeder and judge of Airedale terriers, she resides in Martha's Vineyard.*

Q. You're probably in every TV show that I'm profiling in my book, so I wanted to start with your early influences. I know you studied with Stella Adler.

A. Well, actually I never wanted to be an actor. I found I was really good at it and there were really no places for directing or anything else back in my day. I loved acting and it was easy and it was marvelous and I loved doing characters, but it never occurred to me I could make a living doing it. Then I found out it was probably the only way I could make a living in the industry at that time. So I decided to try to be very, very good at it. I did lots of stock, Shakespeare, everything known to man. I did Off-Broadway at the Circle in the Square when Jose Quintero was there and Ted Mann was running it. While there I did *The Balcony* and another play and then I did Broadway. I found that even though I was starring on Broadway, I was still not making a living and so I went to Hollywood and that's how it started. I borrowed $750 from AFTRA. That was my stake and off I went.

Q. You had such a broad range of experiences in television. You were working constantly in the seventies. Did you see dramatic changes over the years?

A.   In the seventies, I was doing both major pictures as well as television. Television had less of an ego, I found, than features did, which made it a more pleasant environment. I also wanted to play every kind of role and not be typecast, which happened hugely in major motion pictures. You had truly brilliant people directing television that didn't have egos big enough to be trying film. You had people directing films that weren't as good as the people you worked with in television. In the sixties, it was bleak. Most of the studios were down. It was going through a bad period. Theater was going through a very bad period also. When I first went out there, I remember being in the only show that was shooting at MGM – a TV show called *Dr. Kildare.* I remember being slightly incensed -- and he became a good friend afterwards, so I wasn't that incensed --- that my leading man Raymond Massey was a Canadian actor. While everyone was starving in Hollywood, why did the Canadian get a job and not an American? Anyway, that was just me learning about everything.

Q.   What was one of your most satisfying roles that you've done?

A.   I think all of them. I really don't have one. I've never had just one. They're all fascinating. I think the hardest thing to do in our industry, whether it's the theater or movies or television, was moving on to the next thing and losing all those people you became family with and yet kept running into again and again and again. There was a marvelous group of character actors you worked with constantly. You didn't get to meet many women, because you very rarely worked with them. You were usually the only woman in this show of ten. Occasionally you got there and it was really great to work with women, but it was very, very hard, especially in the sixties and seventies to find more than one woman in the show.

Q. When you were interviewed for Emmy Legends, you said, "You learn very quickly how to save yourself physically and mentally in Hollywood." How did that apply to your experiences in television?

A.   Good question. In Africa where I was shooting for a year doing *Born Free*, I was working on the Equator. Sixteen hours we could shoot because it was the equator and I finally said, "You're going to have to use me less." We could work at that time, there were no days off. Finally, the British crew said we need one weekend every two weeks, because they were shooting it, so that's what we ended up getting, but just trying to stay together, stay focused and put up with that schedule --- it was very interesting, but I finally was able to pull it off. Also if I had to run through a field where there were very, very poisonous snakes, because somebody had flown in from Hollywood and thought it would make a great scene, I would refuse to do it. Little things like that. When I would talk to Hollywood, I would say, "I ain't going in that field, because I know what's in that field and they're all over the place and I ain't going into there. Why don't you pound down the grass?" "Because it would ruin the shot," said he. And I said, "Well, then get another shot, because I'm not going in there." You just had to stand up for yourself. I got blown up on the *Gunsmoke* set where my ear got punctured. You know, I'm hiding behind a watering trough and they put a squib in there to look like a bullet had hit, but in the water, it all expanded and blew up and knocked me halfway across the street, so I was very careful after that. I made certain that they didn't use me for the rough stunts. I could ride, I could do a few things, but I refused to do the heavier duty things. You just had to say no.

Q.   Tell me about your experiences on *McCloud* as Chris Coughlin, Mc-Cloud's love interest.

A.   Well, I did the pilot and the character was not in the series. After I did the pilot, they wanted her to be in the series and I didn't want to sign for it, because I wanted to leave myself open to other things, so I never did sign, but I would usually do one scene every *McCloud* for a couple years and then I did *Born Free* and went off and starred in that for a year. When I came back, all of a sudden, they wanted me to be starring in *McCloud* where I'd have the leading part. And so that was a lot of fun. That was much more fun than having the one scene, but the one scenes were fun, too. Dennis Weaver was a great actor. The set was terrific.

Diana Muldaur during her *McCloud* days. Photo courtesy of Eva Alfhild Jonsson.

Q. It was a great show.

A.   It was heaven. His wife thanked me at the end when I called her when he died. "He loved you so much, because you made him a leading man from a character actor," she said. A character actor [is what] he was in *Gunsmoke*. So it was such a great relationship.

Q. When you did the pilot for *Charlie's Angels*, did you have any idea how it would take off? What were your feelings about that?

A.   That was fun, because I played a drunk. I loved playing drunks. (laughs) But I had no idea it would take off. Each girl had their own hairdresser, their own makeup artist and I'd never seen that in my entire life. I was very impressed. They were all being spoiled to death very happily, so no, I had no idea. And they couldn't have been nicer. They were just a nice group. Really nice group.

Q. I'm going to name a few shows and if you could share your memories about working on them. *Hawaii Five-O*.

A.   *Hawaii Five-O*, I did a couple of them. Totally different parts. A lot of doing television is being moved by your location. We shot out on the Memorial for World War II and on the ships where it was bombed in Honolulu harbor and I remember that as just an extraordinary experience. And the crew were these really beautiful Hawaiians who brought fresh sushi from their brother's boat that they caught that morning and we'd all eat sushi together. It was a fabulous, fabulous time. Jack Lord was a little hard to work with, but he did a nice job. God knows it was a big hit. He put in his time. You know, you couldn't do this and you couldn't do that. You had to have this whole instruction about how you could kiss him because he didn't think people would like this move or that move. I think I was eventually hired to make people kissable. There was no question in my mind I was flown in to relax them and make them happy with themselves. (laughs) As I said, the Hawaiians have a history and there was the tsunami that they'd had; they showed me one of our locations, which was over this area where the tsunami had come in and wiped out the whole village. The fascinating thing is to be on location and to get into the history of the people there, as well as enjoy your work and what's going on.

Q. What about *Mannix*? I know you were on a few of those.

A. *Mannix* I did two or three. I was on a film where we shot at Paramount — it never went anywhere. Once again, nice people, nice studio. There was one near the very end, I think, of the *Mannix* series. What was it called? We were all being murdered one by one, I think. Does that ring a bell for you? It was like *Twelve Little Indians* or *Ten Little Indians,* but it was a *Mannix.* It was fascinating and we all gave each other numbers. We couldn't remember anybody's names, I can't remember why, but again we were calling everybody by one, two, three, four -- it was crazy. That's all I remember of *Mannix.*

Q. What about *Ellery Queen*?

A. I don't even remember. Of course, I did an *Ellery Queen.* What was the guy's name?

Q Jim Hutton.

A. Yeah, my God. Jim Hutton. I have no memory of that. Something about a cat. I wonder if he had a cat in his dressing room. Jim Hutton, I do remember. I can't remember the story at all. We were all in period and we were all called into the same room or something. This is fun. I don't even remember all these things.

Q. How about *Streets of San Francisco*? Did you go to San Francisco?

A. Yeah, I went to San Francisco and Michael Douglas I saw very little but I saw a lot of the guy who became governor, Arnold Schwarzenegger. It was a show on body builders. Like ten real body builders and he being the biggest one and he could barely speak English. It was like he had eighteen marbles in his mouth. He couldn't have been nicer and we flew up together and flew back together. His dream at the time was to have gymnasiums, a series of gymnasiums. That was all before he met a Kennedy and his whole life changed. But just a very sincere, lovely man. And Michael Douglas I barely worked with. He was just starting out at that time. He was a young pup!

Q. What about *Ironside*?

A. *Ironside*, same thing. Raymond Burr was a terrific actor and then I did one of his shows in Delaware, a movie-of-the-week. That was a Perry Mason in color, not the old black and white. I remember they did that revival. He was just a gentleman, became a good friend. It was always fun. You're beginning to understand that I would get there at six every morning happy. I had one makeup man say I don't think I've ever had an actor sit in my chair this many times with a smile on their face at six a.m. I just loved working - loved the crew, loved the actors, loved the whole idea of how it's done, loved the studios. It was fascinating to me.

Q. What was the key to being so prolific as an actress?

A. I always hit my marks, I usually got it on the first hit and God gave me a pretty face and I could act. That was a comment Bill Cosby made about me when I did his show, that I could act. I wasn't just another pretty face. That's what it had to do with. I have no idea. I just was gifted. I must have done more shows than anybody living possible.

But what I loved doing was moving on to the next and the next and the next thing. I think the most fun part for me in many ways, because I could wear jeans and be myself, was *A Day in the Life* with Richard Kiley. It was closer to me, I think, than anything else I did; I didn't really do too many things that were close to me. We shot it in Seattle, which back then was a fabulous town. Now it's overcrowded, but wonderful back then. Good people. It was just great.

Q. Tell me about your experiences as the president of the Academy of Television Arts and Sciences. You were the first woman to serve as president. How did that come about?

A. That came about because I was on the board and had somehow become Vice President. I had nowhere to go, but to run for president or drop out and so I ran for president, because I really did think I could get a few things done. I actually did get a lot of things done that no one else had been able to do. I wasn't in the good, old boys' club which irritated the heck out of them. There was talk in New York that they'd bring me down in a year which they didn't. In fact, I brought the person who said that down. I learned from them. I learned about business and machine gun nests.

Q. Machine gun what? Sorry?

A. Machine gun nests. There were all these machines, there were always those trying to bring you down, which fascinated me, because I wasn't in the good, old boys' club and I was bringing in the NEA. In fact, they just had a misprint where this guy [Frank] Hodsoll died the other day. They said the other Academy had given him an honorary, which I don't think they did. We gave him an honorary Emmy for the work the NEA was doing which was all happening through him. It was the last time where the grant money was happening, it was going to the right places. My husband had said I could run again, but as a single woman and so I thought, "Well, maybe I don't need to keep doing that." (Laughs) Maybe I'd done enough, I'd pulled off the things I wanted to pull off. I brought the two Academys -- the local one in New York that wouldn't talk to anybody in Hollywood and the one in Hollywood, which is the national -- back in and got all of that straightened out. They were very happy to be part and parcel of us again. I brought the Daytime Emmys back on the air, nighttime primetime, which back then was important -- it was huge -- and now it doesn't exist anymore. They've taken it all off the air or something. I did do a lot of things that no one else had been able to do and I was really proud of that.

Q. Is there any stone left unturned for you?

A. Well, that's what I'm looking for. I'm looking for it. I haven't found it. I don't know what I should be doing. I started an animal shelter on Martha's Vineyard. It's wonderful. We placed over 800 animals in the five years we've been doing this and found wonderful homes and medical care and spayed and neutered, etc. etc. So that's kept me busy. It's not that I'm not busy, it's just that what am I going to do next? But I don't know. I used to have some ideas that I wanted to produce, particularly with little girls instead of little boys, because that was important to me, to try to maybe bring out one of the great new little girls and that's sort of old hat now. I didn't do it when I should have done it. Plus everybody I knew in Hollywood who was raising money or at the NEA are on the other side. They're all dead. It's very difficult to see where I might like to go. Of course, everything has changed so much in the world. We're so lucky to have been born when we were, because I don't know that I would have been able to make a living in today's world. I'm sure I would have, but would it have been the same? I don't know.

Q. Do you still have Airedales?

A. I do. I have two crazy ones. They are now racing around my property - Auntie Mame and Harry. They're my two Airedales. They're always in trouble, always doing the wrong thing, and they love mud. And I love them both dearly.

Q. You had such a fabulous career. I can't think of many more things you could've done.

A. I was busy. I also served on the Screen Actors Guild. There were almost no women and minorities when I did. That was fascinating. As you can tell, people fascinate me. That's why, I guess, I became an actor. Although I became an actress. I became an actor later, much to my chagrin like, "What are you talking about, actor? I'm an actress!" Anyway, now I'm an actor. So there you are.

Q. Do you feel that you became the sort of actor you wanted to be?

A. Yes. There were a few things I would've like to have done that I didn't do. At the time, I turned a lot of things down. It was very important to me that even if she was a falling down drunk that there was dignity in her as a human being, whoever she was that I was playing. If I couldn't find that dignity, I didn't do those things. I don't know if that makes any sense to you. I'd find dignity in everyone and if it's not there in the script, I just wasn't that interested. If fifty people got shot down in the first hour, I wasn't interested. There were a few things that I maybe might have been able to do, but I didn't do, but I think I basically had the overview. I met so many incredibly wonderful people. It was a wonderful life.

Television writer and producer Tom Sawyer.
Photo courtesy of Tom Sawyer.

Tom Sawyer ~ Writer

Born and raised in Chicago, Illinois, Tom Sawyer is a writer and producer who has worked on a number of television shows of the seventies, including Quincy *and* Wonder Woman *and the TV specials* How to Survive the 70's and Maybe Even Bump into Happiness *and* The Carpenters…Space Encounters. *He was head writer and showrunner for the popular series* Murder, She Wrote, *for which he scripted 23 episodes and produced 79 episodes. His documentary* Reunion *received national theatrical release and honors and he is co-librettist/lyricist of* Jack, *a musical drama about John F. Kennedy that enjoyed acclaim in the United States and Europe. In addition to teaching writing at UCLA and other universities, he has written several thrillers, including* The Sixteenth Man, No Place to Run *and the first book of a mystery series,* Cross Purposes. *He currently resides in Malibu.*

Q. What was your early creative life like? Did you want to be a writer as a child? Were you drawn to television?

A. I drew mostly human figures from the time I learned how to hold a pencil. By age 5 or 6, I was putting dialogue balloons above their heads, already hooked on the syndicated story-comic strips then so common in daily newspapers, and read to me by my parents. Television didn't begin until I was in my teens, but by age 12, I had become focused on my career – to draw and write a syndicated, realistically-illustrated comic strip. My hero/model: Milton Caniff, who drew and wrote *Terry and the Pirates*, and later, *Steve Canyon*. At that time, it meant relocating from Chicago to New York City (all of print-publishing and advertising was based there).

Q. What was your first professional gig as a television writer? Who or what helped you evolve in the field?

A. Lila Garrett gave me my start. I'd been directing back in New York: TV commercials, a couple of short films, an off-off Broadway play. Loved directing, especially film, decided to give Hollywood a try. I knew nobody in the biz. My plan -- direct and produce a low-budget film as a calling-card/sample (I was aware before the move that the above-credits would mean zip in Tinseltown). Found a writer, moved with Holly and two small kids to California. Writer fell through, so I wrote the screenplay. I had, in my first career as a cartoonist/illustrator, written a couple of comic book scripts which I then illustrated. Anyway, I shot the film (originally titled *Gosh!*, later *Alice Goodbody*) and began screening it for distributors and for the players with whom I'd been networking at parties over the two years since we'd relocated.

A short time after our first social encounter, I invited producer/writer Lila Garrett and her companion, similarly successful comedy writer Mort Lachman, to one of my once-or-twice-a-week screenings of *Gosh!* I tried to salt each of these with an audience of ten or so, in hope that their communal laughter would sway whichever distributor I was romancing. When the lights came up, I was flattered to learn from both Lila and Mort that they'd

genuinely enjoyed the film. But before I could even respond to their compli-
ments, Lila emphatically – her *only* mode – added: "You should be writing
for television."

Mort agreed.

"Thank you. Really. But – um – I only wrote the script because I had no
other---"

Lila cut in: "Well, you should really think about it." She and Mort departed. And that was it. End of *The Moment – Part One*.

And quickly put aside as, necessarily, I turned my attention to other at-
tendees, particularly the distributor.

I should explain here that the concept of working in television in *any*
capacity – but *especially* as a writer – wasn't just not on the table. I had *never*
considered TV even as an outside, fallback possibility! As mentioned earlier,
I'd *decided* on my goal, *saw* it. To the exclusion of all else. Very similar, I later
understood, to my childhood fixation on becoming a comic-strip artist.

But it became apparent within a short time that the movie studios were
not exactly clamoring for my services as a film director. Disappointing, yes.
Frustrating, but far from crushing. Moreover, I had been thinking about
what Lila said after that screening. And I began – very tentatively – to toy
with the possibility of working in television. As a stepping-stone, of course.

But still – as a...*writer?*

Invited to another party several nights hence, I learned that Ms. Garrett
would be present. I resolved to set her straight about my preference for *running* the show – for being the *boss.*

As I would come to realize, this was the threshold of *The Moment – Part
Two.* Shortly after Holly and I arrived that evening, I cornered Lila, and, re-
minding her of her advice, I added a challenge: "But I mean – I'm a *director.*
So – why shouldn't I direct for TV?"

"Forget it. You don't wanta *direct* television. I mean – they've gotta shoot
what, seven – eight pages a day." She sipped her wine while allowing that to
sink in, following it up in her characteristic witty, dazzlingly articulate cut-to-

the-chase style: "They haven't got *time* to do anything creative. Hell, they're mostly just traffic cops, trying to keep the actors from bumping into the set."

Then Lila, like *all* good writers, gave it her button: "Besides – *all* those producer-credits you see at the top of every series episode? Those're *all* writers. In TV, *they* run the show." While I was processing that, she added: "So – how it'll work, you'll write a few episodes, then they'll start hiring you on staff."

I actually did a real-life double-take, a la W.C. Fields (or, as I prefer to think of myself, more like Cary Grant). It was one more head-slap revelation. An earth-shift from the no-accident assumption – and truth at least in terms of then-and-still-accepted mythology – that film was "The *Director's Medium*."

Even as I was further digesting Lila's alien concept – one that I had *never* heard, nor read about – my lips were moving: "So – ah – okay – what would I – how would I, you know, get started? As a writer?"

Lila casually waved an upturned palm: "I've got a production deal… Y'come up with an idea, call me."

And she moved off.

Two weeks later, I did phone her. It was morning, and she was rushed: "I can't talk now. I'm on my way out to a meeting. Can you call me tonight?"

But I was too stoked to let go. My words came in a rush: "Lila, I'll just give you one line. A gang-comedy on a tacky used-car lot in the Valley."

There was this two-or-three-second silence, then: "I love it. You'll write it, I'll produce it. Talk to you later." Followed by the *click*.

While leaving me in suspense, and with dozens of questions, *The Moment, Part Three.*

Buttoned.

I hung up the phone, went to the kitchen, and told Holly what had just taken place.

She was delighted, but… "So… What does that mean?"

"I have no idea."

Ten days later, we learned its *stunning* meaning.

I had my *first* gig in Hollywood! I was writing *Mother's Motor City*, a comedy series pilot – for *CBS Television*!

My zero-perspective knee-jerk? Way cool. But – with a shrug: "Oh? Okay. So – this is how the Business works…"

Not.

It would be several years before that sank in. But what did *I* know? Over the following decades I became acquainted with dozens of working writers who would've killed for the chance to ever write a pilot.

My conclusion -- and advice: Put yourself in luck's way -- and when it comes along, grab it by the throat!

Q. Tell me about your television work in the seventies on shows such as *Quincy* and *Wonder Woman*.

A. The following short excerpts from my memoir, *The Adventures of the REAL Tom Sawyer*, address both of these questions:

> Writing for *Quincy* gave me my first experience with a lead actor (Jack Klugman) having a serious "say" about the scripts.

> Early in my TV career, my then-writing partner, Reyn Parke and I got a chance to pitch a *Quincy* episode.

> The *Quincy* pitch gave me my first up-close experience, albeit once-removed, with an actor-with-clout. The hit series starred the magnetic Jack Klugman as a coroner who solved murders, and the house rule for scripts was that *all* of the clues had to come from the corpse. Writer/Producer David Shaw (brother of famous novelist Irwin) listened to our somewhat farfetched-but-doable premise: "A Howard Hughes-type reclusive gazil-lionaire is murdered by his corporate heirs – killed seven years earlier, frozen and then thawed in time to frame someone in present-time."

David reacted instantly: "I love it. You've got a sale. But there is one thing. Jack's got to approve it, and the only way he's gonna do that is if I can convince him it's got some social relevance." Off our questioning looks, David smiled and added: "So, all you need is to come up with a scene, or an overriding theme, that I can sell. One that makes a Statement, preferably Liberal." He suggested we think about it for a day or two, and phone him.

A problem that proved to be minor, as we were driving past the guard gate five minutes later, leaving the Universal lot, I had it. I could *see* the scene. Almost taste it, in fact, because it spoke *for* me. I ran it past Reyn, who agreed, and as soon as I got home, I phoned David.

"Okay, there's this moment in the boardroom of this giant company. Just Quincy and this guy who's murdered the Hughes-character and is now running the business. And Quincy's pissed off, accusing him of using crooked means to get the body released, so they can cremate it before the investigation is complete. Bribery, pressure on judges and Congressmen, and like that. And Quincy concludes by saying: 'I mean who the hell d'you guys think you are, anyway – y'think you're bigger than the government?' And this executive pulls himself to his full height, and says: 'I've got news for you, Dr. Quincy. We *are* the government. We and a few other corporations like ours.' And he points to the door and says: 'Now get *out!*'"

That was as far as I got. David interrupted with: "Perfect. Jack's gonna love it. I'll get back to you." Next day, we had the assignment.

And then, a funny thing happened on our way to finishing the script, which was titled "Gone But Not Forgotten." An interview with Klugman was published in one of the trade papers, wherein he stated that *all* TV writers were hacks, unable to write anything "meaningful." Thus, he added, for next season's shows he would be checking out colleges in an effort to find quality writers.

Amused, I couldn't resist including the following for Jack's final, just-before-FADE OUT, show-ending speech:

QUINCY
(Meaningful curtain-line to be provided
by college-writer of Jack's choice.)

We dropped off the teleplay, and waited. Next morning, between laughs, David Shaw informed us that the writing staff and producers were on the floor. However, probably wisely, they chose not to show it to their leading man.

When I ran into Klugman in Malibu 30 years later and reminded him about it, he laughed: "Yeah. I took a lotta heat for that one."

Interestingly and, I suspect, in keeping with the characteristic passion of Jack's acting performances, he didn't retract what he'd said about TV writers.

Wonder Woman was for me an early example of a delightful phenomenon I continued to encounter: Series Writer Producers virtually "teaching" me how to write.

"My only note – your Bad Guy talks too much. The thing with Bad Guys – they've got tight, thin mouths and they don't say a lot – except for their aria."

Think about it – the conciseness, the awesome, nailing-it truth. I somehow doubt that that is taught at, say, the *Iowa Writers' Workshop*, or at other bastions of Literary Integrity. But it should be.

Instead, Bruce Lansbury, commenting on the first-draft of my *Wonder Woman* teleplay, spoke those piercingly insightful words to me. Bruce had found himself at Warner's, producing the series, and offered me a chance to write an episode. I'd grabbed it, and my matriculation continued. The highlight of this particular "class" coming in the form of that breathtakingly clear, no-frills, and *certainly* non-theory, take-it-to-the-bank lesson from Bruce.

Receiving that sort of writing advice, such priceless nuts-and-bolts knowledge, was a commonplace of my early scripting experience in TV. This is what you *should* do, and *this* is what you shouldn't – all of it supplied by the solid, zero-nonsense veteran staffers on the shows for whom I wrote scripts.

Invaluable gems, like Lansbury's, on the order of:

"Write to the Money – never have your star absent from two consecutive scenes."

"The smarter your heavy, the brighter your protagonist has to be. Dumb villains only work in comedies."

"Never dump stuff in your hero's lap. Make your good guy earn it – make 'em the engines of their own salvation."

"Limit your scenes that take place in one room to three pages – max."

And perhaps *the* most important lesson – one that applies to *any*one who writes, whether it be poetry, advertising copy, fiction or nonfiction, no matter how lofty our intentions: "*Never* forget – we are *entertainers.*"

There were many more, virtually inarguable, every syllable instantly etched into my head. Were all of these people great writers? No. But they were *professionals*. Without pretension. They'd learned what *works* and what does *not*, what techniques grab and hold an audience, and those that deliver viewers to the commercial break (our mandate). This was driven home by the image of every TV writer's bogeyman: a guy in his tee-shirt, tired after another day at a job he probably hates. He's got a beer in one hand, the remote in the other. And if we bore him for *one* second, we've lost him.

Talk about words that *every* writer should live by!

And rather than, as in so many fields, people jealously guarding their power and expertise, these guys were eager to pass such information along to me. They wanted to teach, to help. And man, was I delighted to absorb it!

I was being paid to *learn*. The reason for their generosity: as mentioned, simple self-interest. The small staffs of most TV series were rarely able to write all twenty-two yearly episodes in-house. They had no choice but to employ a few freelancers like myself. And because of the Writers Guild contract, the writer could only be asked for two drafts of the story outline, and two of the teleplay. After that, it was in the staffers' court. Ergo, it was clearly to their benefit to hold the freelance writer's hand. To guide and nursemaid the process so that, when they had to take over and begin their final tweaks, the script wouldn't require a rewrite from page one.

The *Wonder Woman* episode was fun and, as with each of the other scripts, a stretch for me to write. And yes, part of me was continuing to furtively glance over my shoulder, wondering when they were going to catch on that I was faking it. And wondering why the hell it was taking them so long. I mean – it was sure as hell obvious to *me*.

This self-doubt continued for awhile, partly because I was not yet aware of how much I actually understood about the form. It was additionally fueled by my surprising, fluke-seeming, relatively quick acceptance as a professional. Gradually however, it did begin to sink in: maybe they *weren't* going to discover that I was a fraud! Which was very tentatively followed by the realization that during this sneaky apprenticeship, I had *learned* how to write reasonably well. Maybe not art, but craft. Though I must make it clear that getting to the place where I regarded myself as a *real* writer – whatever that implies – took a much longer time.

And – for what it's worth – arriving at that point did *not* and will *never* include taking *myself* seriously – what I think of as *The Ernest Hemingway Syndrome*.

Also, and amusingly *not* incidental, that teleplay titled "Death in Disguise" turned out to be – until *Murder, She Wrote* – residual-wise, one of my most enduring projects. Not, I'm sure, because it was so artfully-written. Rather, it was something few of us understood about the long-term appeal of that Lynda Carter vehicle. *Wonder Woman* was – in the guise of just another run-and-jump adventure series – a superbly executed prime-time Tits-and-Ass Show.

Sometimes it *was* possible to sneak stuff past 'em…

Q. I know you also worked on *The Carpenters - Space Encounters* in the 70's. I adore The Carpenters. What was that experience like and what did it entail?

A.   It was their third TV Special, and I have no anecdotal recollections, other than Karen being adorable.

Q. You were head writer and showrunner on the popular series Murder, She Wrote. Is it difficult to maintain a character working with multiple writers?

A. Not really, in part because back then – unlike the present – almost no series included long-term character arcs. The major characters were usually described in a page or less. Oh, sure, as with Donald Bain having Jessica Fletcher driving a car in one of his early novels[1], occasionally we'd buy an episode-pitch from a writer, and in his story-outline, he'd reveal a misunderstanding of Jessica or one of the other core characters, and we'd have the writer correct it before he finished the teleplay.

Q. Were there any conflicts regarding material or ideas for the show?

A. Each writer, whether on staff or freelance, brings his/her own sensibilities and/or style to a series, but that's where the Showunner brings his/her overall approach and style to a series in their final edits on every script. I never encountered any major, deal-breaker type conflict.

Q. What is the key to writing great mysteries, specifically for a television audience? How do you generate fresh ideas consistently?

A. Stealing helps. There are no new ideas. Those were all used up before Shakespeare picked up a pen. It's why so many one-line story-pitches are so effective. A few of mine: My own favorite of my 24 episodes of *Murder, She Wrote* was "No Laughing Murder." The pitch: "Martin and Lewis meet Romeo & Juliet." Another of my faves was "Dead Eye." The pitch: "Jessica Fletcher solves the Murder of the Century – almost." And on a more overall level, on the day I was asked to write for *Murder, She Wrote*, before it was even in production, the following brief anecdote from my memoir, *The Adventures of the REAL Tom Sawyer*, illustrates the point quite well, I think:

---

1   Author Donald Bain once mentioned that when he did his first *Murder She Wrote* spin-off book, *Gin and Daggers*, he had Jessica Fletcher driving a car, but fans immediately reminded him that Jessica does not drive.

Oddly, though not entirely unusual, the way I became a writer for *Murder, She Wrote* before it began production, was the result of my agent sending Peter Fischer a *non*-mystery series pilot script I'd written for CBS, my one-hour WWII drama titled "Cody's War." Peter "saw" something in it – presumably, that I could write scenes that worked – and he gave me a "blind assignment" to write an episode. Meaning, I had to first come up with a story that was acceptable. He invited me to come in and view the very impressive half-hour film they'd produced in lieu of a full-on pilot, and to me, anyway, Angela Lansbury's specialness, her presence, were awesome. As was the prospect – the honor and privilege, really – of writing for her.

So Peter and I met. Pleasant, witty, like myself a former East Coaster, I have to say – in terms of instant impressions – that what struck me most tellingly about him was his spotlessly clean desktop (in contrast to my own, which has always been a colossal mess of scraps and disorganized piles that periodically reaches critical mass, requiring a half-day or more for me to clean up). Peter's had not a single sheet of paper, not a pile anywhere – and it remained that way for seven years I worked with him. Which is not, incidentally, a knock. A direct corollary of this clearly anal trait, I would learn, was that unlike any other showrunner with whom I'd been associated, Peter *always* had several scripts in the drawer, finished and ready to shoot. In series TV, this is rare to the point of nonexistence. On most shows, they're constantly hanging on by their fingertips, often writing the scripts *as* they're being shot.

All that aside, *MSW* looked to me like a hit, and I said so. I also offered that given my limited writing credits in the genre (a *Quincy* and a *Mike Hammer*), he'd probably have to hold my hand. He assured me that that wouldn't be a problem and, in response to my question about the approach, the show's style, Peter explained – as I feared – that he envisioned it in the mold of traditional Agatha Christie puzzle mysteries – what are known in the mystery genre as "cozies". You know – the character who behaves badly toward all the other players, and is detested by all, who is then – surprise, surprise – murdered – and all of them have motives which at the end are tediously, routinely – for me, anyway – explained by the sleuth, who has gathered them all in the drawing-room. Which prompted – with no hesitation – a remark from me, the sheer chutzpah of which I really didn't wonder at until I recalled the incident several years later. And having wondered, I fully realized that it was pretty much the way I've operated for most, if not all, of my life: "Peter, I have to tell you, when I was a kid, I read a couple of Christies and one or two locked-room mysteries, and they bored the shit out of me. I'm not going to write that for you."

His response betrayed no sign that I'd offended. "Okay. What *will* you write?"

"I'll write *The Maltese Falcon*."

Peter replied without missing a beat: "That'll be fine." And that's what I did for the next twelve years – seven of them with Peter's on-the-job blessing.

Q.   I've always been a writer and cartoonist and see you are a very gifted illustrator as well as an accomplished writer. What was it like trying to juggle the two crafts? Have you kept up with both equally?

A.   Once I decided to begin another career (in film and TV), I gradually phased out of it. And because I knew I would never become any better at my niche (was known in the *Mad Men*, advertising art world as "The Norman Rockwell of line illustration"). That challenge was gone, so it was an easy choice for me to simply abandon drawing and move on.

Q. Tell me about some of the fascinating novels you've written dealing with the JFK assassination and 9-11.

A. The reason for the topics: I guess you could call me a conspiracy-nut. I'm not. But I'm definitely a doubter, having seen over and over in my own lifetime how history gets written to fit a comforting narrative that provides closure for the masses – and more importantly, prevents questions from being asked (examples: Pearl Harbor, the CIA, the battleship Maine, Vietnam, etc., etc.). And once written that way, the accepting public is loath to revisit it, to face the possibility that they might have bought into bullshit. Both Dallas and 9/11 are in those categories, and I felt passionate about trying to make my point via as entertaining a medium as possible: mystery-thriller novels.

Q. What made 70's television mysteries special, in your estimate?

A. For me, the better ones (*Rockford Files, Quincy, Kaz* are my faves) had great writing and featured wonderful actors whom we eagerly welcomed into our living rooms. And all of them were, in their way, ground-breaking.

Michele Weiss with her late mother, television comedy writer Harriett Weiss in Palm Springs, California. Photo courtesy of Michele Weiss.

Harriett Weiss ~ Writer
(As Told by her Daughter Michele Weiss)

I remember the day my mom Harriett Weiss got the call that she was hired as a comedy-writer for the second *Laugh-In*. Producer George Schlatter had stated my mom's writing was some of the best he had ever read and asked where she got all her bitterness and cynicism from. This particular *Laugh-In* was the show that was produced in 1977 that included comedienne/actor Robin Williams (prior to his role on *Mork & Mindy*) and such incredible guest star greats as Bette Davis, Bea Arthur, Tina Turner, Rich Little, Flip Wilson, Wayland Flowers and Madame, Marcel Marceau, etc. That day, which was the beginning of what would become a long wonderful writing career for my mom in the "Entertainment Industry," was also the day she received a letter in the mail from an Agent who had read her "spec scripts" (sample scripts) that she had written. The letter from this Agent informed my mom that he was not interested in taking her as a client and recommended she "go back to school and learn to write."

After *Laugh-In*, my mom got hired to write for *In the Beginning* which was a show created by Norman Lear and produced by Tandem Productions starring McLean Stevenson. From there, an opportunity knocked and my mom and Patt Shea became a power female writing team. (This was a time when gender and age wasn't an issue like it is now in the industry.) They were hired as staff-writers for *All in The Family*. One day Patt's Agent (who was making a nice bundle getting 10% from Patt's income) visited her at the studio. As fate would have it, it was the same Agent who had originally told my mom to "go back to school and learn to write." Because the sweetest revenge is success, my mom went up to him and with her Chicago ballsy attitude, told him, "Schmuck, you could have had 20%." From that day, she never looked back.

My mom Harriett Weiss' writing credits include *All in The Family, Archie Bunker's Place, Gloria* starring Sally Struthers, *In the Beginning, Valerie* starring Valerie Harper, *Golden Girls, Lou Grant, Happy Days,* T.V. Movies of the week, etc.

In Memoriam Harriett Weiss
(10/30/1927 - 02/23/2010)

Just One More Thing: Epilogue

The author (center) and her two sisters as children.

Just One More Thing: Epilogue

By Donna Marie Nowak

As a kid in Catholic school, I used to pass around mysteries I'd written in cliff-hanger installments. By age twelve, I had created over 100 short stories, four novels, countless reviews and over 100 cartoons. In addition to standalone cartoons and individual strips, my sisters and I crafted cartoons and stories of all kinds featuring child versions of six of our favorite television stars that we called "Little People." My favorite star was Stefanie Powers whom I watched religiously in reruns of *The Girl From U.N.C.L.E.* and in numerous made-for-TV movies and we each had our own version of "Little April Dancer." As I look over my childhood short stories, I recognize the influence of 1970's television, particularly the *ABC Movie of the Week* and the warm and fuzzy excitement it generated in us. Weaned on secret agents, spies, the supernatural, whodunits, wiseacre detectives, Gothic houses and stormy nights, like so many kids of the 70's, I was mad about mystery. So was every kid I knew.

The 1970's represented one of the Golden Ages of television, a time when there were fewer stations outside the big three networks (ABC, CBS and NBC), less technology and unlimited imagination. Independent producers working in conjunction with major Hollywood studios came to dominate much of seventies prime-time, such as Quinn Martin and the wildly prolific Aaron Spelling. Many stars who had appeared in silent films and "classic" films of the 30's and 40's made the transition to television and popped up as "guest stars" and sometimes "special guest stars" in broadcasts of the day, particularly in the mystery and detective genre. Roddy McDowall who had been a

Author's cartoon featuring a character
based on Stefanie Powers plus Disney scene.

"Little People" cartoon by author at age 11
with Stefanie Powers as April Dancer.

"Little People" with Stefanie Powers as
April Dancer.

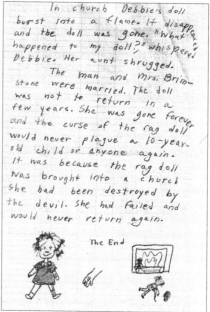

One of author's stories from age 11 inspired
by 1970's television movies.

sweet child star in *Lassie Go Home* became a helmet-haired villain on *Columbo*. Ida Lupino, who was a trailblazing producer and director in male-dominated Hollywood of the 50's, made a wonderful tremulous victim on the series *Ellery Queen*. Classic detectives from Golden Age fiction and radio like Queen, Sherlock Holmes, Nick Carter and Charlie Chan found a resurgence in 70's TV, as did staples from Agatha Christie novels like spiritualism, parapsychology and the gathering of suspects in one room "where all would be revealed." An old-fashioned classicism remained intact at a time when the culture was experiencing radical social shifts with burgeoning civil rights movements and growing cynicism from the Vietnam War. There were always strong women in Hollywood, but now more and more women were entering fields that traditionally had been the domain of men, giving way to series like *Police Woman* and even *Charlie's Angels*. Television mysteries of the 70's ran the gamut and mixed issues and changing mores of the day with classic conventions, all the while remaining family friendly and providing old-fashioned fun. It was a very exciting time and the wealth of creativity in the genre of detection and mystery was proof of the pudding.

As I revisited detective shows and made-for-TV movies profiled in this book, certain things became clear. Every television show followed a format and formula. Rather than making the show stale, these formulas were the key to the show's success. Within the formula which usually featured dynamic protagonists with specific eccentricities or character traits, the plot lines allowed for lots of diversity and ingenuity. Car chases were a staple of 70's television and many private eyes participated in speed chases, shoot outs and fights (sometimes tongue-in-cheek). The tropes used in made-for-TV movies and programs were not always realistic, but that's what made them so entertaining. Even one of the greatest detective series of all times, *Columbo*, used such tropes, such as the prerecorded message that the killer uses to fool others into thinking his or her victim was still alive at a specific time. Usually the prerecorded message was electronically programmed to play when the mark answered the phone, thereby creating a witness who would testify that the victim was still alive at a particular moment. Woody Allen brilliantly spoofs this trope in *Manhattan Murder Mystery* where he and his friends try to blackmail a murderer with a series of prerecorded messages. When the messages are played via phone, the murderer asks unexpected questions and Allen and his friends become frantic, hissing to each other, "We don't have a response for that!" At one point, they play the wrong response to the killer's utter confusion and Allen is left with a handful of tangled answering tape, trying to find the right section of tape.

The 70's was the age of the detective/cop show and amateur sleuth, replacing espionage and spy shows from the 60's. The red phones, trench coats and quirky gadgets of secret agents gave way to cruisers, leisure suits and answering machines. There were endless spins on crime-solving protagonists and among this great output were some of the finest detective shows and characters ever created. The supernatural was also a huge factor in made-for-TV films of the period, possibly owing to the popularity of Hammer and Amicus horror films and the daytime spookfest *Dark Shadows*. Some highly influential classics were generated in this niche, including *Tales of Terror* and *Duel*, along with countless other delicious chillers. The 70's also had its share of misses among the hits, but most mysteries produced were imminently watchable, even the silliest made-for-TV films. The occasional rawness or blooper like seeing a "vampire" stumble over weeds as she pursued her quarry only added to the fun; it was like detecting zippers in the monster suits in sci fi films of the Atomic-themed 50's. Rich atmosphere and settings were evoked in "movies of the week," even those with small budgets, and a number of productions had a certain cinematic polish, perhaps because they were made under the helm of the big studios. Those of us who were kids during this period ordered movie/TV tie-in novels from Scholastic with photos from the shows on the cover. We had pages of titles to choose from and often very hip fare made its way into Catholic schools.

At age eleven, I wrote a three-page handwritten letter to Stefanie Powers from an address gleaned from a movie magazine, possibly "Rona Barrett's

Hollywood." I asked as many critically important questions as possible like "What are your favorite colors? How many pets do you have? Who are your favorite movie stars?" It's taken me all of these years to finally "hear back." Ms. Powers has graciously provided the introduction to my book. Yes, sometimes life does come full circle.

It's been difficult to choose just 100 wonderful television mysteries from the seventies. There are so many. Encapsulated in these mini-masterworks are traces of the decade in varying degrees: disco dancing, shag haircuts and shag rugs, machete plant holders, bell bottoms, lava lamps, hippies, feathered hair, Afros, groovy vernacular ("Freeze, turkey!"), survivors from "Nam," cults, radicals, spit curls and squealing roadsters. There was also some of the cleverest mysteries ever penned. For mystery lovers, it was not just a Golden Age of television, but a Golden Age of mystery. The television mysteries of the seventies have more than held up. Upon reacquaintance, they remain simply without parallel. They again remind viewers like myself to create with all the unlimited imagination in one's power and without being stunted by fear of mistakes like the zippers showing in the monster suits. In other words, they are an encouragement to – artistically speaking – let it all hang out.

Scrappy watches Diana Muldaur in the *Ellery Queen* episode "The Adventure of the Judas Tree".

The author with her father Leonard Nowak, a World War II veteran.

The author's darling Maltipoo Scrappy.

About the Author

Donna Marie Nowak is a writer and cartoonist with over 100 publication credits, including national magazines, books and radio. She wrote *Just Joan: A Joan Crawford Appreciation*, the ultimate guide to the ultimate star, and is currently working on a mystery series featuring her indomitable amateur sleuth, Miss Iodine Bell who has appeared on the radio and in short stories. An active member of Mystery Writers of America, she lives with her father Leonard Nowak, a World War II vet, and adorable Maltipoo Scrappy in New Jersey.

Index

Abbott, John – 6, 69

Ackerman, Leonard J. - 18

Ackroyd, David – 41-42

Adams, Brooke – 43, 45, 83-84

Adams, Stanley – 47-48

Adler, Stella - 210

Akins, Claude – 47-48

Albert, Edward -13, 109

Albertson, Mabel - 29

Alda, Alan – 33-34

Alden, Richard - 66

Alderman, John - 65

Alderson, John – 38-39

Allen, Gracie - 138

Allen, Sian Barbara – 63-64

Allen, Woody – 241

Allyn, Bill - 183

Allyson, June – 9, 110

Ames, Leon - 69

Anderson, Barbara – 116-117, 129

Anderson, Carl - 41

Anderson, Michael, Jr. - 29

Anderson, Richard – 3, 42

Andreas, Luke - 24

Andrews, Tige - 70

Andrusco, Gene - 65

Antonio, Jim - 62

Arbus, Allan - 63

Archer, Anne – 38-39

Arden, Eve – 80-81, 102, 172

Armendariz, Pedro, Jr. - 38

Arnaz, Lucie – 83-84

Arthur, Bea - 234

Arvan, Jan - 65

Ashley, Elizabeth – 50-51, 83

Asner, Ed – 29 49, 75

Astin, John – 70-71

Astin, Patty Duke – 9-10, 67-68, 77, 157

Atkins, Susan - 26

Atwater, Barry – 3. 47

Atwater, Edith - 106

Aubrey, Skye – 18, 80

Avalon, Frankie - 32

Avery, Val – 73, 134

Ayres, Lew – 58-59, 67

Bacall, Lauren - 150

Bacharach, Burt - 176

Badham, John – 33 53

Badiyi, Reza S. - 20

Bagetta, Vincent - 43

Bain, Barbara – 24-25, 44

Bain, Donald - 230

Bain, Sherry - 80

Baio, Scott - 203

Baker, Diane – 36-37, 49

Baldacci, David - 185

Balin, Ina - 158

Ball, Lucille - 84

Balsam, Martin – 49-50

Bankhead, Tallulah – 68, 126

Banks, Jonathan - 68

Barbeau, Adrienne – 71-72

Barbera, Joseph – 152-153

Barnett, Barbara - 82

Barrett, Rona - 241

Barry, Donald - 20

Barry, Gene - 173

Barry, Patricia - 8

Barrymore, Drew – 95, 103

Bartlett, Bonnie – 35-36

Barton, Dan - 51

Barty, Billy - 78

Basehart, Richard – 40-41, 72-73, 99

Baum, Bobby - 24

Baumes, Wilford Lloyd - 164

Baur, Elizabeth - 116

Baxter, Anne – 45, 56-57, 99

Baxter, Meredith - 6

Beal, John - 35

Beatty, Ned - 17

Bedelia, Bonnie - 58

Beery, Noah Jr. – 62, 148-149

Beggs, Hagan - 32

Beir, Fred - 78

Bellamy, Ralph – 38-39, 43

Benedict, William - 69

Benjamin, Christopher - 4

Bennett, Joan - 20

Bennett, Marjorie - 69

Benson, Lucille – 16, 19, 53-54

Benton, Barbi - 162

Beradino, John - 14

Bergen, Polly – 13, 43-44

Bernard, Ed – 140-141

Bernard, Joseph - 12

Berti, Dehl - 56

Bessell, Ted – 63-64

Best, James - 62

Bethune, John - 83

Beswick, Martine - 39

Biggers, Earl Derr - 54

Bikel, Theodore - 43

Birman, Len - 66

Birney, David – 71-72

Bisoglio, Val - 144

Bixby, Bill - 19

Black, Karen – 76-77

Blackman, Honor - 99

Blair, Linda – 43, 78

Blake, Sondra - 26

Blanch, Jewel – 4-5

Bloch, Robert – 6, 10

Blondell, Joan – 10, 12-13

Blyth, Ann - 5

Bochner, Lloyd – 8, 23, 60, 75

Bodeen, Patty - 52

Boileau, Pierre - 54

Bonaduce, Danny - 43

Bonar, Ivan - 52

Bondi, Beulah – 67-68

Bono, Sonny – 43-44, 80

Booke, Sorrell - 2

Boone, Randy - 62

Boone, Richard – 24-25

Borden, Lizzie – 35-36

Borelli, Carla - 56

Borgnine, Ernest – 194, 197

Bosley, Tom – 13-14, 83-84, 93, 118

Bostwick, Barry - 42

Bottoms, Sam - 62

Bourne, Peter - 61

Bowles, Billy - 31

Boyer, Chance – 171, 173, 178

Bradbury, Ray - 65

Braeden, Eric - 34

Brand, Neville – 2, 78

Braugher, Andre - 120

Braverman, Bart – 160-161

Brennan, Claire - 40

Brennan, Walter – 28, 78-79

Bridges, Jeff - 17

Bromilow, Peter - 38

Brooks, Martin E. - 49

Brooks, Ray - 4

Brooks, Stephen – 78-79

Brothers, Dr. Joyce - 102

Brown, George Stanford - 56

Brown, Murray - 15

Brown, Pamela - 15

Brown, Roger Aaron – 3

Bruce, Nigel - 70

Bryant, William - 73

Buchanan, Morris - 46

Buckner, Susan - 105

Bugliosi, Vincent - 26

Bull, Richard – 23, 73

Bullock, Sandra - 5

Bundy, Brooke – 2-3

Buono, Victor – 24-25, 106

Burke, Paul - 8

Burke, Walter - 24

Burnett, Carol - 135

Burns, Catherine – 78-79

Burns, George - 102

Burns, Marilyn - 25

Burr, Raymond – 116-119, 216

Burrafato, George - 55

Burrell, Jan - 41

Burton, Norman – 164

Burton, Robert – 9, 76-77

Burton, Wendell - 44

Bush, Billy Green - 70

Bush, Owen - 20

Buxton, Lord Aubrey - xxii

Cabot, Sebastian - 134

Cacavas, John - 66

Caesar, Sid – 9, 162

Cain, James M. - 185

Calfa, Don - 24

Callahan, James - 67

Calvet, Corinne - 68

Campanella, Joseph – 27, 44, 70-71, 128-129

Campbell, Graeme - 54

Caniff, Milton - 221

Cannell, Stephen J. - 148

Cannon, J.D. – 132-133

Cannon, Orin - 76

Captain & Tennille – 162

Carey, Macdonald - 83

Carey, Michele - 48

Carnell, Cliff - 46

Carpenter, John – 71-72

Carpenter, Karen - 229

Carr, Darleen - 158

Carradine, John – 6-8, 12-13

Carroll, Dee - 65

Carter, Lynda – 164-167, 229

Carter, Terry - 132

Cary, Christopher - 41

Case, Allen - 45

Cash, Johnny - 98

Cason, Barbara – 6-8

Cass, David - 196

Cassidy, Jack – 99, 134, 188

Cassidy, Shaun – 104, 106-107

Castle, William - 64

Cavanaugh, Page - xi

Cavanaugh, Thomas - 121

Chamberlain, Richard – 206, 209

Chandler, Jim - 62

Chandler, [Raymond] - 184

Chaplin, Sydney - 84

Chapman, Lonny - 64

Charles, Lew - 45

Charleson, Leslie - 55

Charney, Suzanne - 126

Chen, Tina - 51

Chermak, Cy - 124

Chicoine, Michelle - 83

Chihara, Paul - 42

Christie, Agatha – 13-14, 101, 184, 232, 240

Christine, Virginia - 49

Christopherson, Stefanianna - 152

Chun, Dennis - 114

Clark, Byron - 82

Clark, Dane - 43

Clarke, Gary – 20, 55

Clayburgh, Jill - 150

Clifton, George - 19

Clouzot, Henri-George - 53

Cobb, Julie - 58

Cobert, Robert - 77

Coburn, Sandra - 53

Cohen, Larry - 175

Cole, Michael – 162, 182-183

Coleman, Dabney – 3, 17, 52

Colen, Beatrice - 164

Colla, Richard A. - 38

Collins, Jackie - xxiii

Collins, Joan – 102, 187

Collins, Johnnie III - 63

Collins, Robert E. - 140

Colon, Miriam - 75

Comer, Anjanette - 21

Conforti, Gino - 73

Conley, Corinne - 11

Connell, Richard - 40

Connors, Mike – 87, 128-131

Conrad, Michael - 61

Conrad, Robert – 2-3, 21, 82

Conrad, William – 88-91

Constantine, Michael – 13-14, 78

Conti, Vince – 120, 122

Conway, Gary – 34

Coogan, Jackie - 69

Cook, Elisha Jr. – 47, 58-59

Corbett, Glenn – 38-39

Corbett, Gretchen – 68-69, 148-149

Cordic, Regis – 23, 56

Corey, Jeff - 9

Corsaut, Aneta – 3, 24

Coryell, John Russell - 2

Cosby, Bill - 216

Costello, Tony - 50

Cotten, Joseph – 64-66

Coufos, Paul - 23

Cox, Ronny - 83

Cox, Ruth - 105

Craig, David - 174

Craig, Helen - 35

Cramer, Douglas S. – 6, 10, 83, 160, 164

Crane, Bob - 106

Crane, Les - 32

Crawford, Broderick - 2

Crawford, Joan - 113

Cristal, Linda – 10-11

Crosby, Bing – 46, 158

Crosby, Cathy Lee - 165

Cross, Dennis - 8

Culp, Robert – 7, 98

Cummings, Quinn - 102

Cunningham, Sarah - 45

Cunning, Joyce - 65

Curtis, Dan – 9, 15, 47-49, 76-77, 125

Curtis, Tom - 38

Curtis, Tony – 160-161

Curtis, Tracy – 9, 76

Cutell, Lou - 24

Cyphers, Charles - 71

Dainard, Neil - 54

Daley, Jan - 24

Daly, Tyne - 31

Dane, Lawrence - 29

Dannay, Frederic – 18, 100

Danova, Cesare - 13

Danton, Ray - 80

Darden, Severn – 70-71

Daugherty, Herschel – 66, 81

Davenport, Nigel - 15

David, Thayer – 45-46

Davidson, John - 158

Davis, Barbara - 14

Davis, Bette – 34-35, 63-64, 234

Davis, Elizabeth - 56

Davis, Jim - 61

Davis, Phyllis – 160-161

Davison, Bruce - 41

Day, Doris – 80, 137

Day, Laraine - 43

Day, Lynda – see George, Lynda Day

Day, Robert – 29, 42, 56, 78

Dayton, June - 8

De Closs, James - 39

De Havilland, Olivia – 64-66

De Vries, Marc - 13

DeBenning, Burr - 29

DeCaro, Frank - 143

DeHaven, Gloria - 83

Deigh, Khigh – 114

DeLano, Michael - 9

Delevanti, Cyril - 8

DeMille, Cecil B. - 196

Demyan, Lincoln - 39

Denver, John - 135

Derr, Richard - 81

Deuel, Geoffrey - 29

DiCenzo, George – 25-26
Dickinson, Angie – 47-49, 102, 140-143, 176-177
Dierkop, Charles – 140-141
Diller, Barry - 183
Dillman, Bradford – 20-21, 39, 55
Dillon, Brendon - 10
Dimitri, Nick – 48-49
Disney, Doris Miles - 14
Dobson, Kevin – 120, 122
Dodd, Molly - 30
Dolan, Trent - 31
Donat, Peter - 54
Doran, Ann - 82
Douglas, Jerry - 10
Douglas, Michael – 83, 156-159, 215-216
Douglas, Sarah - 15
Douglass, Amy - 16
Doyle, David – 92-93
Doyle, Sir Arthur Conan - 69
Drake, Charles – 63-64
Dreier, Alex - 73
Dreyfuss, Richard – 78-79
Dubin, Charles - 44
Duff, Howard – 36-37
Duke, Daryl – 52, 54
Duke, Patty – see Astin, Patty Duke
Dulo, Jane - 48
Dunaway, Faye – 68, 99
Duncan, Lanny - 41
Dunn, Liam - 33
Dunn, Michael – 24-25
Dusenberry, Ann - 73
Dynarski, Gene - 16
Dzundza, George - 58
Eastham, Richard – 52, 164
Easton, Robert - 80
Eastwood, Clint – 24, 196, 199-200
Ebsen, Buddy – 52, 193
Eccles, Ted - 3
Eden, Barbara – 31-32, 72-73, 84-85
Edmiston, Walker - 38
Edwards, Blake - 196
Edwards, Sam - 27

Edwards, Vince – 14, 40
Egan, Richard – 29-30
Eggar, Samantha - 111
Eilbacher, Cindy – 3-4, 8
Eilbacher, Lisa – 3-4, 106
Ekland, Britt - 134
Elcar, Dana - 7
Elliott, Ross – 8, 51, 81
Elliott, William - 49
Enefer, Douglas - 90
Englund, Robert - 41
Erwin, William - 31
Espinoza, Jose Angel - 38
Evans, Linda - 150
Fabares, Shelley – 78-79
Fabiani, Joel - 50
Falana, Lola – 161-162
Falk, Peter – 96-99, 186-188
Farrell, Henry – 20, 31
Farrell, Mike – 38, 66
Farrell, Sharon – 20, 112, 142, 171-180
Farris, John - 83
Farrow, Mia - 21
Faulkner, Edward - 38
Fawcett-Majors, Farrah – 43, 92-95
Feinberg, Ron - 17
Feldshuh, Tovah - 63
Ferguson, Frank - 3
Ferragher, Lou - 40
Fiedler, John – 3, 83, 126
Field, Lizabeth - 39
Field, Sally – 28
Fielding, Jerry - 18
Fields, W.C. - 223
Fink, John - 28
Fiore, Bill - 42
Firestone, Eddie - 16
Fischer, Peter – 100, 181-193, 231-232
Fisher, Cindy – 3-4
Fisher, Gail – 87, 128-130
Fisher, Terrence - 77
Fitzpatrick, Jerry - 40
Fix, Paul - 29

Flanagan, Fionnula – 35-36

Flanders, Ed – 35-36, 58

Fleming, Ian - xvi

Flippen, Jay C. – 49

Flora, Fletcher - 80

Flory, Med - 28

Flowers, Wayland and Madame - 234

Fong, Kam – 112, 114

Ford, Glenn – 199, 201

Ford, President Gerald - 141

Forest, Irene - 9

Forsythe, John – 44, 92-93

Fox, Charles - 165

Fox, John - 71

Fox, Michael – 34, 78

Frame, Dawn - 75

Franciosa, Tony – 9, 173

Francis, Anne – 99

Francis, Ivor – 20, 45

Franciscus, James – 39-40, 46, 50-51

Franklin, Pamela – 60, 90

Frazer, Dan – 120, 122

Freed, Bert - 97

Freedman, Jerrold - 7

Freeman, Leonard - 112

French, Bruce - 9

Frizzell, Lou - 16

Frontiere, Dominic - 56

Frye, Virgil - 6

Fudge, Alan - 23

Funicello, Annette - 32

Furlong, John - 81

Gage, Patricia - 54

Gail, Max - 9

Gale, West - 13

Gallagher, Richard - 90

Galloway, Don – 116-117

Garber, B. Hope - 66

Gardner, Ava - 39

Gardner, Erle Stanley – 76, 116, 185

Garner, Jack – 150-151

Garner, James – 148-151

Garr, Teri - 134

Garrett, Eddie – 144

Garrett, Leif - 167

Garrett, Lila – 221-223

Garrison, Sean - 2

Garro, George - 26

Gaynes, George - 76

Gazzara, Ben – 40-41, 83

Geer, Will - 33

Gehring, Ted - 83

Genge, Paul - 27

George, Christopher – 19, 29

George, Lynda Day – 29, 66-67, 78, 162

Gerber, David - 140

Gerritsen, Lisa – 31-32

Gerstad, John - 45

Gest, David - 43

Giardot, Annie - 11

Gibbons, Robert - 12

Giftos, Elaine - 73

Gilbert, Edmund - 48

Gilford, Gwynne - 60

Gillard, Stu - 66

Gillette, Anita – 144-145

Gilliland, Richard – 136, 139

Gillin, Linda - 80

Gilroy, Frank D. - 45

Gimbel, Norman - 165

Ging, Jack – 11-12

Gish, Lillian - 78

Glass, Ned - 2

Gless, Sharon - 150

Goff, Ivan - 92

Goldberg, Leonard – xxii, 92, 108-109

Golden, Bob - 51

Goldwyn, Samuel - xiii

Golonka, Arlene - 157

Goodier, Robert - 66

Gordon, Don - 54

Gordon, Ruth – 33-34

Gores, Joe - 122

Gorman, Mari - 9

Gossett, Louis Jr. - 150

Graham, William A. - 23

Grahame, Gloria - 19
Granger, Farley – 102, 187
Grant, Cary – 110, 223
Grant, Lee – 34, 46
Grauman, Walter – 8, 23, 49, 51, 75
Graves, Peter – 52-53
Graves, Teresa – 22-23,140
Gray, Coleen - 18
Greenhalgh, Ted - 54
Greenstreet, Sydney - 25
Gregg, Virginia – 3, 8
Gregory, James - 80
Grey, Elizabeth - 9
Gries, Tom - 25
Grieves, Russ - 10
Griffin, Jack - 41
Griffith, Andy – 62-63
Grimm, Maria - 69
Grinnage, Jack – 124, 126
Grisham, John - 185
Grossman, Richard - 180
Gruner, Mark – 36-37
Guardino, Harry - 23
Guevara, Che – 171-172
Gulager, Clu - 27
Gunn, Rocky - 54
Gwynne, Michael C. - 7
Hack, Shelley – 92, 95
Hackett, Joan – 21, 30-31, 53-54, 72-73, 172, 201
Hagen, Kevin - 82
Hagen, Uta - 210
Hager, Jim – 78
Hager, Jon - 78
Haggerty, H.B. - 0
Hagman, Larry – 31-32, 102, 157-158
Hale, Barbara - 119
Hall, Don Ray - 41
Hall, Huntz - 19
Hamilton, George - 10
Hammett, [Dashiell] - 184
Hammond, Nicholas - 106
Hampshire, Susan – 4-5
Hanna, William – 152-153

Hansen, Al - 12
Hansen, William - 23
Harada, Ernest - 54
Hardester, Crofton – 9, 12
Harens, Dean - 51
Hargrove, Dean – 11, 188
Harper, Valerie - 235
Harrington, Al – 112, 114
Harrington, Curtis – 6, 10, 30
Harris, Julie – 28-31, 199
Harris, Robert H. - 31
Harrison, Gregory - 76
Harrison, Noel – xii, 111
Harrold, Kathryn - 150
Hart, Christina - 25
Hartman, David - 32
Haskell, Peter – 20
Hasso, Signe - 69
Hastings, Bob - 80
Hatch, Richard – 156, 158
Hatfield, Hurd - 48
Hawn, Goldie – 134, 180
Haworth, Jill - 28
Hay, Alexander - 64
Haydn, Richard - 54
Hayes, Helen – 14-15, 115
Haynes, Gary - 52
Heatherton, Joey - 161
Heckart, Eileen - 81
Hedison, David - 6
Heffley, Wayne - 41
Heflin, Van - 183
Helmond, Katherine – 35-36
Hemingway, Ernest - 229
Herbert, Pitt - 8
Herbert, Tim - 16
Herrmann, Bernard – 59, 175
Herron, Bob – 2, 194-197
Hessler, Gordon – 63, 70
Hewitt, Alan - 35
Hicks, Chuck - 19
Hill, Marianna – 12-13
Hillerman, John – 73-74, 100-101

Hindy, Joseph - 54

Hines, Grainger - 71

Hingle, Pat – 73-74

Hitchcock, Alfred – 44, 117, 172

Hoag, Mitzi - 27

Hodsoll, Frank - 217

Hoffman, Angela - 3

Holbrook, Hal - 42

Holden, William – xi, xiii

Holliday, Judy - 161

Holliman, Earl – 140, 142

Holm, Celeste – 13-14

Holmes, Lynne - 23

Homeier, Skip - 78

Honing, Howard - 9

Hooks, Robert - 78-79

Hooper, Tobe – 58-59, 204

Hope, Bob - 172

Horner, Penelope - 15

Horsley, Michael - 41

Horton, Peter – 68-69

Houston, Whitney - 23

Houts, Marshall - 144

Howe, Jeannette - 31

Hoyt, John - 45

Huang, Pearl - 54

Huddleston, David - 69

Hudkins, Ace - 194

Hudson, Rock – 136-139

Huffman, Rosanna - 34

Hughes, Howard – 224-225

Hume, Edward – 88, 156-157

Hunter, Kim – 3-4, 23

Hurst, David - 45

Huston, John – 69-70, 196

Hutton, Jim – 75-76, 100-102, 188, 215

Hutton, Lauren - 71

Hyams, Peter - 24

Hyde-White, Wilfrid - 56

Hyland, Diana – 56-57

Ibbotson, Peter - 122

Ihnat, Steve - 73

Ingersoll, James - 73

Ito, Robert – 144-145

Izay, Victor – 46

Jackson, Cornwell - 76

Jackson, Kate – 12-13, 60, 92-94

Jacobi, Lou - 34

Jacoby, Scott – 3-4

Jaffe, Nicole - 152

Jaffe, Sam – 49-50

Janssen, David – 23-24

Jarrett, Renne - 6

Jason, Rick - 83

Jauregui, Victor Hugo - 84

Jensen, Karen – 32-33

Jenson, Roy - 27

Johns, Milton - 4

Johnson, Dale - 38

Johnson, Don - 163

Johnson, Janet Louise – 104-105

Johnson, Melodie – 32-33

Johnston, John Dennis - 11

Jones, Carolyn – 164, 166

Jones, Henry - 83

Jones, Judy – 39-40

Jones, Marcia Mae – 5, 90

Jones, Tom - 161

Joplin, Janis - 177

Jordan, Glenn - 50

Jourdan, Louis – 16, 56-57

Joyce, Jimmy - 56

Jubert, Alice - 29

Jue, George - 81

Jurado, Katy - 36

Justice, Edgar - 71

Kamekona, Danny - 112

Kamen, Milt - 34

Kaplan, Sol - 24

Karlen, John - 76

Kasem, Casey - 152

Katzin, Lee H. – 3, 62, 196

Katzman, Len - 196

Kauhi, Gilbert Lani – 112, 114

Kaye-Mason, Clarissa - 58

Kazann, Zitto - 61

Keale, Moe - 112
Keller, Michael - 81
Kellerman, Sally - 115
Kellogg, John - 46
Kelly, Gene - 113
Kelly, Roz – 9-10
Kennedy, Arthur - 52
Kennedy, George - 118
Kerwin, Lance – 53-54, 58-59, 198-208
Kerwin, William - 38
Kibbee, Roland – 11, 188
Kiley, Richard – 44, 188, 216
King, Stephen – 16, 59, 199
King, Wright - 3
Kirkland, Sally - 73
Kleeb, Helen - 36
Klugman, Jack – 50, 144-147, 224-226
Knotts, Don – 32-33
Knox, Richard Alan - 56
Kobe, Gail - 35
Kosleck, Martin - 39
Kovack, Nancy (Mehta) - 102
Kowalski, Bernard L. - 78
Kramer, Stanley - 196
Krasny, Paul - 2
Kruschen, Jack – 38-39
Kulik, Buzz - 3
LaBell, Gene – 195
Lachman, Mort - 221
Ladd, Cheryl – 92, 95
Laemmle, Nina - 185
Lafferty, Marcy - 51
Lake, Florence - 38
Lamaz, Fernando – 43-44
Lamour, Dorothy – 12-13
Lancaster, Burt - 210
Landau, Martin - 99
Landers, Judy – 160-161
Lang, Doreen - 29
Langdon, Michael - 202
Langdon, Sue Ane - 81
Lange, Hope - 8
Lansbury, Angela – 15, 181, 190-192, 231

Lansbury, Bruce - 227
Larch, John - 3
Larson, Glen A. – 104, 132, 144
Lasser, Louise – 33-34
Latham, Louise – 17, 73-74
Laurence, Michael - 71
Lauter, Ed - 61
Lawford, Peter - 18
Lawrence, John - 24
Lawrence, Kenneth - 31
Leachman, Cloris – 17, 165
Leacock, Philip – 4, 17, 83
Lear, Norman - 235
Le Bouvier, Jean - 71
Lee, Bruce – 171, 180
Lee, Johnny Scott – 51, 55
Lee, Leonard - 3
Lee, Manfred Bennington - 100
Lee, Ruta - 31
Lee, Virginia Ann – 54-55
Leeds, Phil - 42
Leigh, Barbara - 52
Leigh, Janet – 4, 29, 51, 99
LeMaire, George - 35
Lenya, Lotte - 167
Lepone, Jill - 165
Lerner, Michael - 53
Lesser, Len - 71
Levin, John - 53
Levine, Larry - 20
Levinson, Richard – 42, 96-97, 100-101, 128, 182, 187-188
Lewis, Fiona - 15
Lewis, Geoffrey - 58
Lewton, Val – 5-6
Liberace - 161
Lindheim, Dick - 193
Lindley, Barbara - 15
Link, William – 42, 96-97, 100-101, 128, 182, 187
Linville, Joanne – 29, 172
Linville, Larry – 47, 130
Little, Rich - 234
Lloyd, Harold - 12

Locke, Rosanna - 9
Lockhart, June – 9, 83-84
Lockwood, Alexander - 16
Lombardo, Guy – 102, 187
London, Frank - 78
Long, Richard – 13-14
Lord, Jack – 29, 97, 112-115, 139, 177, 214
Lord, Phillip - 32
Lormer, Jon - 23
Lorre, Jr., Peter - 6
Lowy, Otto - 54
Loy, Myrna – 14, 109
Lucas, Lisa - 102
Lucero, Enrique - 84
Luft, Lorna - 134
Lukather, Paul – 29, 41
Luke, Keye – 6-7
Lumley, Terry - 60
Lund, Deanna – 32-33
Lupino, Ida – 32-33, 102, 240
Lupton, John - 34
Luther, John - 36
Lyn, Dawn - 167
Lynch, Ken - 132
Lynley, Carol – 47, 82
MacArthur, James – 112, 114-115
MacDonald, Ryan - 73
MacLeod, Gavin - 114
Macnee, Patrick – 1, 69-70, 109
MacRae, Elizabeth - 122
MacRae, Michael - 11
Macy, Bill - 12
Maguire, Mady - 78
Maharis, George – 43, 81
Mahon, John - 71
Majors, Lee - 82
Malden, Karl – 156-159
Malone, Nancy – 70-71
Mamakos, Peter - 32
Mancini, Al – 4
Mancini, Henry - 137
Mandan, Robert - 48
Mankiewicz, Tom "Mank" – xx, 109

Mann, Abby - 120
Mann, Delbert - 67
Mann, Larry D. – 14
Mann, Michael - 160
Mann, Ted – 210
Manson, Charles - 26
Mantee, Paul - 2
Marceau, Marcel - 234
Margolin, Janet - 183
Margolin, Stuart – 148-149, 206
Markham, Beryl - xviii
Marks, Larry - 153
Marlowe, Scott - 46
Marmelstein, Monique - 126
Marshall, E.J. – 18
Marston, William Moulton – 165-166
Marth, Frank - 60
Martin, Dean - 162
Martin, Kiel – 38-39
Martin, Pamela Sue – 104-107
Martin, Quinn – 29, 88, 156, 238
Martin, Ross – 17, 54, 70-71
Mascolo, Joseph – 72-73
Mason, James – 58-59, 204-205
Mason, Marilyn - 19
Mason, Tom - 45
Massey, Raymond – 52, 211
Matheson, Richard – 16-17, 77, 125
Mathews, Carmen - 76
Mayberry, Russ – 72, 80
Mayo, Raymond - 46
McAdams, James Duff - 120
McAlpine, James - 71
McAndrew, Marianne - 68
McBain, Ed - 185
McCallum, David - 67
McCambridge, Mercedes – 52, 78-79, 83-84
McCarey, Rod – 73-74
McClure, Doug – 34-35, 61-62
McClure, Jacqueline Allan - 33
McCormack, Patty - 37
McDevitt, Ruth – 50-51, 70-71, 124, 126
McDowall, Roddy – 75, 111, 134, 238

McEachin, James - 10

McFadden, Barney - 58

McGavin, Darren – 47-48, 124-127

McGee, Vonetta – 48-49

McGowan, George - 43

McGraw, Charles - 47

McGuire, Biff - 45

McGuire, Dorothy - 67

McIntire, John – 39-40

McKinley, J. Edward - 35

McLaglen, Andrew V. - 38

McMartin, John - 56

McMillan, Kenneth - 58

McMullan, Jim – 68-69

McQueen, Steve – 171-172, 179-180

McRae, Alan - 83

McVeagh, Eve - 42

Meeker, Ralph – 10, 47

Menard, Tina - 29

Merrill, Dina - 106

Messick, Don - 152

Mettey, Lynette – 144-145

Michaels, Barbara - 30

Michel, Frannie - 102

Miles, Vera – 4-5, 31, 38

Milland, Ray – 10, 20, 103, 111

Miller, Nolan - 110

Mills, Donna – 9, 38, 83-84

Mills, Juliet - 110

Mimieux, Yvette - 27

Mineo, Sal – 102, 177

Minnelli, Liza – 43, 161

Mitchell, Don – 116-117

Mitchell, Thomas - 97

Mitchum, Robert - 206

Monroe, Del - 27

Monroe, Marilyn – 142, 145

Montagne, Edward J. - 18

Montalban, Ricardo – 114

Montez, Maria - 85

Montgomery, Belinda – 56-57

Montgomery, Elizabeth – 35-36, 81

Montgomery, Ray - 65

Mook, David - 153

Moore, Irving - 196

Moore, Lisa - 19

Moore, Roger – 1, 69-70

Moreno, Rita - 150

Morgan, Harry - 18

Morgan, Jaye P. - 2

Morita, Pat - 80

Morley, Christopher - 162

Morris, Greg - 160

Morrow, Lissa - 70

Morrow, Vic - 9

Moss, Stewart - 38

Mossman, Doug - 112

Moxey, John Llewellyn – 19, 28-29, 47, 75

Muldaur, Diana – 115, 132, 134, 169, 209-219

Munoz, Aurora - 84

Murray, Mike - 4

Murray, Noel - 163

Murtaugh, James - 71

Nadder, Robert - 9

Nagy, Ivan - 41

Nalder, Reggie – 10-11, 59

Narcejac, Thomas - 54

Natwick, Mildred – 14-15, 136

Nelson, Ed – 3, 36-37, 64-65

Nelson, Ricky - 106

Nelson, Tracy - 118

Nettleton, Lois - 82

Newcombe, James - 53

Newmar, Julie – 80, 138

Newton, Wayne - 162

Nicholas, Denise - 21

Nicholson, Jack - 89

Nielsen, Leslie – 43, 46, 54, 75-76, 166

Nimoy, Leonard – 4-5, 89

Niven, Kip – 40-41

Noguchi, Thomas - 144

Nolan, Jeanette - 39

Nolan, Lloyd - 33

Noland, Ann - 60

Norris, Chuck - 180

North, Heather - 152

North, Sheree – 40-41
Novak, Kim – 61-62
O'Brian, Hugh - 43
O'Brien, Edmond - 33
O'Brien, Pat - 2
O'Brien, Richard - 23
O'Byrne, Bryan – 9, 48
O'Connell, Arthur - 75
O'Connell, William - 10
O'Connor, Tim – 23, 29
O'Hanlon, George Jr. - 105
O'Hara, Shirley - 16
O'Kelly, Tim - 114
O'Leary, John - 45
O'Neal, Patrick – 78, 134
Oakes, Randi - 78
Oakland, Simon – 47, 124-125
Oh, Soon-Tek - 54
Oland, Warner – 54
Oliver, Edna Mae - 80
Olmstead, Nelson - 67
Olson, James – 51, 134
Oppenheimer, Alan – 25-26
Ortega, Francisco - 27
Page, Geraldine - 38
Page, LaWanda - 73
Paine, Cathey - 25
Palance, Jack - 15
Parfey, Woodrow – 8, 80
Parker, Eleanor – 28, 68
Parker, Lara – 125, 150
Parkins, Barbara - 75
Parsons, Milton - 10
Parton, Dolly - 21
Pataki, Michael - 76
Patrick, Alain - 13
Patten, Robert - 51
Paul, Lee - 23
Paull, Morgan - 180
Pearson, Karen - 83
Pellett, Christopher - 83
Perkins, Anthony – 4, 30-31
Perry, Roger - 55

Peters, Bernadette - 133
Petrie, Daniel - 31
Pevney, Joseph - 83
Pflug, Jo Ann - 75
Phalen, Robert - 71
Philippe, Andre - 32
Phillips, Barney - 39
Phillips, Michelle - 162
Picerni, Paul - 49
Picon, Molly - 43
Pidgeon, Walter – 29, 38, 43, 64
Pierce, Charles - 167
Playdon, Paul - 124
Pleasance, Donald - 98
Pleshette, Suzanne - 3
Polanski, Roman - 26
Porter, Don - 35
Post, Ted – 14, 21, 46, 200
Potts, Cliff - 38
Powell, Dick - 110
Powell, Michael - 33
Powell, William - 109
Power, Udana - 80
Powers, Stefanie – xi-xxiii, 18, 21-22, 51-52, 70, 73-74, 108-111, 135, 238-239, 241-242
Pravda, George - 15
Pravda, Hana Maria - 15
Preece, Mike - 196
Price, Vincent - 102
Prine, Andrew – 3, 41, 46, 172
Pryor, Rain - 175
Pryor, Richard - 175
Purcil, Karen - 3
Quade, John - 24
Quillan, Eddie - 34
Quinn, Bill – 60, 136
Quinn, Pat - 33
Quintero, Jose - 210
Raffill, Stewart - 40
Raffin, Deborah – 41-42
Ragin, John S. – 144-145
Railsback, Steve – 25-26
Rainey, Ford - 31

Rains, Jessica - 63
Raleigh, Ben - 153
Rambo, Dack - 27
Ramos, Rudy - 26
Rampling, Charlotte - 69
Randolph, John – 34-35, 45, 166
Rapf, Matthew - 120
Rasey, Jean - 105
Raye, Martha – 136, 139
Reddy, Helen - 43
Reed, Robert - 130
Rees, Angharad - 4
Reese, Della - 133
Reese, Tom – 100-101
Reid, Kate – 66-67
Reinking, Ann - 102
Revere, Anne – 78-79
Revill, Clive - 68
Rey, Alejandro - 61
Reynolds, Burt - 29
Reynolds, Kathryn - 76
Reynolds, Larry - 83
Rhoades, Barbara – 34-35, 78
Rhodes, Jordan - 47
Rhue, Madlyn - 126
Rice, Jeff – 124-125
Rich, David Lowell – 34, 60
Richman, Peter Mack - 29
Rifkin, Ron - 23
Rigg, Diana - 109
Riley, Rex - 41
Rinehart, Mary Roberts - 60
Ritter, Thelma - 137
Robards, Jason - xiii
Roberts, Ben - 92
Roberts, Davis - 23
Roberts, Ewan - 4
Roberts, Pernell - 2
Roberts, Rachel – 4-5
Roberts, Tanya – 92, 95, 162
Roberts, Tracey - 23
Robertson, Cliff - xiii
Robertson, George A. Jr. - 153

Robinson, Charles Knox – 64-65
Robinson, Chris – 73-74
Robinson, Edward G. – 49-50
Rockwell, Norman - 232
Roddenberry, Gene - 210
Rodrigues, Percy – 49-50
Roley, Sutton - 73
Rollins, Alden - 180
Roman, Joseph - 144
Roman, Nina - 100
Roman, Paul Reid - 41
Roman, Ruth - 49
Romano, Andy - 23
Romero, Ned - 29
Rorke, Hayden - 35
Rosenberg, Meta - 148
Rosenthal, Laurence - 13
Ross, Katharine - 42
Rossen, Carol - 55
Rubinstein, John – 31, 68-69
Ruby, Joe - 153
Rucker, Dennis – 80
Runyon, Damon - 109
Rush, Barbara – 20, 174, 187
Russell, Bing – 60, 75
Russell, Jackie - 65
Russell, Mark – 120, 122
Russo, Barry - 39
Russo, Gianni – 24-25
Ryan, Linda - 41
Sagal, Boris - 69
Saint James, Susan – 136-139
Saltzman, Philip – 96
Sangster, Jimmy - 75
Santos, Joe – 148-149
Sargent, Joseph - 39
Saunders, J. Jay – 71
Savage, Brad - 58
Savalas, George – 120, 121
Savalas, Telly – 66-67, 120-123, 191
Sawyer, Tom – 220-233
Schallert, William – 19, 105
Schifrin, Lalo - 128

Schlatter, George - 234

Schmidtmer, Christiane - 63

Schott, Bob - 48

Schreiber, Avery - 19

Schuck, John – 136-137

Schwarzenegger, Arnold - 215

Scott, Brenda - 73

Scott, Jacqueline - 16

Scott, Pippa - 3

Seaton, Aileen - 66

Seel, Charles - 16

Segall, Ricky - 155

Seitz, Matt Zoller - 149

Sellecca, Connie - 68

Selleck, Tom - 151

Selzer, Milton – 3, 8, 50

Senensky, Ralph - 13

Sepinwall, Alan - 149

Serling, Robert J. - 53

Serling, Rod – 53, 183

Server, Eric - 23

Severn, Maida - 52

Shalet, Diane - 14

Shaw, David – 224-226

Shaw, Irwin - 224

Shaw, Lou - 144

Shaw, Reta – 44-45

Shea, Christopher – 36-37

Shea, Patt - 235

Shear, Barry - 18

Sheen, Martin - 90

Sheindlin, Judith – 122-123

Sheiner, David - 70

Sheldon, Sidney – xx, 108-109

Shepherd, Harvey – 190, 193

Sherbanee, Maurice - 13

Sherman, Bobby – 70-71

Shirriff, Cathie - 68

Short, Elizabeth - 84

Sidney, Sylvia - 12, 14

Sierra, Gregory - 82

Signoret, Simone - 201

Silver, Ron - 11

Simmons, Richard - 174

Simpson, O.J. - 196

Sims, William - 6

Sinatra, Tina - 134

Skaff, George - 71

Slezak, Walter - 126

Smart, Patsy - 4

Smight, Jack - 64

Smillie, Bill - 10

Smith, Bill – see Smith, William

Smith, Dwan - 80

Smith, Jaclyn – 92-95

Smith, James B. - 52

Smith, Kent – 6, 30, 34, 47

Smith, Kevin Burton – 90, 129

Smith, Paul - 14

Smith, William – 112, 178-179

Smith-Jackson, Jamie - 60

Snively, Robert - 71

Snyder, Arlen Dean – 11-12

Sommars, Julie – 21, 102

Sondergaard, Gale - 6

Sorel, Louise – 23, 52, 54

Soul, David – 58-59, 90, 203, 205

Soule, Olan - 29

Spader, James - 206

Spanier, Frances - 39

Sparks, Don - 53

Spears, Ken - 153

Spelling, Aaron – xx, xxii, 8-9, 21, 30, 49, 75, 78, 92, 108-109, 160-161, 183, 238

Spielberg, Steven – 16, 172-173

Sprang, Laurette – 40-41

Springfield, Rick - 105

Spurlock, Shelley - 3

St. John, Jill - 111

Stack, Robert – 43, 173, 177

Stacy, James – 51-52

Stander, Lionel – 108-111

Stanwyck, Barbara – 29-30, 75

Steinem, Gloria - 134

Stephens, Laraine – 2, 64-65

Sterling, Tisha - 46

Stern, Leonard B. - 136

Sterne, Morgan - 18

Stevens, Leslie – 32, 132

Stevens, Morton - 67

Stevens, Naomi – 49-50, 160

Stevens, Pat - 152

Stevens, Paul - 23

Stevens, Stella - 111

Stevenson, McLean - 235

Stevenson, Parker – 104, 106-107

Stewart, Fred Mustard - 49

Stewart, James - 101

Stewart, Kay - 65

Stockwell, Dean – 2, 51-52

Stockwell, Guy - 175

Stohl, Hank - 61

Stoker, Bram - 62

Stoler, Shirley - 94

Stone, Ezra - 80

Stone, Sharon - 72

Stoppelmoor (Ladd), Cheryl – see Ladd, Cheryl

Storch, Larry - 84

Storch, Norman - 84

Storm, James - 76

Stout, Rex - 45

Strasberg, Susan – 134, 150

Stratemeyer, Edward – 104-105

Street, Elliot - 51

Strickland, Amzie – 13, 35

Stroock, Gloria - 136

Struthers, Sally - 235

Sukman, Harry - 59

Sullivan, Barry - 29

Sullivan, Ed - 193

Sutton, Pelly - 55

Swackhamer, E.W. - 12

Swanson, Bob - 184

Swenson, Karl - 31

Swofford, Ken - 100

Symonds, Robert - 35

Talbot, Nita – 76, 99, 126, 134

Tapscott, Mark - 19

Tata, Joe E. - 3

Tate, Sharon – 13, 26

Tayback, Vic - 76

Taylor, Elizabeth - 39

Taylor, Jud – 55, 81

Taylor, Marc Scott - 144

Taylor, Sue - 51

Taylor, Valerie - 4

Taylor, Vaughn - 76

Tedrow, Irene - 38

Temple, Shirley - 5

Terhune, Shannon - 65

Thaw, John – 156-157

Thinnes, Roy – 48-49, 60

Thomas, Robert - 51

Thomas, Terry - 32

Thorson, Russell – 46, 65

Tigar, Kenneth - 23

Tolan, Michael - 90

Toler, Sidney - 54

Tone, Franchot - 172

Toner, Jeff - 66

Torn, Rip - 52

Townes, Harry - 76

Trikonis, Gus - 68

Tristan, Dorothy - 33

Troy, Louise - 8

Trump, Donald – 111

Tryon, Thomas - 37

Turner, Tina - 234

Turner, William - 53

Turow, Scott - 185

Tuttle, Lurene - 38

Uhnak, Dorothy - 23

Urich, Robert – 160-163

Vaccaro, Brenda – 11-12

Valentine, Nancy - 46

Vallaro, Vic - 24

Van Ark, Joan – 34-35

Van Dine, S.S. – 101

Van Dyke, Dick - 189

Van Fleet, Jo - 60

Van Scoyk, Bob - 184

Vandis, Tito – 23, 61

Vaughn, Robert – xvi, 84-85

Vernon, Glen - 65

Vernon, John - 19

Vickers, Yvette - 10

Victor, James - 78

Vincent, Virginia - 46

Vinson, Gary - 14

Vint, Bill - 31

Waggoner, Lyle – 164-166

Wagner, Lindsay - 150

Wagner, Lou - 24

Wagner, Robert "R.J." – xvii, xxii, 12, 108-111

Wainwright, James - 52

Walberg, Garry – 50, 144

Waldman, Marian - 83

Walker, Nancy – 136-137

Wallach, Eli - 7

Walsh, M. Emmet - 11

Walsh, Raoul – 196

Walston, Ray - 187

Walter, Jessica – 28, 68, 75-76, 90, 117, 146

Walton, Jess - 81

Ward, Sandy - 23

Ward, Simon - 15

Warner, Robert - 83

Waterson, Sam – 53, 201

Watkins, Linda – 3-4, 136

Watson, James A. Jr. - 49

Waxman, Albert S. - 83

Wayland, Len – 51, 73

Wayne, Carol - 161

Wayne, David – 100-101

Wayne, John - 210

Weaver, Dennis – 16, 132-135, 178, 213-214

Weaver, Fritz – 35-36

Webb, Clifton - 101

Webb, Jack - 29

Webster, Bryon - 50

Wedemeyer, Herman - 112

Wegge, Inger - 32

Weiss, Harriett – 234-235

Weiss, Michele – 234-235

Weld, Tuesday – 53-54, 201

Welker, Frank – 152-153

Wendkos, Paul – 35-36

Werber, Vic - 26

West, Adam - 20

Westgate, Murray - 66

Weston, Jack – 32-33

Weston, Steve - 83

Wetherell, Virginia - 15

Whately, Kevin - 157

White, Betty - 102

White, David - 78

White, Robb - 62

Whitman, Stuart – 6, 55-56, 84-85

Whittington, Dick - 16

Widdoes, Kathleen - 54

Wiggins, Russell – 64-65

Wilcoxon, Henry – 38-39

Wilkie, Robert J. - 75

Willard, Fred - 58

Williams, Johnny - 56

Williams, Robin - 234

Willis, Penelope - 41

Wilson, Flip - 234

Windom, William – 19, 29 32, 75, 91

Windsor, Marie – 58-59

Winger, Debra – 164, 166

Wingreen, Jason - 51

Winn, Kitty – 29-30

Winters, Shelley – 2, 55

Wise, Bob - 196

Wodehouse, P.G. - 45

Wolfe, Nancy – 25-26

Wood, Lana - 83

Wood, Natalie - 110

Wood, Ward - 130

Woods, Lesley – 3, 11

Wright, Patrick - 48

Wyatt, Jane - 82

Wynn, Keenan – 27, 29, 177

Wynn, Tracy Keenan - 27

Wynter, Dana – 118-119

Yardum, Jet – 11-12

Yarnall, Celeste - 34

York, Francine - 32

York, Susannah – 23-24

Yoshioka, Adele - 54

Young, Clint - 41

Young, Collier - 116

Young, Gig - 69

Young, Otis - 78

Yuro, Robert - 49

Zee, John A. - 12

Zimbalist, Efrem Jr. – 83-84

Zuckert, Bill - 18

CPSIA information can be obtained
at www.ICGtesting.com
Printed in the USA
BVOW08s2240230118

505930BV00008B/91/P